FUNDAMENTALISM
AND INTELLECTUALS
IN EGYPT,
1973–1993

FUNDAMENTALISM AND INTELLECTUALS IN EGYPT,
1973–1993

David Sagiv

Routledge
Taylor & Francis Group

LONDON AND NEW YORK

First published 1995 by
Routledge

2 Park Square, Milton Park, Abingdon, Oxon OX14 4RN
711 Third Avenue, New York, NY 10017, USA

Routledge is an imprint of the Taylor & Francis Group, an informa business

First issued in paperback 2016

Transferred to Digital Printing 2007

British Library Cataloguing in Publication Data

Sagiv, David
    Fundamentalism and Intellectuals in
    Egypt, 1973–93
    I. Title   II. Svirsky, Gila
    297.0962

        ISBN 978-0-7146-4581-0 (hbk)
        ISBN 978-1-138-99182-8 (pbk)

Library of Congress Cataloging in Publication Data

Sagiv, David.
    Fundamentalism and intellectuals in Egypt, 1973–1993 / David Sagiv
    ; translated by Gila Svirsky.
        p.   cm.
    Includes bibliographical references and index.
    ISBN 0-7146-4581-8
    1. Islamic fundamentalism – Egypt – History – 20th century.
    2. Intellectuals – Egypt – Religious life.   I. Title.
    BP64.E3S24   1995
    322'.1'0962 – dc20   95-15888
                                                                          CIP

Typeset in 11/12½ Berling
by Vitaset, Paddock Wood, Kent

Cover Photograph: The Star of Jericho: Daniel G. Pinkerton

Publisher's Note
The publisher has gone to great lengths to ensure the quality of this
reprint but points out that some imperfections in the original
may be apparent

To
my wife Marcelle

Contents

Acknowledgements

I would like to thank the Truman Research Institute for the Advancement of Peace of the Hebrew University of Jerusalem, and the head of the Institute, Professor Moshe Maʻoz, for assistance through the years of preparation of this study. I would also like to thank Bar-Ilan University for its assistance, with special thanks to Professor Michael Winter, who gave advice and encouragement throughout until the completion of this work. Special thanks also to the head of the Arabic Department at Bar-Ilan University, Dr David Doron, from whom I received the utmost encouragement and support.

My gratitude to Professor Shimon Shamir, head of the Tami Steinmetz Center for Peace Studies, Tel Aviv University, to Professor Jacob M. Landau of the Department of Political Science at the Hebrew University of Jerusalem, who read the manuscript, gave insightful comments, and recommended publication of the study, and to Professor Michael Bruno of Hebrew University, who furnished me with statistical data about economic conditions in Egypt. Heartfelt thanks to Ms Chaia Beckerman, director of publications at the Truman Institute, for her arduous efforts to coordinate the various elements required for publication. I am deeply grateful to Ms Gila Svirsky, an able editor and translator with whom I labored to produce the English version of this book, for the quality of her work and her meticulousness.

I would like to express my appreciation to my wife Marcelle and to my family for their encouragement and understanding throughout the years of this research, which required a great deal of time, including many absences for gathering material and for conducting interviews in Egypt and elsewhere. Without their encouragement, this work could not have been completed.

Before its publication, this work was awarded the Michael Landau Prize of Mifal HaPayis for political science and Arabic studies, in 1990, at the recommendation of Bar-Ilan University.

David Sagiv, Jerusalem

Introduction

The Egyptian people are a religious people who revere their faith. They perceive religion as being of paramount importance, an integral facet of the nation's culture, folklore and society. Islamic groups, each according to its doctrine, capitalize on this, using all their strength to undermine the state and attain the common goal: application of Islamic law (*Shari'a*) and the installation of Islamic rule free from all Western influence. Such was the case, these groups believe, in the time of Muhammad the Prophet and his early followers; they idealize the period of the genesis of Islam, and – according to their teachings – only a return to this golden age can cure the ills of modern Egypt. Arguing that Western influence, beginning with the invasion of Napoleon, is at the root of the evil, they support their writings and declarations with interpretations of Quranic passages by Ahmad Ibn Hanbal and Ibn Taymiyya, both of whom call for close textual reading of the Quran and Hadith, and a rejection of all interpretations, philosophies and accompanying texts.

Even the non-religious dare not castigate religion or its representatives in public. They undertake any such criticism cautiously, with moderation. They preface their words with an apology, explaining that it is not their intention to attack religion or the religious spirit, but merely to remove some of the dust that has clung to it over the generations. This is the approach that most Egyptian intellectuals adopt in criticizing their country's religious extremists.

This apologetic attitude does not spare them the wrath of the religious zealots, but the intellectuals will not overstep the line, since the majority also consider themselves religious. Examples are legion. Most of Egypt's leading writers publish books or articles demonstrating their religious faith before or shortly after the start of their literary careers, in order to defray in advance a debt to their readers and society. No matter whether they are liberals or socialists (with the exception of fully-fledged communists who define themselves as *ilmaniyyun* [secular]), they show respect and courtesy toward religion.

Such was the course followed by Egypt's first great modern writer, Muhammad Husain Haikal, and after him, by Taha Husain, Ahmad Amin, 'Abbas Mahmud al-'Aqqad, Tawfiq al-Hakim, Naguib Mahfouz, 'Abd al-Rahman al-Sharqawi, Yusuf Idris and others. Even though some of these writers did not address religious issues, many found themselves under attack or boycott by the religious establishment; in some cases one or more of their books may have been proscribed for certain periods, and works considered anti-religious permanently banned. Traditionally, though, the clerics, and their chief representatives, the *'ulama* of al-Azhar, knew where to draw the line. It was rare to encounter threats or the actual use of physical violence against intellectuals, nor was it common practice to confiscate or burn their books.

Bernard Lewis has written:

> Modern Western man, being unable for the most part to assign a dominant and central place to religion in his own affairs, found himself unable to conceive that other peoples in any other place could have done so, and was therefore impelled to devise other explanations of what seemed to him only superficially religious phenomena . . . We are prepared to allow religiously defined conflicts to accredited eccentrics like the Northern Irish, but to admit that an entire civilization can have religion as its primary loyalty is too much. Even to suggest such a thing is regarded as offensive by liberal opinion always ready to take protective umbrage on behalf of those whom it regards as its wards. This is reflected in the present inability, political, journalistic, and scholarly alike, to recognize the importance of the factor of religion in the current affairs of the Muslim world and in the consequent recourse to the language of left-wing and right-wing, progressive and conservative, and the rest of the Western terminology, the use of which in explaining Muslim political phenomena is about as accurate and as enlightening as an account of a cricket match by a baseball correspondent[1].

The past two or three decades have seen the intensification of religious extremism in Egypt and a growing propensity toward violence. In the mid-1980s, the Egyptian press reported the existence of 44 militant religious organizations; now it reports about 200 such groups. These, of course, are only the groups which have been uncovered by the Egyptian security forces; there may well be other militant organizations which will become known only when, or if, they are tracked down.

The first few chapters of this study concentrate on the resurgence of Islam. A number of basic concepts and their connection to fundamentalism as explicated by Western scholars are explained, including *al-sahwa al-Islamiyya* [the Islamic awakening or revival], *al-salafiyya* [ancestral heritage], *al-jahiliyya* [the pre-Islamic state of ignorance] and *al-jahiliyya al-jadidya* [the new state of ignorance]. These concepts are crucial for understanding the slogans and arguments of the leading preachers and organizations that have been calling for a return to the ancestral heritage. We shall endeavor to elucidate the idea of *Shari'a* and its relationship to Muslim justice, *fiqh*, its place in Islamic society and its relationship to the Quran, the Hadith – the recorded tradition about the Prophet Muhammad – and the various interpretations of the Quran. Also important is the idea of the Islamic state [*al-dawla al-Islamiyya*], in contrast to the idea of nationalism. Islamic preachers throughout the Muslim world are trying to revive 'the rule of God' [*hakimiyyat Allah*].

The fundamentalist Wahhabi movement emerged in Saudi Arabia at the end of the eighteenth century, though at the request of the Ottoman Sultan, the Egyptian ruler Muhammad 'Ali succeeded in eliminating it during his rule. However, through the Saudi royal family, the Wahhabis regained power in the last quarter of the nineteenth century in the Najd and the Hijaz.

Muhammad 'Ali concentrated his efforts on steering Egypt on to a path of modernization. He developed a modern military apparatus, strengthened by Western technological assistance, and promoted Western education, culture, science and technology. To assist him in achieving these aims, he sent working groups for five years of study in France, under the supervision of the learned al-Azhar graduate, Shaikh Rifa'a Rafi' al-Tahtawi. Upon their return to Egypt, the members of the study groups, including al-Tahtawi himself, established Western-style schools. These schools taught that there was no contradiction between borrowed Western values, especially in scientific methodology, and the teachings of the Islamic *Shari'a* based on the Quran and the teachings of the Prophet. Thus, there were two parallel education systems in Egypt, one influenced by al-Azhar and *al-kuttab*, the other by Western educational traditions.

The rise of Western influence in education, and throughout society, engendered a sharp dispute between the two streams of thought. Islamic reformists Jamal al-din al-Afghani, Muhammad 'Abduh and Rashid Rida, anxious about the fate of Islam, began to employ Western methods in its defense. This was particularly true of al-Afghani and Rida; 'Abduh saw less danger in implementing reforms in Islam. It was he who instituted reforms at al-Azhar, although he remained faithful to pan-Islamic notions.

This debate between the two major schools was abandoned for a time as the pro-Westernization school gained strength and support. With the rise of Ataturk came the dissolution of the caliphate, the supreme Islamic symbol, causing tremendous distress among the faithful. Three men in particular became central participants in the debate over the caliphate: Shaikh 'Ali 'Abd al-Raziq (in favor of its abolition), and Shaikh Muhammad Bakhit and Rashid Rida (against).

The liberal strain began to flourish in the 1920s as writers, thinkers, journalists and others influenced by Western culture emerged to support the liberal cause. In spite of these developments, in 1928 an Islamic opposition group appeared on the stage of modern Egyptian history: the Muslim Brothers, under the leadership of Hasan al-Banna. At first, the movement preached a return to Islamic spirit and values, and organized its activities with the aim of social unification. As the organization gained strength, however, the Muslim Brothers became more aggressive. By the time of their fifth conference in 1938, Islam was defined by the leadership as religion and state, book and sword. The Brothers called for a return to the heritage of Islam as it had been in the days of the Prophet. The aim of pan-Islam was thus defined as establishing a state, Islamic in every way, devoted to the caliphate and to the commandment of jihad to spread Islam throughout the world.

It was during this time that the Muslim Brothers played the most active role in its political life in Egypt. In 1941 the movement established a secret paramilitary underground, which had at its core a unified command and a network of underground cells. The movement developed a totally anti-Western and anti-colonial character, which quickly took the form of an all-out war against the British occupation. The Brothers took a hostile stance toward both Jews and Christians, and members of the organization fought against Israel in the 1948 War, as a special division.

In the political conflict between the government and the Brothers, several incidents stand out, including the murder of the judge Ahmad al-Khazindar, who had sent dozens of members of the Brothers to prison. Following al-Khazindar's death in late 1948, Egyptian Prime Minister al-Nuqrashi Pasha decided to disband the organization. Days after his decision, he met his own death. King

Farouq, himself endangered by the Brothers, joined forces with the new government and together they had Hasan al-Banna killed. Hasan al-Hudaibi succeeded him as leader of the movement.

Rapprochement talks between the Wafd government and the Muslim Brothers were interrupted by the Free Officers Revolt, led by Muhammad Neguib and Jamal 'Abd al-Nasir in 1952. The Brothers assisted the Free Officers, hoping that Nasir would allow them to participate as equal partners in the new government. Nasir refused and the Brothers retreated into angry opposition. The rift reached its peak in October 1954 when the Brothers made an attempt on Nasir's life in Alexandria, during talks with the British on the withdrawal of British troops from Egyptian soil. Nasir, rescued from the assassination attempt, began to pursue the Brothers in earnest. He sent thousands of members to jail, including Hasan al-Hudaibi and, later, Sayyid Qutb, who from then on was to have tremendous influence on the Muslim Brothers and on other extremist Islamic groups.

Sayyid Qutb began as a secular author and journalist. In the course of the 1940s, he began to change his direction and wrote several books on Quranic interpretation. In 1948, he went to the United States to study and remained there two years. Upon his return, he became vociferously anti-American and anti-Western, and strengthened his ties to the Muslim Brothers, which he had not previously joined. He had been one of the supporters of Nasir's revolt, but became strongly opposed when Nasir began his persecutions of the Brothers. He was sent to jail several times. It seems that under the influence of the works of the Islamic Pakistani thinker al-Mawdudi, Sayyid Qutb became more extreme, to the point of blaming society as a whole, labeling it *al-jahiliyya al-jadidya*. He preached clearly and forthrightly for a radical change in Islamic life. The gist of his thoughts is reflected in his book, *Ma'alim fi al-Tariq* [milestones], which has become tantamount to a covenant for all militant Islamic organizations. Qutb was executed in 1966 but his influence continues to spread to this day.

After Nasir's death, his successor, Anwar Sadat, made efforts to appease the Muslim Brothers and other Islamic organizations, in order to balance the influence of the Nasirists and communists. At first they were willing to be reconciled with Sadat, but as their strength grew, some of the organizations used force to oppose him. Among those groups was the National Liberation Party, under the leadership of the Palestinian Salih Siriyya, which attempted a coup with the help of sympathizers from the Cairo Military Technical College. Sirriyya argued that jihad was the only way to establish an Islamic state. The plot was discovered and leaders of the organization were executed.

The movement, *Al-Takfir wal-Hijra* [accusations of ignorance and *hijra*] was led by Shukri Mustafa, who consolidated his thought while in jail, under the influence of 'Ali 'Abduh Ismail, founder of the *Jama'at al-Muslmin* [Muslim society] organization. Both men preached the need for distance from heretic Muslim society which was under Western influence. Although his mentor abandoned and dispersed the organization, Mustafa carried on in his stead. In his book *The Caliphate*, influenced by Sayyid Qutb's *Ma'alim*, Mustafa declared that because Islam became alienated in its own homeland, it was necessary for the faithful to depart, as did Muhammad when he left Mecca for Medina, and return to take power, as did Muhammad after ten years of exile from Mecca. Mustafa's followers retreated for a time to regroup. Following the October War, they returned to the cities where they carried out several spectacular acts of defiance, including the execution of Shaikh Muhammad Hasan al-Dahabi, former Minister of the Religious Endowment. Following this murder, Shukri Mustafa was caught and executed in 1977.

The most dangerous of all the organizations was *al-Jihad*, which had branches in Cairo, Alexandria and several smaller towns. This organization declared Sadat a heretic for signing a peace agreement with Israel and for his persecution of members of militant Islamic organizations. The organization's leader wrote a book, *Al-Farida al-Ghaiba* [the missing commandment], detailing his claim that the 'missing commandment' is the jihad. Striving to establish an Islamic state led by a reinstated caliphate is thus imperative as an alternative to all forms of secular rule in Egypt. The leaders of *al-Jihad* were eventually captured and killed.

The credo, then, of the Muslim Brothers and of the other militant Islamic organizations which emerged in the two decades following Nasir's death is the imperative of establishing an Islamic state led by a caliph who will implement the *Shari'a* and restore the rule of Allah through jihad. From these major themes emerge hatred of the West and scorn for Jews, Christians, the State of Israel, and all Western scientific and technological developments. Yet it should be noted that some of the organizations and individuals, most notably Sayyid Qutb, did not object to borrowing useful scientific technology to strengthen Islam and help attain its goals.

Many intellectuals and liberals have attempted to block the fanaticism of these Islamic organizations, and to temper the violence they use against the state, society and any individuals who oppose their views. These leading writers, intellectuals, thinkers and journalists, who oppose religious radicalism, espouse instead Western-style progress, urging Egypt to take advantage of twentieth-century science and technology and prepare itself for the twenty-first century. The latter chapters of the book survey the attitudes of more than 20 intellectuals on such issues as the implementation of the *Shari'a*, the rule of Allah and the Islamic state, the caliphate, jihad, the West, Jews, Christians, Israel and science. The work is divided up according to these themes, and opinions are presented, for the most part, in the intellectuals' own words, to avoid unintentional distortion. No one intellectual is entirely representative, nor is there any umbrella group that unites the various attitudes on all issues. The ideas of these intellectuals are contrasted with the responses of Islamic thinkers who call for the establishment of an Islamic state and the imposition of religion on the state.

Many intellectuals claim that the Quran and the Prophet Muhammad did not dictate a specific form of government that should rule in all Islamic states. Most accept the teachings of preachers that the Quran and the Prophet apply to all people in all situations, but believe that it is necessary to adapt the teachings to the needs of the times. It is impossible, they say, for the law to remain exactly as it was in the days of the Prophet Muhammad and the first four caliphs; thus it is legitimate to borrow laws from the West when they are not in opposition to the *Shari'a*. These intellectuals base their ideas on those of the Islamic modernizers of recent generations, such as Rifa'a Rafi' al-Tahtawi, Muhammad 'Abduh and others. Moreover, some intellectuals state that the Quran refrains from setting out a legal system. Ashmawi and others maintain that *Shari'a* comes from the grammatical root *shar'a* which appears in the Quran only a few times and which means not law, but way of life or recommended path. In addition, the quranic use of the word *hukm* [rule] does not signify rule in the modern sense of 'govern', but rather means 'judgment'. Thus, when Islamic preachers talk of the rule of Allah, the intent is not a state ruled by Allah, but rather, through the judgment of Allah. Ashmawi and others declare that it was Judaism that first produced a legal system and that Islam never intended to do the same – Islam is a religion of mercy, justice and good works. Only 80 of 6,000 verses of the

Quran can be considered to be dealing with law; thus the Quran borrowed from legal judgments in Judaism.

The intellectuals argue that because there was no system for choosing a caliph, the caliphate has been a controversial and inconsistent institution and not a 'missing commandment'. As we shall see, they cite the following history to back their claim: Following the death of Muhammad, Abu Bakr was chosen by residents of Medina after a heated dispute with al-Ansar (Muhammad's followers in Medina), who opposed his election, and chose someone who never accepted Abu Bakr's rule. 'Umar Ibn al-Khattab was personally appointed in writing by Abu Bakr before his own death. 'Umar recommended that six of his people decide on a caliph from among themselves after his death. Among the six were 'Ali Ibn Abi-Talib and 'Uthman Ibn 'Affan. The six voted and chose 'Uthman, who was later killed and succeeded by 'Ali. Mu'awiya Ibn Abi Sufian challenged 'Ali's rule and fought him. In the course of the battle 'Ali was murdered by a sect in his own camp who resisted 'Ali's acceptance of arbitration between himself and Mu'awiya. This sect is known in Islamic history as Khawarij, and upheld the slogan 'No rule but the rule of Allah', which to them meant that once 'Ali had received acceptance of his rule by Allah, any compromise was unacceptable. As for Mu'awiya, he appointed his son Yazid to succeed him, and from this point on, the caliphate continued in that bloodline.

Intellectuals argue that there is no well-established commandment regarding implementation of the jihad, except when the Islamic state must confront aggression. This is supported by verses of the Quran and the teachings of the Prophet. The intellectuals even argue that the Prophet declared that the main struggle is not the war against the enemy but the war against the evil instincts within. Above all, jihad emerged at a time when Islam was faced with widespread paganism and idolatry, phenomena which the intellectuals claim are practically obsolete.

The attitude of the intellectuals toward Jews and Christians is rife with controversy. Most say that they are not opposed to Jews and Christians, since Islam recognizes them as 'People of the Book'. However, the opposition to Jews among some intellectuals, Haikal and Yusuf Idris for example, stems from leftist ideology or Nasserist nationalism emerging from anti-Zionist and anti-Israeli sentiments. Occasionally, these intellectuals have vehemently and poisonously incited opposition against Israel and Zionism. Even their opposition to Western influence is ideological, and not religiously motivated. For the most part, intellectuals support the borrowing of ideas from the West, particularly in the fields of science and technology and even culture, as long as it is for the strengthening of Egypt. Intellectuals maintain a bitter debate with Islamic preachers who would return Islam and Egypt to an earlier era.

The power of the group of new intellectuals remains an open question. The concern that they voiced in the 1980s was that their country was liable to become an Islamic *Shari'a* state ruled by the clerics, akin to Shi'ite Iran under Khomeini or Sunni Saudi Arabia. Can this group counterbalance the Islamic preachers? The prospects have not seemed promising while contemporary Egypt suffers poverty, a sense of deprivation and a deep sense of alienation. Against this backdrop, increased radicalization has been the trend. But the war in the Gulf at the beginning of 1991 opened a new page in Middle East history. In its wake, violence as a strategy appears impractical. The United States has shown that it is not a paper tiger and that it can maintain order. If it succeeds in its efforts to bring peace to the region, moderates may gain the upper hand. A march of the Middle East toward a new era of cooperation may cause fundamentalists to think twice before starting out on new adventures, given that religious zealotry and violence flourish amid instability and want. There is no doubt that in such circumstances, Egypt's intellectuals can contribute greatly toward increasing stability and moderation in the region.

NOTE

1. Bernard Lewis, 'The Return of Islam', *Commentary*, January 1976, pp. 39–49.

Part I
Fundamentalism:
The Resurgence of Islam

1 Origins of Fundamentalism from Ibn Taymiyya to the Muslim Brothers

For over two decades, slogans such as *al-Usuliyya al-Islamiyya* [the roots of Islam, Islamic fundamentalism], *al-Salafiyya* [the ancestral heritage], *al-Sahwa al-Islamiyya* [the Islamic awakening], *al-Ihyaa al-Islami* [the Islamic resurgence], or *al-Badeel al-Islami* [the Islamic alternative][1] have attracted millions of young people in the Muslim world in general and in Egypt in particular. Slogans like these are regarded as a return to the pure sources of Islam and to the divine message of the Prophet Muhammad (570–632), which reached a zenith in the days of Muhammad and the first caliphs – Abu-Bakr al-Siddiq (573–634), 'Umar Ibn al-Khattab (d. 644), and 'Ali Ibn Abi-Talib, cousin of the Prophet and his son-in-law (d. 661). In his book *Ma'alim fi al-Tariq* [milestones], Sayyid Qutb (1906–65) notes, '*al-Da'wa* [the message] – This [Islamic] preaching created a generation of people – a generation of followers of Muhammad – which is special in the history of Islam and of the human race in general'.[2] Their devotion to the divine calling in the full sense of the word is what gave them the power to bring two giant empires to their knees with the growth and dissemination of Islam as the new religion, the religion of the supreme God which was heir to the other monotheistic religions – Judaism and Christianity.[3]

Islam was perceived by most Muslims not only as the supreme religion or a faith with rites and ceremonies, but as a way of life and culture capable and worthy of organizing human society in its entirety.[4] The Quran and the Hadith [the tradition of the Prophet] comprise a kind of constitutional order according to which the faithful must behave and which is appropriate to all people in all places in all periods of time. In this, there is almost no dissension between religious extremists and those who interpret the Quran and the Hadith in a liberal vein.[5] The reason for the decline of Islam was a weakening of religious faith. After the defeat of Egypt in the Six Day War, a plethora of books and articles appeared – written not only by Islamic preachers – which advocate a return to the original, 'pristine' sources of Islam.[6] Those who preach an Islamic resurgence claim repeatedly that all types of regimes have already been tried – monarchy, capitalism, Western forms of nationalism, democracy, Nasir's socialism, monarchical dictatorship, secular dictatorship – except for the Islamic alternative which has not yet been tried and which, in their opinion, will cure the ills of Egypt.

Islamic interpreters stress that the decline began at the height of the Abbasid rule (750–1258), and was followed by defeat as a result of the hedonism of the Abbasid caliphs in the grand palaces as well as waning faith among the believers. Hence the Islamic empire in the Abbasid era fell prey to the Persians, Turks, Mongols, Tartars and so on. During this period, preachers appeared who encouraged Muslims to return to the sources of Islam. The first was Ibn Hanbal (Abu 'Abdullah Ahmad Ibn Ahmad) (780–855). Those in the Islamic resurgence movement today think of Ibn Hanbal as the spiritual father of this movement because of his zealotry and adherence to the sources in his exegesis of the Quran and the Hadith.

Ibn Hanbal lived at the time of al-Maamun (786–833), the Abbasid caliph who, at the end of his life, came to believe that the Quran is a *khalq* [creation], a concept based on the thought of al-Mu'tazila[7] which was itself influenced by the *Imam* Bishr al-Marisi (d. 833). Ibn Hanbal and orthodox schools of thought viewed this concept as heretical. Ibn Hanbal was persecuted relentlessly by Maamun and jailed several times until the period of al-Mutawakkil (821–61), who released and honored him. Ibn Hanbal was considered a very strict interpreter of the law and founder of the Hanbali school of thought, which became one of the four main schools of Sunni Islam.[8] Ibn Hanbal was:

> an extreme fanatic in his thoughts and he angrily opposed every *bid'a* [religious innovation]. He demanded that every verse be taken at face value, and he also accepted literally the attributes of God, his physical features, so to speak, and his characteristics. Ibn Hanbal vehemently opposed the concept of free will and every rational consideration concerning the religious codex, and also limited the *ijma'* [the consensus of scholars] to the first few generations only.[9]

No less important in the movement of Islamic resurgence was Ibn Taymiyya (Taqi al-Deen Ahmad) (1263–1328). Ibn Taymiyya was born after the great tragedy in the history of Islam when the Mongols under Kublai Khan conquered Baghdad in 1258. The appearance of the Mongols from central Asia on the stage of Islamic history presented a major problem. Although the Mongols accepted Islam, their faith was weak in the eyes of Muslim religious leaders, who asked if the mere avowal that one is Muslim is sufficient. Despite Mongol acknowledgement of Islam, Ibn Taymiyya called for a jihad to defend Damascus against them, claiming the Mongols were only paying lip service to Islam as a way of consolidating their conquest. When, during their siege of Damascus, the Mongols flaunted copies of the Quran on their spears in an attempt to persuade the defenders to lay down their arms, Ibn Taymiyya admonished the Muslims of Damascus that this was a trap intended to vanquish Islam under the ruse of faith in it. Like Ibn Hanbal, Ibn Taymiyya was mercilessly persecuted for his views and thrown into prison several times in Alexandria and Damascus, but he would not renounce his beliefs, and indeed upheld them vigorously. He declared a fight-to-the-finish against the sects and the various theological, philosophical, and mystical groupings, including those under royal protection.[10]

Ibn Hanbal and Ibn Taymiyya had a profound influence on those who sought to revive Islam in the modern era. The Wahhabiyya movement (1703–1878) appeared in the Arabian peninsula under the banner of Muhammad Ibn 'Abd al-Wahhab. 'Abd al-Wahhab denounced the Ottoman Empire (1300–1918) and, after many efforts, saw his exegesis – based on Ibn Hanbal and Ibn Taymiyya – become all-powerful. Like them, 'Abd al-Wahhab called for a return to the original sources of Islam and an uprooting of the undesirable innovations. Under the army of Ibn Saud, the exegesis of 'Abd al-Wahhab dominated all of the Najd region. Ten years after the death of Ibn 'Abd al-Wahhab, Ibn Saud conducted a military campaign in the deserts of Najd, Hijaz, Tuhamma and Iraq. He reached the Shi'ite city of Karbalaa, destroyed the dome of the mosque of *Imam* al-Husain (the son of 'Ali Ibn abi-Talib), and took control over all the valuable property in the city. Four years later, he undertook another campaign to Medina where he destroyed the domes of the mosques and graves of holy people. Subsequently he invaded and plundered Mecca.[11] The Ottoman rulers viewed the Wahhabiyya movement and Ibn Saud as a grave danger, because of their belief that Islamic rule must be returned to the Arabs as in the days of the Prophet and his followers.

Thus the problem was not only religious, but also ethnic-national, and therefore the Ottomans turned to Muhammad 'Ali (1769–

1849), then ruling Egypt, and asked him to recapture all the provinces that had fallen to the Saudi-Wahhabis. 'Ali defeated the Saudi-Wahhabi state in September 1818. The Wahhabiyya movement did not, however, die out with the defeat of its government and, late in the nineteenth century, it again managed to establish the Saudi-Wahhabi state, which was the Arab-Islamic challenge to the Ottoman-Islamic Empire. But from then on, the Saudi-Wahhabi state was limited to Najd and then Hijaz, and its leaders did not seek to expand this domain.[12] Writing of the imamate, Albert Hourani notes that the Saudi-Wahhabis felt that: 'if it is to be conferred by choice at least "The Arabs are worthier of it than the Turks". Its appeal was to Islamic not Arabic solidarity'.[13]

Egypt, on the other hand, underwent a process of modernization under Muhammad 'Ali, from his rise to power in 1805 until his death in 1849, as pasha of Egypt under the aegis of the Ottoman Empire. His rule began some three years after the end of the French occupation of Egypt by Napoleon, and following 300 years of Ottoman rule over Egypt. The regime in Egypt, although not defined by Islamic doctrine, was, however, consonant with the general Islamic outlook. The primary division of society was between rulers and their subjects. The former enjoyed the accoutrements of power, while the latter operated almost independently within traditional institutions.

The subjects were organized into small and close-knit religious-social-economic units. In villages, the unit was the village itself; in cities, the guilds. Heading the units were *shaikhs* who were responsible for the collection of taxes and for the good conduct of their followers. The villages and the guilds had scout-like orders which conducted their affairs according to the ancient traditions and were led by the *shaikhs* of these orders and the legal pronouncements of the *qadis*. The *shaikhs* were also the only connection between the rulers and the ruled. Relations between the two were minimal, as long as the rulers did not interfere in social affairs. The real leaders of the religion were the shaikhs and the *'ulama* [the representatives of the clerics] who had control over al-Azhar. Harmony was achieved between ideology and reality as a result of the agreement of those in power to allow society to function autonomously on the basis of independent institutions and pre-scriptions of the *Shari'a*.[14]

Muhammad 'Ali began to bring Egypt into the modern Western world. In 1811, he eliminated the Mamelukes (at the massacre of al-Qal'ah), whom he viewed as the main threat to his rule, built a modern army with a modern fleet trained by French officers and others, developed industry, built the al-Qanatir al-Khayriyya dam on the Nile, introduced new systems of agriculture and irrigation, sent delegations of students to study in Europe, opened modern schools, established the first publishing house in Bulaq and put out the first official newspaper of Egypt as a way to publicize his injunctions.[15] According to the liberal Islamic thinker Husain Ahmad Amin, who has studied this period, Ottoman rule in Egypt prior to Muhammad 'Ali had somewhat weakened loyalty to an independent Egyptian entity and strengthened the connection of Egypt to the Islamic state embodied by Ottoman rule. This is not to suggest, however, that Egypt became more Islamic in that period. On the contrary. According to Ahmad Amin, before Muhammad 'Ali's rule Egyptians had abandoned or were indifferent to Islamic education. The common people tried to apply Islamic interpretations to the ancient religions then practiced in Egypt – pagan, Pharaonic and Coptic – seeking to preserve the ancient character of Egyptian culture. The study of Islamic tradition became limited to a small group among the illiterates. Ahmad Amin sums up the period by saying that Ottoman Egypt was characterized by a stronger connection with the large Islamic state, a weaker perception of an independent Egypt, the absence of an awareness of Arab identity or nationalism, meager knowledge of the Islamic tradition and absolute ignorance about what was happening in the Western world.

The occupation of Egypt by Napoleon, followed by the rule of Muhammad 'Ali, introduced a new element into Egypt, that of Westernization. Ever since, there has been an constant struggle between a new, imported way of life and tradition, rather than between a new, imported way of life and religious faith. The standard-bearer of the Western orientation which encompassed Egyptian nationalism was Shaikh Rifa'a Rafi' al-Tahtawi (1801–73). Tahtawi had studied at al-Azhar and, in 1826, was appointed head of the delegation of students sent to Paris at the recommendation of the head of al-Azhar, Shaikh Hasan al-'Attar (d. 1834). Tahtawi spent five years in Paris and was greatly influenced by the concept of nationalism which was fundamentally different from the concept of loyalty to one Islamic nation. He maintained that there is no inherent contradiction between the Islamic Shari'a and the modern Western values of equality, social justice and so on. Thus religion should be no obstacle to adoption of these Western values. In this spirit, Tahtawi wrote several essays, including *Qalaid al-Mafakhir* [The necklace of glory] and *Takhlis al-Ibriz* [Purifying gold from dross]; and he called for the giving of rights to all citizens, including Christians. Thus, the jihad on behalf of the homeland came to replace the jihad on behalf of Islam. And in its wake, there was no way to avoid dissemination of the secular approach which separated religion from state.[16]

This approach won supporters in Egyptian society, but could not but arouse skepticism and dissent. From the 1860s, authors, journalists and thinkers began to become involved in these debates, asking questions like: What is a good society? What are the norms on which a good society is based? Should these norms rest on Islamic law or on a modern European model? Questions such as these engaged the attention of some writers of the time who viewed it as their responsibility to enact certain reforms, but who were simultaneously upholders of Islamic tradition, emphasizing that modern reform is not just legitimate, but a vital part of the social teachings of Islam itself.[17]

Subsequently, however, the interference of the Great Powers – Britain, France, and to some extent Russia as well – in the affairs of the Ottoman Empire reined in the spread of Western thought. The conquest of Tunisia by France in 1881, and especially the conquest of Egypt by Britain in 1882 seemed to threaten the entire Muslim world. The political thinking of the Middle East underwent a radical transformation.[18] Opposition to Western influence increased, with religion serving as the primary weapon. The Sultan of Istanbul welcomed the trend, emphasizing the Muslim character of the Ottoman empire. He sought to have himself appointed caliph of all Muslims, both in countries within the Ottoman Empire and of Muslims in Western countries. This pan-Islamic trend found support in Egypt for a few generations.[19]

An important group of Islamic preachers appeared in this period, foremost among them Jamal al-din al-Afghani (1839–97) and Muhammad 'Abduh (1845–1905). The group also included Sa'd Zaghlul (1857–1927) who was to head the Wafd Party and lead the popular rebellion against the British, known as the Revolution of 1919. The origins of Afghani are shrouded in mystery. He himself claimed that he was born in Afghanistan and was a Sayyid descendant of the Prophet Muhammad.[20] His detractors, however, claimed that he was of Iranian descent, and it was indeed proven beyond doubt that he was a Shi'ite.[21] Afghani travelled to India where he studied various sciences and mathematics and also learned about modern Europe. He tried to become involved in Indian politics, but without much success, and he left for Istanbul. On his way, he made a short visit to Egypt where he met Muhammad 'Abduh, a few years younger and still a student in al-Azhar, and the two developed a bond of friendship. In Turkey, Afghani was supported by 'Ali Pasha, a politician of considerable influence in the Ottoman Empire of that period. However, Afghani gave a lecture about Islamic philosophy which compared it with the prophecy of Muhammad, and this so aroused the ire of many religious leaders that he was forced to leave Turkey in 1871. Afghani returned to Egypt where he spent the next eight years under the patronage of a liberal minister, Riadh Pasha. In Egypt, Afghani cultivated a group of disciples, of whom Muhammad 'Abduh was the leading light. Afghani taught them theology, Muslim law, scoutcraft, and philosophy, most of the instruction being given at his home. He emphasized the dangers of the West and its interference in the Muslim world, stressing the need for unity among Islamic peoples in order to repel this danger. He encouraged his followers to disseminate their ideas in writing. At one point, he became friends with Tawfiq, the son of Ismail, who was the governor of Egypt, but when Tawfiq himself came into power, he expelled Afghani to India, apparently under pressure from the British, as Afghani's views were not compatible with British needs. Afghani remained in India for several years, and then went to Paris in 1884, where Muhammad 'Abduh joined him. Together they formed a clandestine group that worked for Islamic unity and the introduction of reforms. The activities of the group were veiled in secrecy, although it is known that there were branches in Tunisia and elsewhere. During this period, the two founded an important journal called *Al-'Urwa al-Wuthqa* [the strong bond], but only 18 issues were published. The journal preached a return to the values of Islam as interpreted by Ibn Taymiyya, it fought against the caliphs and the *'ulama* who do their bidding, and it even condoned the use of force to attain this goal, including acts of murder. It was thought that Afghani might have incited the assassination of Nasr al-Din, Shah of Persia, as he did not conceal his delight when the Shah was assassinated by one of Afghani's own pupils.[22]

Afghani's thought – expressed in the passionate style of Muhammad 'Abduh – analysed the impact on the Muslim world of the policies of the world powers of the time, especially the effect of

British policies upon Egypt and the Sudan. Even though the publication was banned in the countries under British rule, it was widely read and had considerable influence among intellectuals.[23]

Muhammad 'Abduh (1849–1905) was born into a traditional rural family in one of the villages of the Nile Delta near Tanta. His father was apparently of Turkish stock and his mother claimed she was descended from one of the heroes of early Islam.[24] The families of both his parents were forced to abandon their homes in the village due to the burden of taxes upon them. 'Abduh studied the principles of religion with several *shaikhs* and began his studies at al-Azhar in 1866, where he met Afghani and the friendship developed. In 1879 'Abduh was given a teaching appointment at the seminary of Dar al-'Ulum, which was an extension of al-Azhar, but he was expelled for his political views, which differed sharply from those of the rulers of that period. (This was the same year that Afghani was expelled from Egypt.) 'Abduh was ordered to return to his village and to refrain from political activities. Two years later, he was called back to Cairo to edit the official bulletin, *Al-Waqai' al-Misriyya* [the Egyptian bulletin]. Although this was an official publication, 'Abduh managed to publish in it some of his political, religious and social views. At the outbreak of the revolt in 1881 led by 'Urabi Pasha (1841–1911) 'Abduh was not sympathetic to him or to his officers, but when the British attacked Alexandria in 1882, 'Abduh did everything in his power to help organize a civilian rebellion against them. Following British victory and restoration of the khedive (viceroy), 'Abduh was arrested. His maltreatment in prison and the defeat of nationalist aspirations before his very eyes affected him deeply. Following his release from prison, 'Abduh was expelled from Egypt for three years. After spending some time in Beirut, 'Abduh joined Afghani in Paris where, as noted, they together put out the influential journal *Al-'Urwa al-Wuthqa*. 'Abduh travelled to Tunisia in an unsuccessful attempt to re-enter Egypt incognito, in hope of joining the Mahdi in the Sudan. When this failed, he returned to Beirut, where he taught for three years in the religious seminary established by an Islamic charitable institution. Here he gave his most important lectures about Islamic theology, which he later collected in a book, considered his most important work about Islam. 'Abduh's home in Beirut became a meeting place for intellectuals of all religions, including Jews. In 1888, through the mediation of some influential individuals, including the British government, the khedive allowed 'Abduh to return to

Egypt. He wanted to continue teaching, but the khedive would not allow him to hold a lectureship from which he could influence young people. So he was appointed a judge and then Mufti of Egypt (in 1899) until his death in 1905. As Mufti, 'Abduh enacted reforms in the *Shari'a* courts and in the administration of the Waqf holy places. His *fatwas* (relogous decisions) helped many adapt Islamic law to the spirit of the time. In 1895, 'Abduh persuaded the khedive to convene an administrative council for the purpose of reorganizing al-Azhar. He was a member of this council for ten years and here, too, introduced reforms into this old and staid institution.[25] Although Muhammad 'Abduh owed to Afghani his vision of a new Islam and its endless possibilities, it was 'Abduh who framed the new conception and disseminated it beyond the borders of Egypt.

We know, then, that Jamal al-Din al-Afghani adopted the pan-Islamic conception and conveyed it to Muhammad 'Abduh, who was initially skeptical of Tahtawi's view of the need for far-reaching, Western reform. 'Abduh, however, wholeheartedly accepted Tahtawi's contention that there is no inherent contradiction between such reform and the spirit of Islam. Indeed, in time Muhammad 'Abduh became one of the important defenders of this view. When asked if adoption of Western culture necessarily leads to loss of religious identity, faith or tradition, 'Abduh absolutely denied the link. The core of the teachings of Muhammad 'Abduh and his disciples is that Muslims must take from both Western culture and Islam what is right for them, seeking a golden mean in which the cultures will not be in conflict. According to this approach, Muslims are in the fortunate position of not having to choose between Western culture and Islamic faith. Since Western civilization is based on science, materialism and daily practice, there is nothing to prevent a Muslim from accepting all these and consecrating them with the spiritual character of Islam. There are no reservations for a Muslim to learn from Western experience about industry, agriculture, medicine, commerce, engineering and the like. After all, Europe surpassed the Muslim East in its achievements not because it was Christian, but because it ensured the development of technology, neglected by Muslims. It is not shameful to learn from the West. In fact, Western progress has itself taken advantage of Muslim knowledge, which preserved the Greek and Roman heritage. Indeed, Islam encouraged Muslims 'to trudge as far as China for the sake of knowledge'. This, then, is the crux of the reformers' call for *tawfiqiyya* [a conciliatory approach] between Western culture and Islam.[26]

Husain Amin criticizes those he calls *al-tawfiqiyyun* [accommodators], who seek to reconcile the two approaches described above, considering themselves to be following in the footsteps of Shaikh Muhammad 'Abduh, but knowing little about Islam and having pretensions of defending him and renewing his thought. In this they are only defending their own liberal views which they believe – sincerely or otherwise – are the true teachings of Islam. As for the Messenger of Allah, they redrew his picture in keeping with twentieth century values, and they chose from among thousands of stories about him those that suit them and prove their claims, calling the other stories Israeli inventions [*Israiliyyat*] or weak stories, as if this were a condition for adherence to their religion and their Prophet after having been influenced by Western values.

According to Amin, even the conservatives were affected by the trend spread by Shaikh Muhammad 'Abduh. He claims that 'Abduh's disciples painted Islamic history in a romantic light, ignoring objective criteria of scientific historical research and the values of truth and honesty in their survey of historical events, in favor of choices made arbitrarily which only reflect one's personal mood. Their actions destroyed part of the historical structure of Islam. In studying Muslim history or the Quran and the life of the Prophet, the arbitrary choice of stories reveals immaturity and lack of trustworthiness. This was precisely the blunder of the reformers of Islam who sought to coordinate Islamic education.[27]

One cannot discuss Muhammad 'Abduh and his school of thought without taking into account an important disciple and admirer, one who wrote his biography and exegesis of his work: Muhammad Rashid Rida (1865–1935). Rashid Rida was born in Tripoli, then part of the Syrian district, where he received his *'Alim* diploma in 1897. He read many of Muhammad 'Abduh's works and was greatly influenced by them, especially by the writings published in *Al-'Urwa al-Wuthqa*. After completing his studies in Syria, he immigrated to Egypt where he became friendly with Muhammad 'Abduh and remained close to him until the latter's death. Rashid Rida founded an Islamic journal called *al-Manar* [lighthouse], in which he expressed his views about Islam and the reforms that it must undertake. Most of the articles appearing in *al-Manar* were written by Rashid Rida, though other intellectuals contributed some pieces. Muhammad 'Abduh had called for the purification of

Islam from later accretions, the improvement and reform of higher Islamic education, and the defense of Islam from external attacks. For Rida, the latter was the most important issue. He and 'Abduh defended Islam primarily against Christian thinkers who, in their eyes, were to blame for the inferior status of Islamic countries. Rida was aware that 'Abduh could be interpreted to justify those who support Western culture, even though his main goal was the defense of Islam. This was the critical difference between the two. Rida tried desperately to eliminate support for Western culture, without simultaneously getting rid of the reforms necessary to Islam. He also differed from Muhammad 'Abduh in wishing to restore the institution of caliphs, writing that the Muslims had notable accomplishments under the leadership of 'appropriate caliphs'. The Quran and the Hadith as interpreted by the followers of Muhammad include a system of rules, an institutional constitution, and the best of all virtues because they are the product of 'divine wisdom'. This was actually a rejection of the sophistry of theology and religious philosophy. In contrast with Muhammad 'Abduh who ignored the issue of the caliphate, Rashid Rida believed that it must not be abandoned when reforming Islam. This subject became particularly important to him after the abolition of the Ottoman caliphate with the fall of the Ottoman Empire, as he viewed the caliphate as a practical alternative to the nationalism that he so opposed, which was being espoused by pro-Western intellectuals. Rida wrote a book in this vein called *al-Khilafa wal-Imama al-Uzma* [the caliphate and the great imamate], published in 1923, which is a collection of essays written several years earlier. The fundamental premise in the thought of Rashid Rida was the superiority of Islamic rule, as it is derived from divine inspiration.[28] There can be no normal or contented life except under such a regime. To those who bemoan the fall of Islamic rule and the Islamic caliphate, he responded that this was brought on by the Muslims themselves, who did not adhere to a regime based on *shura* [consultation], starting from Mu'awiya whose son Yazid succeeded him by dint of bribes and threats through the Abbasid period. The worst were the Turks who took the caliphate from the Abbasids, the descendants of Quraish who had been selected by divine providence to disseminate the message of Islam and Arabic (the language of the Quran) and the followers of the Prophet. Rashid Rida did not object to the fact that the caliphate was in the hands of the Ottomans, so long as Mecca was the center with branches throughout the Muslim countries. In his view, the caliphate was important for warding off the assault of nationalist ideology, which he regarded as a threat to Islamic ideology.[29] There is nothing more dangerous, he claimed, than shedding Islamic sentiment and sense of solidarity in favor of the nationalist solidarity promoted by the Westernizers 'in whose eyes a Muslim is thought of not as an Arab but a foreigner if he does not belong to the same country as they do and thus for them the Sherif of Hijaz or of Syria is no better than an idol-worshipper in China'.[30]

Rashid Rida stresses that Muslims cannot truly think that their religion exists without a strong and independent Islamic state conducted according to the laws of Islam and protected from foreign opposition or hegemony.

Despite this, Rashid Rida and his colleagues from the journal *al-Manar* fully accepted Muhammad 'Abduh's call to adopt the sciences and modern technology of the West, as they are for the public good. They even interpreted the concept jihad [struggle, holy war] as the obligation to pursue and accept the progress of foreigners so that the Muslims can, when the time comes, ward them off.[31] Nadav Safran graphically summarizes the message of Rashid Rida as follows:

> His reforms were so daring to the conservatives, his puritanism was so arid to the simple masses, his proscriptions were so rigid and stringent to those advocating adoption of western culture, that his views were not accepted by anyone until the day of his death in 1935, an event which was hardly noticed.[32]

The subject of the caliphate continued to agitate the Muslim world, especially Egypt which had the oldest and most respected religious institution, al-Azhar, and its large number of *'ulama*. After the revolution of the young Turks and the rise to power of Mustafa Kamal Ataturk in Turkey, the sultanate was abolished in 1922 and the caliphate was retained only as a symbol with vague spiritual authority. Two years later, in 1924, the caliphate was entirely abolished. The Turkish People's Council published a semi-official announcement defending its abolition on the grounds that the conditions for the caliphate existed only during the period of the first four caliphs. Kamal Ataturk openly explained his motivations for eliminating the caliphate, asserting that it undermined the foundations of the Turkish people because the caliph was absorbed in an ideal that was not compatible with the national interest, not to mention that the institution was impossible in and of itself. Thus, in 1926, *'ulama* from all over the Muslim world gathered in Cairo, in a council convened by the head of al-Azhar. The council stressed the need for an active caliphate.

In 1925, Shaikh 'Ali 'Abd al-Raziq (1888–1966) published a book that evoked considerable controversy called *al-Khilafa wa Usul al-Hukm* [the caliphate and the basis of rule] in which he spoke in favor of abolishing the caliphate. Because of the importance of the subject, which is controversial to this very day, we shall present here something about him and the book. 'Ali 'Abd al-Raziq was born in Lower Egypt into a very well-connected family. His father was the first chairman of the People's Party in Egypt. He himself was educated in al-Azhar where he studied from age 10 to 23, and graduated with the title *shaikh*. In 1912, 'Abd al-Raziq travelled to England where he lived for two years, but he returned to Egypt with the outbreak of the First World War. Upon his return, he was appointed judge in a *Shari'a* court and he was a lecturer in Muslim law at the Islamic Institute of Alexandria. He also edited the journal *al-Rabita al-Sharqiyya* [the eastern association], was elected to the Senate council, and continued his research on Muslim law. In his book, 'Ali 'Abd al-Raziq raises a key question, namely, is the institution of the caliphate truly necessary for Islam? He analyses the situation of the *Umma* at the time of the Prophet Muhammad and concludes that Muhammad had absolutely no political function apart from his role as a prophet and preacher of the truth. For 'Abd al-Raziq, the Prophet was not sent to exercise political authority, and he did not. His role was exclusively spiritual: to lead people in the way of the Almighty. With his special qualities, Muhammad created an *Umma*, but not of the type familiar to us as a state. This is an *Umma* which has no connection or tie to any form of government or with any particular people. Furthermore, this *Umma* does not have to be united politically, and indeed, it cannot be. But if it could be united, would that be good? It is God's will that there be differences between tribes and nations, which will foster competition so that human civilization will be improved and perfected. The proof of this is that the Prophet established no criteria for the kind of regime that would follow his death. Either it was not part of his mission to prescribe the form of regime to follow him, or the mission of the Prophet was imperfect, which is not conceivable. Naturally, 'Ali 'Abd al-Rizaq espoused the former. Islamic preaching created a Muslim religious community, and, as a by-product, an Arab nation. After the death of Muhammad, the Arabs founded a state in the spirit of the Muslim religious community that the Prophet had created. The first caliph, Abu-Bakr, devoted himself primarily to politics and to creating a monarchy – 'a state which was Arab and based upon religious teachings', in his words. Although this policy fostered the dissemination of Islam, first and foremost it sought to advance Arab interests, something that was not clear to all the Muslims of that period. Abu-Bakr took for himself the title *khalifat rasul Allah* [the caliph of the Messenger of God]. He accused those who rejected his political leadership of abandoning Islam, or apostasy. From that time on, the concept of the caliphate struck root and was cultivated by the absolutist rulers because of their personal interests. And that, in the words of 'Ali 'Abd al-Raziq, was the crime of the kings who tyrannized the Muslims.[33]

As noted, the book aroused considerable anger and controversy. Many *'ulama* wrote at length to refute the thoughts of 'Abd al-Raziq. Members of the al-Azhar Council of *'Ulama* excoriated him and 'disproved' his claims by reference to verses from the Quran and the Hadith. Rashid Rida declared that the book by 'Ali 'Abd al-Raziq, a senior shaikh at al-Azhar, was an attempt by the enemies of Islam to weaken and divide it, and that this attempt came from forces within Islam itself. The harshest critic of all was Shaikh Muhammad Bakhit, who claimed that the premise of 'Ali 'Abd al-Raziq concerning the regime was destructive of one of the two fundamental precepts of Islamic doctrine: the precept of prophecy. Muslim theologians teach, wrote Bakhit, that certain prophets were sent to reveal the truth of the divinity or to bring a constitution, but Muhammad was sent to reveal the divinity and the constitution, and also to implement these revelations. Implementing the constitutional order was an essential part of the mission of Muhammad. The implementation included political power and therefore the religious community of Muslims was from the outset a political community. Further, since the Quran and the constitutional order were not bound to one generation or period, implementation of political power on the *Umma* must continue.[34]

In summary, from the middle of the nineteenth century, four main political currents have appeared: a Western current, which preaches the imitation of the West in all facets of life; a religious, anti-Western current which seeks to restore the glory of Islam by returning to the original founts of the religion; a local nationalist current which does not give priority to general Muslim nationalism or to pan-Islamic unity; and a current of pan-Arab nationalism which appeared in the late 1800s and has intensified through the twentieth century. Many advocates of this last approach were Christians who immigrated to Egypt when British rule granted them broad rights and a wide range of freedom. Both educated Muslims and educated Christians sowed the seeds of Arab nationalism whose fruits have ripened from the middle of the twentieth century.[35]

The liberal ideological approach, influenced by the reformist positions of Shaikh Muhammad 'Abduh, of a kind of integration of local Egyptian nationalism and pan-Arabism grew significantly after the revolution of Sa'd Zaghlul in 1919. This stream included the great philosophers and writers of Egypt, such as Ahmad Lutfi al-Sayyid (1872–1963), Muhammad Husain Haikal (1889–1957), Taha Husain (1889–1973), Tawfiq al-Hakim (1898–1987), 'Abbas Mahmud al-'Aqqad (1889–1964), and a younger generation, including Naguib Mahfouz (born in 1913). This stream fertilized the cultural life in Egypt and created the best of philosophy, literature and poetry. But it rapidly lost momentum, apparently constrained by the political and social forces behind the government corruption, of which these intellectuals were, perhaps unconsciously, a part. In his book *Kharif al-Ghadab* [autumn of the anger], Muhammad Hasanain Haikal notes that the main reason for the slow-down might be the unwritten armistice between this group and the forces of imperialism, which precluded a vigorous struggle against them.[36] This allowed for the growth of greater religious radicalization in the form of both the Muslim Brothers and the pan-Arabism of 'Abd al-Nasir and the officers of the July 1952 revolution. The following chapter examines the development of the Muslim Brothers and the struggle between the religious and the pan-Arab currents.

NOTES

1. In the course of this book, we shall try to explain these concepts and their context as they appear.
2. Sayyid Qutb, *Ma'alim fi al-Tariq* [Milestones] (Cairo and Beirut), 1982), p. 14 (hereinafter, *Ma'alim*).
3. See the verse, 'Lo! religion with Allah [is Islam, or] The Surrender (to His will and guidance).' The Family of 'Imran, 19. This and similar verses are often repeated in Islamic books and preaching.
4. Many sources could be cited for this, but since this book deals with modern Islam, I will

cite two current references: Muhammad Hasanain Haikal, *Kharif al-Ghadab* [Autumn of the anger] (Beirut, 13th printing, 1986), pp. 273–304 (hereinafter, *Autumn of the Anger*); Gunaina Ni'mat-Allah, *The Jihad: An Islamic Alternative in Egypt* (Beirut: American University Press, 1986), p. 17.

5. Modern Egyptian writers and intellectuals voice this opinion almost unanimously, even if some speak hypocritically. Their liberal attitude toward people of other religions is rooted in their approach of humanity and loving-kindness, but this does not detract from their manifest or latent belief in the superiority of Islam.

6. Shimon Balass, *Arabic Literature in the Shadow of the War* (Am Oved, 1978), in particular the second part, pp. 146–336. Balass cites many sources in this spirit.

7. 'Ahmad B. Hanbal', *The Encyclopaedia of Islam* (Leiden and London, New Edition, reprint of 1st edition, 1967), pp. 272–7.

8. Khair al-din al-Zarkali, *Al-A'lam* (Beirut, 3rd printing, 1969), pp. 192–3.

9. Hava Lazarus-Yafeh (ed.), *Studies in the History of the Arabs and Islam* (Tel Aviv, 9th edition, 1984), Ch. 7: 'The Development of the Oral and Written Law in Islam' by the editor, p. 171.

10. Ibid., p. 172; John Alden Williams, *Islam* (New York and London, 1961), pp. 205–10; and al-Zarkali, pp. 140–41.

11. Albert Hourani, *Arabic Thought in the Liberal Age, 1798–1939* (Cambridge, 1983), pp. 37–8.

12. Ibid.

13. Ibid., p. 38.

14. Nadav Safran, *Egypt in Search of Political Society* (Cambridge, MA, 1961), pp. 27–9.

15. Hourani, pp. 51–3.

16. Husain Ahmad Amin, 'The Movement of Islamic Innovation', *al-Hilal*, July 1986.

17. Hourani, pp. 67–8.

18. Ibid., p. 103.

19. Amin, op. cit.

20. Hourani, p. 108.

21. Kedouri asserts with certainty that Afghani was born a Shi'ite. See Elie Kedouri, *Islam in the Modern World* (London, 1980), p. 25; and Nikki R. Keddie, *An Islamic Response to Imperialism* (Berkeley, CA, Berkeley University, 3rd edition, 1983). Muhammad 'Amara, however, insists that Afghani is Sunni, but without solid proof. See Muhammad 'Amara, *Jamal al-Din al-Afghani* (Cairo, Dar al-Mustaqbal al-Arabi, 1984).

22. Hourani, op. cit.

23. Anwar Al-Jundi, *al-Yaqza al-Islamiyya fi Muwajahat al-Isti'mar* [The Islamic awakening in confrontation with imperialism] (Cairo, Dar al-I'tisam, (undated)), first chapter.

24. Hourani, p. 108.

25. Hourani, pp. 108–11, 130–60 and 231; see also Safran, pp. 62–73.

26. Husain Ahmad Amin, *Al-Islam fi 'Alam Mutaghayyir* [Islam in a changing world] (Cairo, 1988), pp. 125–6.

27. Ibid., pp. 127–8.

28. Ibid.

29. Safran, p. 79.

30. Ibid., p. 82.

31. Ibid.

32. Ibid., pp. 82–3.

33. Ibid., p. 84. The paragraph about Muhammad Rashid Rida is based on Safran, pp. 75–84 and on Hourani, pp. 222–44.

34. Hourani, pp. 183–92; Safran, pp. 139–40; and Leonard Binder *Islamic Liberalism* (Chicago, 1988), pp. 128–70.

35. Amin, pp. 122–3.

36. *Autumn of the Anger*, p. 278.

2 From Liberalism to the Resurgence of Religion: The Muslim Brothers and Sayyid Qutb

From the 1920s, liberalism flourished in Egypt and Western culture was regarded as a model for emulation. During this period, many authors and thinkers made significant contributions to the modernization of Egypt patterned after the West, which they deeply admired. A newly emergent enlightenment movement began to translate the best of Western literature and research in various fields. Newspapers and journals published translations of Western writing as well as original writing in genres like those published in the West. A movement began for the liberation of women, which included casting off the veil and traditional garb.

A wave of modernization swept across Egypt during these years, modelled after modern Turkey in the early days of Ataturk's rule and also modern Japan. Both of these countries at this time showed impressive achievements in the wake of their Westernization and neither country is in Europe – under suspicion in both religious and liberal circles of imperialism and exploitation of the East. Both are Asian countries which were seen to have brushed off the dust of the past and built a society based on dynamic, modern foundations. Many liberals such as Ahmad Lutfi al-Sayyid, Sa'd Zaghlul, Muhammad Husain Haikal and others who were disciples of Muhammad 'Abduh relied on him in their writings and advocacy of Westernization.

In the face of these developments, a broad-based counter-movement arose inspired by the 'dangers' of Westernization – the Muslim Brothers, who viewed the movement for the liberation of women as a grave danger to morality, to social tradition and to the character of Islamic society in Egypt. The Muslim Brothers vehemently objected to women working alongside men, to the introduction of women to political and social life, to the decreased numbers of men studying religion at al-Azhar, to reform of the *Shari'a* courts, and to the battle of the liberals against polygamy.

In their minds, Westernization meant anarchy and corruption.[1]

The movement of Muslim Brothers was founded in Isma'ilyya in 1928 by Hasan al-Banna (1906–49) to disseminate Islam on the basis of love, brotherhood and friendship. Hasan al-Banna was born in Mahmudiyya near Alexandria. He grew up in a religious family, completed elementary and high school in Mahmudiyya, and then went to Damanhur to study at the teachers' college. From there al-Banna moved to Cairo where he studied religion at the Dar al-'Ulum seminary, an extension of al-Azhar. During this period, he often attended meetings of the Islamic group associated with *al-Manar*, the journal put out by Muhammad Rashid Rida, which provided the basis for his later struggles on behalf of religion in the spirit of the conservative Rashid Rida. At the age of 21, al-Banna completed his studies and was given a teaching post in the elementary school of Isma'ilyya. It was then that he began to preach Islam in a new style. He taught young men not only in mosques, as was common, but in coffee houses, where he would give a weekly lesson about Islam. Six months later, he had gathered around himself a close-knit group, and in March 1928, this group met in his home in Isma'ilyya and chose him as its leader.[2] Al-Banna named the group 'The Movement of Muslim Brothers', and defined its mission as activity on behalf of Islam and Muslims. This was the beginning of a broad Islamic movement of signal historic importance inside and outside Egypt. Although the establishment of this movement constituted a distinct turning-point in the political, social and economic life of Egypt and possibly the entire region, no events of particular importance were recorded in the year of its founding. Binder notes that no one in the group, including Hasan al-Banna himself, imagined that the movement would grow as much as it did from the middle of the 1930s.[3]

The objectives set out by the members of this group indicate that they do not appear to have had political intentions in the early years, but they struggled to return to *al-Salafi* [ancestral] Islam, which opposes Westernization, in the spirit of the preaching of Rashid Rida.[4] But as it grew, the movement had to define its ideological position concerning the Islamic and political problems on the public agenda. Thus it gradually developed a clear and comprehensive ideology which was fundamentally different from the one with which it started. The ideology was based on tenets that were simple but threatening to the existing political structure.[5] The basic tenets of the Muslim Brothers can be summarized as follows:

1. *The inclusiveness of Islam.* Islam is religion and state, prayer and jihad, obedience and rule, book (*mushaf*) and sword (*saif*).[6]
2. *Islam must be restored to its first teachings.*[7] At the fifth conference of the Muslim Brothers in 1938, Hasan al-Banna stated, 'We must draw the rules of Islam from their original sources and understand Islam as it had been understood by the followers of the Prophet and their disciples from the generation of the good forefathers'.[8]
3. *Pan-Islam.* Al-Banna clearly specified that 'Every millimeter of land on which the flag of Islam waves is the homeland to every Muslim and must be defended. All Muslims are one nation, and the Islamic homeland is one homeland'.[9]
4. *The concept of the caliphate as previously conceived.* At the same conference, al-Banna affirmed that the Brothers believe the caliphate is the symbol of Islamic unity.[10]
5. *Islamic government.* In the Islam of the Muslim Brothers, according to al-Banna, Islamic government is a basic precept.[11]

The idea of organizing members into units who would go on outings together to foster solidarity and learn about the homeland developed by leaps and bounds from 1934 to 1937, until the movement had virtually turned into a paramilitary organization. In July 1937, these units were nicknamed 'the military groups' and they were headed by Sayyid Nusair, a world champion weightlifter. During this period, the Muslim Brothers were ardent supporters of King Farouq, then just beginning his reign, and they organized a rally to welcome him and demand that he be crowned caliph.[12]

In 1938, al-Banna decided to enter political life and, at the same time, to reorganize the paramilitary units. In 1939, all the units were ordered to practise every kind of military activity one day a week. In 1940 during the Second World War, the paramilitary organization entered a new phase, and was registered officially as part of the scouts association so that the Brothers could enjoy various benefits accorded to the scouts. A supreme council of *jawwala* [graduate scouts] was established, headed by Hasan al-Banna himself. The enterprise spread to Cairo, Alexandria and other provincial towns. By the end of the Second World War, they were 45,000 strong, and by the end of 1947, on the eve of the Israeli war for independence, there were 75,000 members.[13]

The first clash between the Muslim Brothers and the government took place in 1941. The British, who were the real controlling power in Egypt, were deeply concerned about the growing strength of the Brothers because of the movement's sympathy with the Axis powers. The British asked Husain Sirri Pasha, of the Sa'diyyin Party and head of the Egyptian government, to cancel all licenses for the movement's publications, including Rashid Rida's journal *al-Manar*, which the Brothers had revived. The printing presses were closed down and on 19 October 1941, Hasan al-Banna and his two assistants were arrested, although released at the intervention of the King himself after less than a month. From that time, al-Banna began to organize himself politically and militarily on two levels, by the avoidance of clashes with the British to prevent them from banning his organization; and by the establishment of *al-Tanzim al-Sirri*, the underground organization.

'Abd al-'Azim Ramadan provides evidence that in this period the Brothers had an unwritten armistice with the British and even cooperation in exchange for ignoring their activities.[14] As for the underground, the precise date of its establishment is not known, but Ramadan says that the estimated date is 1942 or earlier.[15] The underground drew its strength from the Brothers who had undergone military training. Every member of the underground received a special numerical symbol with an acronym of his name. Each was under strict surveillance and treachery would be punished by a death sentence.[16] The organization was composed of many small cells, each called a family and headed by an *amir*. An intelligence operation belonging to the underground monitored all the parties and other organizations, even those considered sympathetic to the Brothers,[17] and was supplied with money, arms, ammunition, vehicles, communications devices and a radio.

In 1942, the government – under the Wafd Party which rose to power despite opposition from the King and the threat of British tanks – closed the branches of the movement. But the Wafd reversed its policy before leaving the government in October 1944. The Sa'diyyin Party then returned to power under Ahmad Mahir Pasha, who did not forgive the Muslim Brothers for cooperating with the Wafd, and he undermined the election of Hasan al-Banna to Parliament. When 'Ali Mahir planned to join the other uncommitted Allies in a declaration of war on Nazi Germany, the Brothers asked him to refrain from this step. Mahir did not heed their warning, and defiantly made his official announcement in Parliament. He was killed on 24 February 1945 while leaving the Parliament building by a man named Muhammad al-'Isawi. The assassin admitted to membership in the National Party, but not to membership of the Muslim Brothers. Nevertheless, two senior Muslim Brothers confirmed that al-'Isawi was in fact a member of the Muslim Brothers, and that the assassination had been carried out under orders from the movement. Indeed, scholars have shown that it was not unusual to be a member of two or more parties.

On 8 September 1945, the general assembly of the Muslim Brothers adopted for the first time a constitution for the movement. This constitution was finalized, in eight sections, on 21 May 1948. According to this constitution, the Muslim Brothers is 'an inclusive Islamic body acting to attain the objectives for which Islam came into being'. The eight sections include:

> Interpreting the Quran according to the original, natural covenant; the inclusiveness of the Quran and its compatibility with the spirit of the times; similarity among the various Islamic schools of thought; defense, liberation, and development of the national treasures; raising the standard of living; social justice and social insurance for every citizen; participation in the national services; war against illiteracy, disease, poverty, and corruption; encouragement of acts of loving-kindness; liberation of 'Wadi al-Nil – Egypt and Sudan' – the liberation of every Arab country and all parts of the Islamic homeland from foreign domination; aid to Islamic minorities everywhere; and establishment of a state with integrity that will function according to the laws and precepts of Islam, will protect Islam from within, will spread the preaching of Islam to all, and will cooperate in international endeavors.[18]

In 1946, the Muslim Brothers began to step up their political activity, organizing conferences against the government then headed by Muhammad Fahmi al-Nuqrashi Pasha and in support of the King. Meanwhile in Egypt, the problem of Palestine was gaining momentum. Claiming a jihad on behalf of Palestine, they managed to acquire many weapons, some openly from the army arsenals. They fought in the war of 1948 against the Jewish population at the side of the Egyptian and other Arab armies.[19] Simultaneously, they took action in Cairo against Jewish property and attacked several British army camps in which Egyptian citizens were also killed. The government arrested many and they were tried before Judge Ahmad al-Khazindar, who meted out harsh sentences. Eight months later, Khazindar was murdered by two Muslim Brothers. By the end of 1948, they had become very powerful and were a 'government within a government'.[20] Al-Nuqrashi Pasha's government which had returned to power a short time earlier set out to disband the

Muslim Brothers organization, but twenty days later he met his death by assassination by one of the Brothers. A new government was formed under Ibrahim 'Abd al-Hadi, who was particularly cruel. Less than two months later, the King began to comprehend the danger of the Muslim Brothers, and – in collaboration with the government and an undercover agent – he had Hasan al-Banna killed on 12 February 1949. The underground unit made an unsuccessful attempt to assassinate 'Abd al-Hadi.[21] A year later, the Wafd Party, which had begun to seek *rapprochement* with the Brothers, returned to power. Meanwhile, Hasan al-Hudaibi was elected head of the Brothers. Hudaibi began to renounce the use of force and violence, but the underground units opposed this. During the guerrilla war against the British in the Suez Canal in 1950–52, with the Wafd back in power, Hudaibi declared that the Muslim Brothers used spiritual power, and only the government used material power. This declaration, an attempt to offset British opposition to the movement, met with scorn and derision among the members of the underground. In al-Hudaibi's words, 'I am certain the west will become persuaded of the advantages of the Muslim Brothers and will cease describing them as terrifying ghosts, in the words of some.'[22]

Rapprochement talks had begun between the Wafd and the heads of the Muslim Brothers,[23] but the internal situation in Egypt was deteriorating. The worst came with the 'burning of Cairo' on 16 January 1952, which incensed the Egyptian populace and paved the way for the *coup d'état*, supported by the Muslim Brothers.[24]

The Free Officers had held secret talks with representatives of the Brothers to request support for the imminent revolt. Al-Hudaibi gave his blessing, and an alliance was forged between them. When the coup began on 23 July 1952, the Muslim Brothers used all means at their disposal to help the military junta. Sayyid Qutb (1906–66) who was then an ardent supporter of the Muslim Brothers, but not officially a member,[25] enthusiastically supported the coup. Qutb demanded freedom for all political prisoners who had been thrown into jail in Egypt, including the communists 'who were fighting tyranny like the other forces . . . we must address their claims one by one and not meet them with iron and fire'.[26] But this demand did not hold for more than three days. Riots broke out in the Kafr al-Dawwar factories and the Revolutionary Command Committee (RCC) accused the communists of having organized the riots. Sayyid Qutb supported the accusations of the military junta and, in a published article, he blamed the communists for the riots, cursing them and calling them 'filth'.[27]

On 10 December 1952, the RCC suspended the Egyptian constitution of 1923 and, soon after, the Party Law, in an attempt to eliminate the Wafd Party, while allowing for the legal operation of the Movement of Muslim Brothers. On 10 February 1953, the RCC issued a provisional three-year constitution, in which it consolidated its legal control over the state. The Muslim Brothers raised no objection. Their sole desire was to remain alone in the political ring so that they could dictate their terms to the RCC. Two representatives of the Brothers met with Nasir and requested that all proposed bills be presented to a committee of the Brothers for approval before final ratification. Nasir firmly refused.[28]

In late 1953 and early 1954, a rift developed inside the Muslim Brothers, primarily between Hasan al-Hudaibi and the head of the underground organization. At the same time, a rift appeared between Nasir, who led the coup, and Muhammad Naguib, president and – in the public mind – leader of the junta. The rift brought the Muslim Brothers closer to Muhammad Naguib. Naguib wished to restore democratic order to Egypt and to hold parliamentary elections. He writes in his memoirs that representatives from the Muslim Brothers contacted him with an offer that they form a united front headed by him. Naguib, however, told them that he wanted to end military rule, to return the army to its barracks, to restore party rule and the Parliament, and to abolish censorship of the press. The Muslim Brothers did not accept these terms; they wanted Muhammad Naguib to be sole ruler with a Revolutionary Command Committee, half of which would be composed of Muslim Brothers. Naguib rejected the terms because he believed that they would lead to the Muslim Brothers taking control over the state, without accepting the responsibilities. Hence talks broke down between them.[29]

While the Muslim Brothers were conducting talks with Muhammad Naguib, Egyptian intelligence learned that the Brothers had renewed their contacts with the British, which incensed the Nasir-controlled RCC, who decided on 14 January 1954 to apply the law abolishing political parties to the Muslim Brothers. A wide series of arrests ensued.[30]

Relations between the junta and the Muslim Brothers had reached an impasse, and the war against the ruling power pushed the Brothers to search for allies. This time the allies were none other than the communists, and the person who represented the Brothers in these contacts was Sayyid Qutb himself. Relations with the junta reached their lowest ebb with the famous attempt by the Brothers to assassinate Nasir during his speech in Alexandria on 26 October 1954, in which Nasir sought to justify his signature on the agreement with the British for their evacuation of the Suez Canal. The assassination attempt was made by Muhammad 'Abd al-Latif, a member of the underground, who managed to fire eight bullets, but missed. The event touched off waves of mass arrests of the Muslim Brothers, especially members of the underground. Among those arrested was Sayyid Qutb.[31] The Muslim Brothers vehemently denied that the would-be assassin came from their ranks.

We have mentioned Sayyid Qutb several times. Because of his importance in Islamic ideology from the early 1940s until his death and to this very day, we briefly set out below his life and the main points of his ideology.[32]

Sayyid Qutb was born in 1906 in the village of Musha[33] in the Asyut district in Upper Egypt (325 kilometers from Cairo) into a family of farmers with sizable land holdings, though not wealthy. His father was a village notable and twice married. He had an elder brother Muhammad and two younger sisters, Hamidah and Aminah. His father would host guests with great generosity, in the style of dignitaries, compelling him to mortgage his land, of which he was eventually dispossessed by creditors. As a boy, Qutb studied the Quran in the *quttab* [religious elementary school] of the village, and then later in elementary school there. At the age of 13 he went to Cairo to attend high school, and entered the teachers' seminary in 1925. In the period 1928–33, he studied at Dar al-'Ulum from where he graduated. Qutb worked for many years for the Egyptian Ministry of Education and taught in a variety of schools. In the 1930s and 1940s, he wrote essays and literary criticism in many Egyptian newspapers and journals. He wrote an autobiography *Tifl al-Qarya* ['village boy'] in which he copied Taha Husain's style in his book *Al-Ayyam*. In these years Qutb lived the life of a normal intellectual, and the motifs and style of his writing were like those of the Egyptian writers of that period – nationalist, liberal, and even secular. Sayyid Qutb was very impressed by the Biblical *Song of Songs* and he used love passages from it in his book *Al-Suwar wal-Zilal fi al-fann* ['pictures and shadows in art'].[34] In 1945, he published his first work showing clear evidence of his turn to Islam – *Al-Tasawwur al-fanni fi al-Quran* ['Artistic perception in the

Quran'] – in which he gave literary expression to his admiration for the style of the Quran. But the final adoption of Islam seems to have come during period of study in the United States in the years 1948–50, where he was sent by the Egyptian Ministry of Education. Qutb did not conceal his repugnance for Western culture. In a postcard to his friend 'Abbas Khadr, Qutb wrote, 'America is fit to be [the factory of the world] so that it will perform its job best, but if all the world were America, it would undoubtedly be the disaster of humanity'.[35] Qutb's first clearly Islamic book was published in 1949, *al-'Adala al-Ijtima'iyya fi al-Islam* ['social justice in Islam']. When he returned to Egypt from the United States, many leaders of the Muslim Brothers came to pay their respects, as they viewed him as a friend, and they discussed with him his book, which aroused great interest. Several Free Officers later confessed that this book had been one of the most influential they had read before the revolution.[36] From then on, Qutb was considered the main ideologue of the Muslim Brothers (even though he was not an official member of the movement). Dr Samir Amin writes, 'Sayyid Qutb was the ideologue of the Muslim Brothers, and the book was a kind of general theory which preceded the appearance of the *salafite* stream'.[37] Some concepts that recur frequently in this book are social justice, limiting property, the redistribution of wealth, and a minimum wage – all frequent in the writings of liberals, leftists, and communists. Qutb declared that European-American culture concentrated on manufacturing, and that this culture would die out before the end of the twentieth century. Before that, he contended, communism would dominate Western civilization, including the United States.[38] In his view, 'communism takes up more ideological space than the principles of the French Revolution in the western world', since 'communism is the natural end of a culture without spirit, ideals or vision'.[39] Qutb asserted with assurance that 'The leadership of humanity will be passed to Islam. If Islam had not existed, humanity would have had to search for it or to create a similar regime, in the wake of the disappearance of the two previous and conflicting trends'.[40] In June 1957, Sayyid Qutb was in Liman Tura Prison together with many members of the Muslim Brothers who had been picked up during the arrests following the attempt on Nasir's life in October 1954. There was a clash between the prisoners and the guards, resulting in the death or injury of dozens of the Muslim Brothers,[41] an event which had a great impact on his thinking.

Ma'alim fi al-Tariq ['Milestones'] is unquestionably the most important of Sayyid Qutb's books, and is considered a constitutional framework for Islamic groups whose goal is to take control of the government by any means, and turn it into a *Shari'a*-ruled Islamic state. The book is divided into twelve chapters and a preface, four of which had already appeared in his large, multi-volume *Fi Zilal al-Quran*['in the shadow of the Quran']. In the introduction, Qutb preached that:

> Humanity is on the brink of a chasm. Not because of the threat of annihilation hanging over its head[42] . . . as this is an early symptom, but because of the bankruptcy of its world of values. It is patently clear that the west does not have additional values to give to humanity. It cannot even persuade its conscience that it deserves to live, after its democracy appears to be bankrupt.[43]

The following passages capture the essence of the thought of Sayyid Qutb in *Ma'alim fi al-Tariq*:

> The world exists today in a state of *jahiliyya* [ignorance] of essential matters, originating in the main elements and systems of life. This *jahiliyya* is based on hostility to the rule of Allah on earth and on the most special attributes of divinity, which are the 'Kingdom of Heaven'. It [*jahiliyya*] attributes this Kingdom to human beings.[44]

> Today we are in a state of *jahiliyya* like the one that existed before Islam, or even worse. Everything surrounding us is *jahiliyya*. The perceptions of people and their art, their habits and traditions, the resources of their culture, art, and literature, their constitutions and their laws, even much of what we consider to be Islamic culture, Islamic sources, Islamic philosophy, and Islamic thought . . . even they are the product of this *jahiliyya*.[45]

> Our main task is to change the reality of this society. This reality is on a collision course with *manhaj* [the Islamic 'way'] and, in the Islamic view, prevents us by coercion and pressure from living according to how the *manhaj* wishes us to live.[46]

> The path is not to liberate God's creatures from a Greek or a Persian *Tagouth* [Satan] for an Arab tyrant. Every cruel tyrant is a tyrant! People should be worshippers of Allah alone. And they cannot be worshippers of Him alone unless they carry high the flag 'There is no God but Allah'.[47]

> The way of Islam is equal to 'truth' and there is no separation between them. No foreign *manhaj*[48] can ultimately realize Islam.[49]

> He who understands the nature of this religion [Islam] will understand the need for the activist push of Islam as a jihad of the sword alongside

a jihad of education. He will also understand that it is not a defensive movement in the limited sense of 'a defensive war' as the defeatists would have it, but a movement of pushing and breakthroughs for liberation of the individual on earth.[50]

If Abu-Bakr, 'Umar and 'Uthman had been protected against the aggression of the Greeks and the Persians on the Arab peninsula, would they have abandoned the dissemination of Islam to all corners of the globe?[51]

Those who seek clearly defensive reasons for the growing movement of Islam have been beguiled by the offensive Orientalist movement at a time when the Muslims no longer had power. On the contrary, there is no more Islam for Muslims. The spread of Islam has no need of moral excuses beyond those borne by the texts of the Quran.[52]

Islam has the right to forge ahead. Because Islam is not a nationalist offshoot or the government of a homeland. But it is the *manhaj* of Allah and his worldly regime. It is the right of Islam to free its 'creations' from enslavement to slaves to the worship of Allah alone. One constitution will apply to all in complete equality.[53]

Wherever there is an Islamic gathering in which the Divine way is revealed, Allah gives it the right to move and forge ahead to assume power and to determine the regime.[54]

But what is the '*jahiliyya* society'? And what is the Islamic way of *manhaj* in grappling with it? The '*jahiliyya* society' is all societies except the Muslim society. In this objective definition, all societies on earth belong to the category of the '*jahiliyya* society'. Jewish and the Christian societies everywhere belong to it. Finally, the category of '*jahiliyya* society' includes all societies who have pretensions of being 'Muslim'![55]

This brings us to the last problem which is the way that Islam grapples with the entire human reality . . . today, tomorrow, until the end of time. As Islam gives a definitive answer to this question without prattle and without a moment's hesitation. Because the testimony that there is no God besides Allah and that Muhammad is the Messenger of Allah is the fundamental foundation of Islam. [Religion] will not arise and will not be fulfilled until this is the foundation.[56]

A society of Islamic culture does not despise materialism in theory (because the universe in which we live is composed of it, influenced by it, and also has an influence on it) and not in the form of 'material creation'. Material creation is one foundation of the inheritance of the earth from Allah, but He does not consider it a supreme value for which the freedom of the individual and his honor should be neglected.[57]

The philosophy of Sayyid Qutb in *Ma'alim fi al-Tariq* can be summarized as follows:

1. Two conceptions are in absolute opposition: Islam and *jahiliyya*, faith and apostasy, the rule of the Kingdom of Heaven and the rule of man, God and Satan. There can be no compromise between them, other than elimination of one, and clearly *jahiliyya* should be eliminated so that the true Islam will prevail in the world.
2. The entire world is one of *jahiliyya* and apostasy, including the Islamic states and their current regimes.
3. Only Islam is the religion of truth. All other religions – philosophies, theories, and ideologies – are futile and misguided.
4. Because faith must be implemented daily in word and deed, one should believe that 'there is no God but Allah and Muhammad is the Messenger of Allah'. This credo is what guarantees the rule of the Kingdom of Heaven on which will be founded the Islamic state.
5. Change will come about by action [*harakah*], a turning-point and fundamental revolution.
6. The revolution will ensue through the faith of someone from outside current society. Many will join forces with him until the new Islamic society has the power to rule on earth.
7. This change is an act of liberating the individual from enslavement to another person. It is an obligation upon every believing and true Muslim. This change will be carried out only by a chosen group which believes with all its heart and soul in the Islam which has come from Allah.
8. The jihad is not as interpreted by Orientalists and their disciples. The jihad is an ongoing precept to liberate the entire world so that only Islam will prevail.
9. Jews and Christians are infidels and none of their interpretations or studies of Islam should be used.
10. One can use their studies in the pure sciences if they are not available from believing Muslims, but in this field only.
11. Islam does not despise materiality, which is part of the universe in which we live, and theories and training for development should not be rejected out of a true belief in Islam.

The later writings of Sayyid Qutb were significantly influenced by the writings of Abu al-A'la al-Mawdudi from Pakistan who was apparently the first to raise the concept of 'the new *jahiliyya*'.[58] Al-Mawdudi was a leader of the Muslim movement in India which demanded independence from Britain. He refused to join the national Indian movement, and demanded a pure Islamic state that would rise on foundations like those of Islam in the days of the Prophet Muhammad and his companions. His preaching was published in the 1940s in a Pakistani journal called *Turjaman al-Quran* which was actually an organ of the Muslim Brothers in Karachi. Islam in India under al-Mawdudi was an irredentist Islam from the (infidel) Indian society. His philosophy is based on the following tenets:

1. All human society is a kind of *jahiliyya*.
2. *Jahiliyya* should be fought by jihad so that Islamic rule can prevail.
3. At first, Islamic society is weak and must gather strength in order to move toward the goal of establishing an Islamic state. This first period will be called the period of *istid'af* [powerlessness] and is similar to the period of Muhammad in Mecca.
4. After it gathers strength, Islamic society can embark upon a jihad, just as Muhammad gathered strength in Medina after his migration from Mecca.

Abu al-A'la al-Mawdudi presents four principles in his book, *The Four Concepts*:

(a) The rule of God versus the rule of man.
(b) The divinity of God versus the divinity of man.
(c) The sovereignty of God versus subjugation to another.
(d) The uniqueness of God versus reliance on human philosophy to organize society.

Al-Mawdudi's concept of *'hakimiyyat Allah* – the rule of the Kingdom of Heaven' and the *jahiliyya* of society in general is a revolutionary concept which means that all human society is comprised of infidels and therefore it is permissible and even obligatory to do battle with it and to forcibly take power and all that entails. There is no obligation of obedience except to the *imam*.[59]

Sayyid Qutb's health was poor, and yet he continued to write from prison and from the hospital ward of Liman Tura Prison. He took advantage of his extended stay in this and other prison hospitals (about ten years) to expound his ideas and to organize the Muslim Brothers, many of whom were in prison during the Nasir regime, and he would engage them in ideological discussions. Meanwhile, factions of the Brothers had begun to reorganize their ranks and store weapons of all sorts to prepare for the moment that they could take their revenge for the wave of arrests in 1954 and the torture in 1957, to assassinate Nasir and take power. The reorganization took place in the utmost secrecy. In 1962, Hasan al-Hudaibi, the 'general guide', was released from prison because of his poor health. And in 1964, Sayyid Qutb was released for the same reason at the intervention of the President of Iraq at the time, 'Abd al-Salam Muhammad 'Arif. Upon his release, Qutb was asked by the leaders of the Brothers to accept command, but he refused, though he continued to work on behalf of the organization. One year after his release, the Egyptian authorities discovered the Brothers' plot, and again carried out widespread arrests, capturing most of the weapons in their possession. Sayyid Qutb was caught, sentenced to death in late 1965 and executed with another group of Muslim Brothers in early 1966.

NOTES

1. 'Abd al-'Azim Ramadan, *Al-Ikhwan al-Muslimun wal-Tanzim al-Sirri* [The Muslim Brothers and the underground movement] (1977), p. 25.
2. In a footnote, Mitchell (1977) says that the group was founded in the month of Zu al-Qa'da 1347 H, which is equivalent to April–May 1929, but the date accepted by most scholars is March 1928.
3. Leonard Binder, *Islamic Liberalism* (Chicago, London, 1988), p. 271.
4. Ramadan, p. 27.
5. Ibid.
6. Hasan al-Banna, *Mudhakkarat al-Da'awa wal-Da'iya* [Memoirs of the preaching and the preacher] (Cairo, Dar al-Shahab, 2nd edition, 1966), p. 145.
7. Ibid.
8. Hasan al-Banna, *Risalat al-Mutamar al-Khamis* [Letter to the Fifth Conference] (Dar al-I'tisam, 1977). The quotation is from Ramadan, p. 28.
9. *Journal of the Muslim Brothers*, 8 Thu al-Qa'da 1352 H.
10. Ramadan, p. 29.
11. Ibid.
12. Ibid., p. 38.
13. Ibid., pp. 38–52. In this context, see also Muhammad Shawqi Zaki, *The Muslim Brothers and Egyptian Society* (Cairo, 1954).
14. Ramadan, p. 43.
15. Ibid., p. 44.
16. Ibid., p. 47.
17. Ibid., pp. 48–50, based upon the court testimony of 'Abdul Majid Hasan who assassinated Egyptian Prime Minister al-Nuqrashi Pasha.
18. Ibid., pp. 112–13.
19. See a comprehensive description in Kamal al-Sherif, *Al-Ikhwan al-Muslimin fi Harb Falastine* [The Muslim Brothers in the Palestine War] (Jordan, Maktabat al-Manar, 1984).
20. Liwaa Hasan Sadiq, *Judhur al-fitna al-Taifiyya fi al-firaq al-Islamiyya* [The roots of strife between Islamic sects] (Cairo, 1977), p. 278.
21. Ramadan, p. 85.

22. Ibid., p. 116.
23. Sadiq, p. 279.
24. 'Abd al-'Azim Ramadan notes that the cooperation actually began when Jamal 'Abd al-Nasir contacted Abu Ruqayyiq Adil, one of the leaders of the Muslim Brothers, and told him that the police were about to search the officers' rooms in the camps where quantities of weapons for the *coup d'état* were concealed. Nasir asked the Brothers to help transfer the weapons to their homes. Hence, while the fire was raging, these weapons were being smuggled through the streets of Cairo. Ramadan, p. 100.
25. Adil Hamuda, *Sayyid Qutb min al-Qaria ila al-Mishnaqa* [Sayyid Qutb from the village to the scaffold] (Cairo, 1987), p. 101 (hereinafter, *From the Village to the Scaffold*). Hamuda notes that Sayyid Qutb says in his book, *Why I Was Executed*, that he was not a member of any party or movement and was therefore able to publish two books and hundreds of articles in all the newspapers of Egypt; Qutb himself claims to have officially joined the Muslim Brothers in 1953.
26. Ibid., p. 113.
27. Ibid.
28. Ramadan, pp. 114–15.
29. Ibid., p. 129, based on the memoirs of Muhammad Naguib, *Kalimati lil-Tarikh* [My words to history] (Cairo, 1975), pp. 211–13. 'Abd al-'Azim Ramadan supports Neguib's version of events and asserts that it is the only one, of several accounts published, that is correct.
30. Ibid., p. 130. In *From the Village to the Scaffold*, p. 113, Hamuda notes that: 'Sayyid Qutb requested freedom for the Brothers by virtue of their being *shurfaa* [noble] and he demanded violence toward others by virtue of their being filth; and he [Qutb] believed that the fire of democracy would merely warm them, while it would burn their enemies . . . He never imagined that the flames would reach them as well, but he was proven wrong and they also reached them.'
31. Ramadan, pp. 9–21. Hamuda, pp. 119–22.
32. This summary is based on many sources, in particular: Hamuda; Sadiq; Emmanuel Sivan, *Radical Islam* (Am Oved, 1986), pp. 32–40; Dr 'Ali [Iraq] al-Kuraishi, '*Mafhum al-Hadara Baina Malik Bin Nabi wa-Sayyid Qutb*' [The concept of civilization in Malik bin Nabi and Sayyid Qutb] *Al-Hilal*, Sept. 1987, pp. 10–125; Sylvia G. Haim, 'Sayyid Qutb', *Asian and African Studies*, Vol. 16, March 1982, pp. 147–57; William E. Shepard, 'Islam as a "System" in the Later Writings of Sayyid Qutb', *Middle Eastern Studies*, Jan. 1989; Binder; Gilles Kepel, *The Prophet and Pharoah* (London, 1985) (trans. from the French). Also see the writings of Sayyid Qutb, especially *Ma'alim fi al-Tariq* [Milestones] (hereinafter, *Ma'alim*); and his preface to the book *Fi Zilal al-Quran* [in the shadow of the Quran], (6th edition, undated, but published 1951–52), Vol. 1, pp. 5–14.
33. William Shepard contends that he was born in the village of Qaha. I tend to accept Adil Hamuda's version, who claims that he visited the village where Sayyid Qutb was born.
34. Hamuda, p. 57.
35. Hanuda, p. 87.
36. Dr Tahir Makki, 'Sayyid Qutb and Three Unpublished Letters', *Al-Hilal*, Oct. 1986, pp. 120–30.
37. Dr Samir Amin, *Azmat al-Mujtama' al-'Arabi* [The crisis of Arab society] (1985), pp. 92–3.
38. Sayyid Qutb, *al-Adala al-Ijtima'iyya fi al-Islam* [Social justice in Islam] (Dar al-Qitab al-Arabi, 1949), pp. 46–61. Recently we have witnessed the incorrectness of his theory with the collapse of the communist regimes and their growing need of the West.
39. Sayyid Qutb, *Nahwa Mujtama'a Islami* [Toward an Islamic society] (Dar al-Shuruq, 8th edition, 1982), pp. 20–33.
40. In his book *Ma'alim*, Qutb notes: 'The social theories led by Marxism which initially attracted large numbers in the east and even the west as a school of thought with the

character of a religion clearly retreated in their ideology in that they limit themselves to just a "state and its systems"', pp. 5–8.

41. According to Sayyid Qutb, the incident was staged by Nasir's people. For the government's version as well as that of Qutb, see Hamuda, pp. 129–32.
42. The reference is to the threat of atomic war.
43. *Ma'alim*, p. 5.
44. Ibid., p. 20.
45. Ibid., p. 21.
46. Ibid., p. 22.
47. Ibid., pp. 28–9.
48. Shepard translates the word *manhaj* as 'system'. I prefer to translate it as 'way', although not every use of 'way' refers to *manhaj*.
49. Ibid., p. 51.
50. Ibid., p. 72.
51. Ibid., p. 73.
52. Ibid., pp. 81–2.
53. Ibid., p. 89.
54. Ibid., p. 91.
55. Ibid., pp. 98–101.
56. Ibid., pp. 103–4.
57. Ibid., p. 121.
58. Sivan shows the clear influence of al-Mawdudi on Qutb through the translations of Abu al-Hasan al-Nadawi, p. 35.
59. Muhammad Hasanain Haikal, *Autumn of the Anger*, pp. 284–90; Hamuda, pp. 134–9; Sivan, pp. 33–4, 62–3, 47–9; Kepel, pp. 47–9, 62–3; Binder; Vatikiotis; Abu al-A'la al-Mawdudi, *al-Qanun al-Islami wa-Turuq tanfidhuhu* [Islamic law and its way of implementation] (Cairo, undated, and apparently translated by Muhammad 'Asim al-Haddad); Dr Muhammad 'Amara, '*Al-Mawdudi Baina al-Taqlid wal-Intilaq, Limadha Hazarat al-Jami'ah Qira'at Kutub al-Mawdudi*' [Al-Mawdudi between imitation and action: why did the university ban the reading of al-Mawdudi?], *Al-Hilal*, March 1987, pp. 38–47; Dr Muhammad 'Amara, '*Al-Islaman wal-Thawra*' [The two Islams and the revolution], *Al-Hilal*, May 1987.

3 From Sayyid Qutb to Militant Islamic Organizations

Although Hasan al-Hudaibi, Sayyid Qutb and thousands of other Muslim Brothers were thrown into prison during the regime of 'Abd al-Nasir, many Islamic preachers read the writings of Qutb and of al-Mawdudi and were greatly influenced by their ideas concerning the *tajhil* [accusations of ignorance] of Muslim society. Among them was 'Ali 'Abduh Isma'il, a young Egyptian graduate of al-Azhar, who founded the organization called *Jama'at al-Muslmin* [Muslim society] while serving time in the famous Liman Tura prison. This was the first religious organization in the spirit of Qutb's ideology whose members did not simply preach it but began to isolate themselves from society, becoming reclusive while still actually in prison. (The ideology of Sayyid Qutb had not at this time progressed beyond the stage of preaching.) Through their reclusiveness they aimed to create the nucleus of a new Islamic society which would become strong and then declare a jihad, in accordance with the preaching of Qutb. Most veteran members of the Brothers who were in prison and many of the younger members rejected the preaching of Isma'il, whereupon he declared them to be part of the society of infidels. This accusation was taken up by other splinter groups, and there was a growth of animosity between them, with charges and countercharges of infidelity often ending in fights and brawls.[1]

In the same period, a young man named Shukri Ahmad Mustafa was imprisoned on the charge of membership in the Muslim Brothers. Mustafa, born in 1942, was from the village of Abu Haras in the Asyut district. Abu Haras is located near the range of mountains extending from Minya to Sohaj, on the west bank of the Nile. Caves and clefts riddle the hillsides and are inhabited by outlaws called *matarid* [fugitives].[2] Mustafa's father was an *'umda* [village head] and his mother was his father's second wife. Mustafa's parents divorced when he was two years old, and his mother took him to live with her wealthy family. However, unlike the children of the wealthy who were educated in private foreign schools, Mustafa attended the school of the Islamic charitable society where the children of the poor studied. His grades in secondary school were not good, so he continued his studies in the field of agronomy, not then regarded as a faculty of importance, at Asyut University. While there, Mustafa was arrested for distributing Muslim Brothers leaflets. This was part of a new wave of arrests by presidential order. In prison, Mustafa joined the *Jama'at al-Muslmin* and became an ardent supporter of Isma'il and his organization.

In prison, the moderate older members of the Muslim Brothers, including al-Hudaibi, tried in vain to convince the young Isma'il and his comrades that their views were too extreme. In response to the rising extremism, al-Hudaibi wrote his famous book, *Du'at la Qudat* [Preachers not judges].[3] Following his release from prison in 1969, Al-Hudaibi tried a new tactic in an attempt to persuade Isma'il to change his approach: speaking to him alone and at length. With the exception of Mustafa, Isma'il and his comrades responded to the appeal. Over time, Mustafa became the *Amir* of a group of Muslims who eventually became known as *Jama'at al-Takfir wal-Hijra* [the group for accusations of ignorance and for *hijra*]. In 1967, Mustafa was transferred to the Abu Za'bal prison and put into solitary confinement until 16 October 1971, when he was released with the rise to power of Sadat and the change in policy toward the Muslim Brothers and other religious groups.[4]

Much has been written – both scholarly works and books for the general reader, including novels – about the extent of the tragedy and disappointment that followed the defeat of Egypt in the June 1967 war with Israel. The defeat revealed the speciousness of the Nasir regime and the illusions on which the Egyptian people had been fed in his attempt to realize his aspirations. Nasir was unable to explain the defeat rationally, and resorted to the mystification of events through religious revival.[5] He attempted to restore the legitimacy of his rule by declaring a war of attrition on Israel and promising social reforms, but he did not succeed in either.

After Nasir's death in September 1970, Sadat was officially appointed president on 15 October 1970, and he inherited a particularly heavy burden. The first crisis he encountered was the suppression of the revolt of 15 May 1971, and elimination of the power centers of the Nasirists and their communist supporters. He arrested many and simultaneously sought other partners to widen his base of legitimacy. He tried to cultivate the support of the Students' Association, which had begun to gather power during Nasir's rule following the demonstrations of February 1968. From 1972, various Islamic streams began to dominate them. Sadat also cultivated support from the religious camp by giving a freer hand to the student organizations at the universities, and by releasing from jail thousands of members of the Muslim Brothers and other Islamic streams. After the October War, the alliance with the religious group was strengthened through the intercession of a friend of Sadat, Muhammad 'Uthman Isma'il, who had been persecuted by Nasir and forced to emigrate to Saudi Arabia. 'Uthman Isma'il returned to Egypt very affluent. Through 'Uthman Isma'il, Saudi Arabia strengthened its ties with Egypt, and gave generous support to Islamic groups and institutions such as al-Azhar. The circulation of *Turath* [heritage] literature became massive, and the Islamic press such as *al-Da'awa* and *al-I'tisam*, which had been outlawed during Nasir's rule was revived, most without license (a situation to which the authorities turned a blind eye).

Sadat's alliance with the religious camp did not prevent Islamic extremists from waging battle with the Sadat regime. One such organization was the *Jama'at al-Muslmin*, whose leader, Shukri Mustafa, had been released by Sadat in 1971. Mustafa returned to intense organizational activity while completing his studies in the agronomy faculty in Asyut. He wrote a 206-page book, *Kitab al-Khilafa* [The book of the caliphate] in which he outlined his thinking,[6] based primarily on the works of Sayyid Qutb, especially *Ma'alim*, with some extremist additions. This philosophy had two main axes: ideology and *haraki* [action].

The principles of the ideology are as follows:

1. *The approach of Islam* – Islam has become alienated. Existing societies will fall. Islam will undergo a renaissance brought about by an elite which believes in leaping from the hills of Yemen brandishing the sword, based on the Hadith, 'Stories from the End of Days'.
2. *The* hijra – The need to abandon existing society in order to begin forming the nucleus of the hoped-for Islamic society through *hijra* to the mountains and the caves.
3. *The concept of stopping and studying* – Refusing to accept that simply by fulfilling the five elements of Islam a person may become a complete Muslim. This is an obligation to distance

oneself from acts forbidden by commandment, otherwise every Muslim will be considered an infidel.

4. *The only sources for the laws and the commandments* are the Quran and the Hadith.

The principles of the action are:

1. *Creating the organizational structure of the group*, the election of Shukri Mustafa as *Amir* (head of the faithful). Thereafter *amirs* were chosen for each region under Mustafa, the chief *amir*.
2. Rental of flats to be used as the *local underground headquarters* in Cairo, Alexandria, and other districts.
3. *Migration* of the group to the caves and clefts of the mountain region in order to implement the ideology.
4. *Recruitment* of as many military men as possible for use in operations and for training members of the organization to use weapons. These military men were to seize the weapons in their military units.

Another source of information about the thinking of Shukri Mustafa was his second work, *Tawassumat* [revelations, distinctions]. This booklet was not printed, but passed around to his followers in Mustafa's handwriting 'so it would not be made impure by the machines of the infidels'. At the beginning of the book, Mustafa describes himself as 'head of the rulers of the faithful, the chosen *Taha*, Shukri Mustafa, *Amir* of the End of Days and inheritor of the land and its inhabitants'. He notes that the great tension between the large blocs in the world will cause a nuclear war and the destruction of the world. But this will not hurt the *Jama'at al-Muslmin*, who are hiding in the caves and the mountains, and thus they will inherit the earth and its inhabitants, and will found the Islamic state and will restore the use of the sword because modern weapons will no longer exist. Mustafa does not, of course, explain how 'the Muslim group' will survive a nuclear war. He explains that:

> The only way to establish an Islamic state is according to the precepts of the Prophet of Islam. Thus, there is no way to avoid the *hijra*, because the death of the infidels and the defeat of their state cannot take place while the faithful still live among them. *Al-Sunna* [the tradition] is that the Muslims will leave the land of the infidels. Only the infidels will remain, and only then will suffering come upon them.

In his book, Mustafa defines the true Muslim as one whose Islam was formed during the period of the Messenger, one who avows that he does not believe in *Tagouth* [Satan], but believes in Allah, in his full perfection alone, witnessing the Prophecy of Muhammad, accepting obedience to Him, carrying out the commandments of God and continuing in His path, and keeping distant from vice. None of these characteristics can exist in reality other than through the *Jama'at al-Muslmin*. All others are infidels.[7] Mustafa expounded his ideas at impassioned length in a military court on 6–7 November 1977. When asked what is the solution to the problems of Islam, his response was that he is the solution. He is the redeemer because the gate of *al-ijtihad* [religious judgment] is closed and *jahiliyya* [ignorance] has been forced on the world, until his coming. Allah has chosen him, has led him in the correct path so that he will reopen wide the gate of *al-ijtihad* and will interpret the Quran as he understands it. The court asked him what would be the position of his group if Jewish forces attacked Egypt, and he replied, 'If Jewish or any forces attack, our group will not fight in the ranks of the Egyptian army. It will flee to safe places for shelter. Our position is to flee from both the internal and the external enemy. We do not oppose it.'[8]

To implement his plans, Mustafa and his companions indeed sought refuge in the mountains in the al-Minya region in September 1973. They equipped themselves with weapons and food supplies, but were caught at the end of October that year and released after the October War with Israel toward the end of April 1974. Mustafa and his companions returned to the underground and even expanded their activity. They decided to draw attention to themselves by kidnapping a public figure. In June 1977, Mustafa and his senior comrades planned to take hostage a senior government official in exchange for the release of their comrades in prison, wide circulation of the ideology of the organization, and other demands. They chose for their victim Dr Shaikh Muhammad Hasan al-Dahabi, former minister of the Waqf, because he had once attacked their organization, calling it misguided and wayward, and thus was an infidel in their eyes. On 3 July, they kidnapped him, publicized their demands, and issued an ultimatum that if their demands were not met within 24 hours, they would kill al-Dahabi. The demands were not fully met, and they indeed killed him. Security forces were brought in and, by the end of July, most of the group had been captured. Mustafa and another four were condemned to death, many were sentenced to various prison terms, and several dozen were released. This incident had a profound impact throughout Egypt and the world. Serious attention was given to the gravity of the activities of the extremist Islamic groups. Saad Eddin Ibrahim writes that this organization had 3,000–5,000 active and well-trained members who were spread throughout Egyptian society. But the Egyptian government, instead of seizing the bull by the horns, accused Moscow and its liberal supporters of encouraging extremist Islamic groups to revolt and undermine the government. At a later stage, even the renewed Wafd Party was accused of assisting these groups.[9] In another article, Saad Eddin Ibrahim claims that Mustafa's organization was forced into this struggle, as the Egyptian authorities had arrested some members of the group and detained them for a long period. When their demand to be put on trial or released was not met, the organization was 'forced' to take a drastic step even though their original strategy was not to engage the regime at this stage, but only after they had gained strength in the mountain refuges, just as Muhammad had gathered strength for ten years in Medina before he attacked the society of infidels in Mecca.[10]

Three years before Mustafa's organization, *al-Takfir wal-Hijra*, was exposed, another militant Islamic organization, the Islamic Liberation Party led by Dr Salih 'Abdullah Siriyya – also known as *Shabab Muhammad* [Muhammad's youths] – was exposed. This came about as a result of the abortive attempt by the organization to take over the building of the Technical College near Cairo in April 1974, six months after the October War, when Sadat was riding the crest of the 'victory of 6 October'. Salih Siriyya was born in 1937 in Haifa, the same city in which Taqi al-Din al-Nabhani was born and lived until the Israeli War for Independence in 1948, when he moved to Jordan and founded the Islamic Liberation Party, apparently in 1950.[11] Siriyya, however, had migrated to Iraq, where he became part of the Muslim Brothers and an officer in the Palestine Liberation Army set up by 'Abd al-Karim Qasim, then president of Iraq. In 1968, Siriyya was elected to the Palestinian National Council. He was forced to flee Iraq in 1971 under suspicion of plotting against the President of Iraq at that time, Ahmad Hasan al-Bakr. Siriyya moved to Egypt, where he attended 'Ayn Shams University, earning his doctorate based on a study of Arab education in Israel, and was appointed lecturer at that university. Although Siriyya made contact with the former leaders of the Muslim Brothers in Egypt, he was rejected by them.[12] He decided to form his own organization, and in 1973 he began to recruit members from among his students at 'Ayn Shams University, as well as students in Alexandria and other universities. He recruited about 100 members, including several students from the Technical Military College.[13] The point of occupying the College was to seize the weapons there and to use them to gain control of key government facilities in Cairo and Alexandria, to capture or kill the President, take power, and declare the establishment of an Islamic state. On 17 April 1974, the action began. Members of Siriyya's organization grappled with those who resisted them at the College. They might have succeeded, at least to begin with, had not one member of the group who at the last minute balked at the enormity of the deed, informed the authorities. Siriyya, confident of initial success, had prepared *bayan raqm wahid* [proclamation number one] to be broadcast over radio and television from the hall of the Coordinating Committee of the ruling party in Alexandria, where President Sadat and top government officials were gathered to address a student conference. Siriyya was planning to announce a curfew and his own appointment as *Amir* of Egypt.[14] The contents of 'proclamation number one' give a clear idea of the objectives of the organization:

On this day, we have been successful, praise God, in taking power and arresting all those responsible for the previous regime and we are about to embark upon a new era. We shall not lavish promises, however, we declare that the new government shall be founded upon the following principles:

(a) The principles of state shall rest upon new foundations which are not ambiguous or self-contradictory.
(b) The revolution shall not be limited to political or military directions. It shall include all parts of economic, cultural, and social life and others.
(c) The state shall be concerned in particular with faith, morality, and virtue.
(d) In its political activities, the state shall be concerned first and foremost with the interest of the nation, and thereafter with covenants and agreements.
(e) The state shall work to liberate all territories stolen from the homeland and to assist the downtrodden and the exploited in each and every place, and shall oppose imperialism in all forms in the world.
(f) The state shall apply all its power to bringing about unity, without regard to verbal attacks, and shall apply all its might to fostering development for raising the standard of living of the residents.

(g) Society shall be free to say whatever it wishes and to criticize the systems of state, with the exception of lies, falsehoods, and libelous statements.

(h) We shall rewrite all the principles [and replace] individuals and positions.

(i) The state shall defend all the principles of justice known to everyone as part of our heritage.

And success is from Allah.

Signed: President of the Islamic Republic.[15]

Salih Siriyya and his comrades did not leave behind any documents or writings from which one could gain a deeper understanding of their views, as the organization was based on absolute secrecy. However in the 1980s, a book written by Siriyya himself came to light. It has 61 small pages and was printed by the Student Association of the Dar al-'Ulum Seminary at Cairo University in 1976–77. The book did not bear the name of Salih Siriyya, perhaps for reasons of caution.[16] The scholar Rif'at Sayyid Ahmad summarizes the ideological-political content of the book as follows:

1. Jihad is the only way to establish the Islamic state.

2. It is not permissible to extend support to infidels or their regimes. One who extends support is himself an infidel.

3. Anyone who dies defending a government of infidels against those attempting to establish an Islamic state is an infidel, unless he was compelled to do so.

4. Anyone participating in an ideological party that is not Islamic is an infidel, as is anyone participating in an international association such as the Freemasons or anyone espousing a different philosophy such as existentialism or pragmatism.

5. The rulers and the *jahiliyya* society are infidels, and should be treated like *dar harb* [enemy territory].

6. It is permissible to participate in political parties, elections to parliament and the cabinet, only if the individual seeks power in order to revolutionize the state to an Islamic state.

7. It is permissible for a Muslim to interfere in the authority of the state by order of an Islamic group and to take advantage of his position to help the group attain power or to extend assistance to it.

8. Anyone who carries out the orders of an infidel state against Islam or the Islamic movement is an infidel.

9. In an election between an Islamic candidate and a socialist, nationalist or Communist candidate, if an individual votes for

the non-Islamic candidate, he is an infidel by virtue of this position.

10. He who fights the preachers of Islam because they combine religion and state is an infidel because he relegates Islam to one aspect and is an infidel in the other aspects.

11. Those who accuse religion of being backward and reactionary are infidels, as are all those who oppose any part of Allah's laws.

12. All laws of the state which oppose Islam are laws of the infidel. Anyone who prepared them or participated in their preparation or turned them into binding legislation is an infidel.

13. Saluting a flag, an unknown soldier, or singing the anthem are ceremonies of *jahiliyya*.[17]

After the members of the organization were arrested, they were tried. Siriyya and the commander of the action at the Military College were both condemned to death and executed. This appeared to bring to an end, at least for the time being, Salih Siriyya's organization of *Shabab Muhammad* or the Islamic Liberation Party. But religious extremism and agitation by young Muslims on behalf of an Islamic state did not come to an end, and indeed continued even more vigorously. For all the extremism and harshness expressed by Sayyid Qutb against existing Islamic governments and the regime of infidels, he preached first and foremost the development of a deep religious faith and only thereafter an attack on these governments. But neither Salih Siriyya nor Shukri Mustafa wanted to delay attainment of their goals, and took up arms against the government before they had fully organized their ranks. In his book *Autumn of the Anger*, Muhammad Husanain Haikal notes:

> There is not the slightest doubt that [Siriyya's] attempt did not stand a chance, and was indeed quickly defeated. Some of the members were killed, Salih Siriyya and some of his comrades were tried, some were executed, and the matter was quickly forgotten. The responsibility for the entire matter was laid upon an unknown party, the Islamic Liberation Party. No one paused for a moment to examine the dimensions of the event.[18]

As a result, under the very nose of the government, there was a proliferation of competing Islamic organizations which aspired to bring down the 'corrupt' regime of Sadat, to introduce Islamic rule through jihad and to return to the caliphate as the integral principle of the Islamic state. For every Islamic organization exposed and eliminated by the government, several sprouted in its place. But unquestionably the most widespread and dangerous group that appeared in the late 1970s and early 1980s was the Jihad Organization, one of whose members, Khalid al-Islambuli, a lieutenant in the artillery, assassinated Sadat on 6 October 1981.

The name 'Jihad Organization' refers to three militant Jihad groups which formed a coalition several months before the assassination of Sadat: the group organized by the engineer Muhammad 'Abd al-Salam Faraj who became head of the coalition; the group which formed around Muhammad Salim al-Rahhal, a Jordanian student at al-Azhar who was expelled from Egypt and passed the leadership to Kamal Sa'id Habib, a graduate in economics; and the group organized by Karam Muhammad Zuhdi, a student in the Institute of Cooperative Studies in Asyut.[19] The final unification of the three factions of Jihad was carried out in June 1981.[20] It is necessary at this point to set out briefly the background and development of these three groups.

Muhammad 'Abd al-Salam Faraj was born in the al-Bhira district in 1952. His father was a member of the radical wing of the Muslim Brothers movement. Faraj graduated from the College of Engineering of the University of Cairo, and worked in Alexandria. In 1978, he found out about the local Jihad Organization headed by Ibrahim Salama, who recruited him. When the security services discovered this organization, Faraj immediately cut off ties with Salama and moved to Cairo where he began setting up a Jihad organization of his own. While working in an administrative capacity at the University of Cairo, Faraj befriended young students there, recruiting many for the movement. In the summer of 1980, he finished consolidating the organization and published his book *Al-Farida al-Ghaiba* [the missing commandment].[21] That year he also visited the mosques near his home where he recruited young people aged 20–30, believing that individuals in this age group are pure of heart and strong of faith. A young man drafted into the organization would immediately begin his ideological education and military training. Faraj demanded of recruits courage and absolute secrecy; only then would they be introduced to the other members of the group.[22] Faraj met Tariq al-Zumur, of Egyptian military intelligence, who eventually became his right-hand man.

Karam Muhammad Zuhdi was born in 1954. In 1980 when Faraj approached him, Zuhdi was the *Amir* of one of the Islamic groups in the city al-Minya. Zuhdi had been a student at the High Institute of Cooperation in Asyut, but he fled from the security services after the clash between the Muslims and the Copts, and hid on the campus of the University of Cairo. Zuhdi agreed to have his group join Faraj's organization.

Muhammad Salim al-Rahhal, a Jordanian student at the University of Al-Azhar, belonged to the Syrian faction of the Islamic Liberation Party. Al-Rahhal, like Faraj, wished to create an organization that would establish an Islamic state, but al-Rahhal advocated the method of military revolution. In 1979, the same year that Faraj began but quite independently, al-Rahhal began to establish his organization. He prepared the structure, and developed a platform and a strategy. He recruited Kamal Sa'id Habib, a graduate of the School for Economics, as well as other students, graduates and others. In July 1981, al-Rahhal was expelled from Egypt by the security forces, and passed the mantle of leadership to Kamal Habib. Several days later, together with his group called *Al-Ahram* [the pyramids], Habib joined Faraj's organization through his friend Tariq al-Zumur.[23]

These three groups united to form the Jihad Organization based on the ideology of Faraj, as expressed in *al-Farida al-Ghaiba*.

In *al-Farida al-Ghaiba*, 'Abd al-Salam Faraj advocated an Islamic state headed by the institution of the caliphate as an alternative to the Egyptian regime. Such a state cannot materialize except by jihad, which is the missing commandment today.

The jihad is the ultimate work of creation in Islam, as expressed by the Prophet Muhammad, 'The best jihad is a word of truth or justice before a tyrannical ruler'. Those who seek to evade the jihad out of fear of defeat sin twice: firstly, by forsaking Allah's commandment to establish an Islamic state, as commanded to every Muslim, regardless of the outcome; and secondly, by not acknowledging that Islam is attractive to the masses. To all preachers who apply their Islamic resources to liberating the holy places of Islam and the countries conquered by the Zionists and the imperialists, the Jihad Organization replies that this is not the direct route. The road to liberating Jerusalem passes through the liberation of one's own country from the rule of infidels. It is these rulers who provide the basis for imperialism in the Muslim country. There is no choice but to eliminate these first and then to leap forth, under Islamic leadership, to liberate the holy places. Imperialism is a distant foe, but the infidel rulers are an enemy that is near. War against our enemy nearby precedes war against the distant foe. The Islamic state will not appear except through war. The trials undergone by Muslims today follow from the deeds of infidel rulers who passed this legislation and led Muslims in their path. The rulers of our period are the rulers of *Ridda* [apostasy]. They were raised on the milk of imperialism – the Crusades, Zionism and communism. They do not partake in Islam other than their names, even if they pray, fast and have pretensions of being Muslims.

Faraj compared the current rulers of Egypt with those during the Tatar conquests at the time of Ibn Taymiyya, and found a great similarity with the earlier period, as viewed by Ibn Taymiyya. He referred to an incident recounted by Ibn Taymiyya, in which a devout Muslim came to Ibn Taymiyya to ask how to deal with the Mongols who had conquered the city of Mardin and were then in control. Ibn Taymiyya replied that part of the city is true Muslim and part is ruled by a mixture of laws taken from Judaism, Christianity and Islam, according to a codex called the *Yesk* which was arranged for the convenience of the rulers, and that this must be fought.

Faraj concluded that there is no choice but jihad to rectify the distortions and that political and ideological justification can be found in today's reality, in the suras of the Quran and in the words of the Prophet, such as: 'Fight them! Allah will chastise them at your hands, and He will lay them low and give you victory over them, and He will heal the breasts of folk who are believers';[24] 'Whoso judgeth not by that which Allah hath revealed: such are wrong-doers'.[25] And from the words of the Prophet: 'Whoso among you who sees an act that should not be done must change it with his hand, and if he cannot [change it], then with his words, and if he cannot [change it], then with his heart, and that is the weakest faith.' Faraj asserted that these verses and sayings permit war against all who present an obstacle to Islam. On the basis of these verses, Faraj permitted attacks on shops belonging to the Copts. He was sharply critical of Sadat for taking a position against the Islamic revolution in Iran. Faraj also vehemently attacked the peace agreement with Israel. In general, the Jihad Organization abhorred Jews and showed particular hostility toward them. They considered Jews to be criminal enemies of the Islamic *Umma*, going so far as to dissociate them from the 'people of the book' in the Quran. As for Christians, they were seen as the continuation of the Crusaders against Islam. Clearly, the Jihad Organization drew its ideology from the writings of Sayyid Qutb, al-Mawdudi, and Ibn Taymiyya. In his book, Faraj censured the other Islamic movements, especially the Muslim Brothers, which sought integration with the political parties, and the *al-Takfir wal-Hijra*, which preached migration to the caves or to other countries until the movement was strong enough to attack society and establish an Islamic state. He asserted that only through jihad can an Islamic state be established.[26]

Faraj set up the institutions of his movement according to a structured division of labor. The Shura Council, with 11 members, was the supreme council of the movement, and included Faraj himself, 'Abbud al-Zumur, Karam Zuhdi, Najih 'Abdullah, Fuad Hanafi, 'Ali al-Sharif, 'Isam Durbala, 'Asim 'Abd al-Majid, Hamdi 'Abd al-Rahman, Usama Hafiz and Tal'at Qasim. He also set up three committees which had the functions set out below:

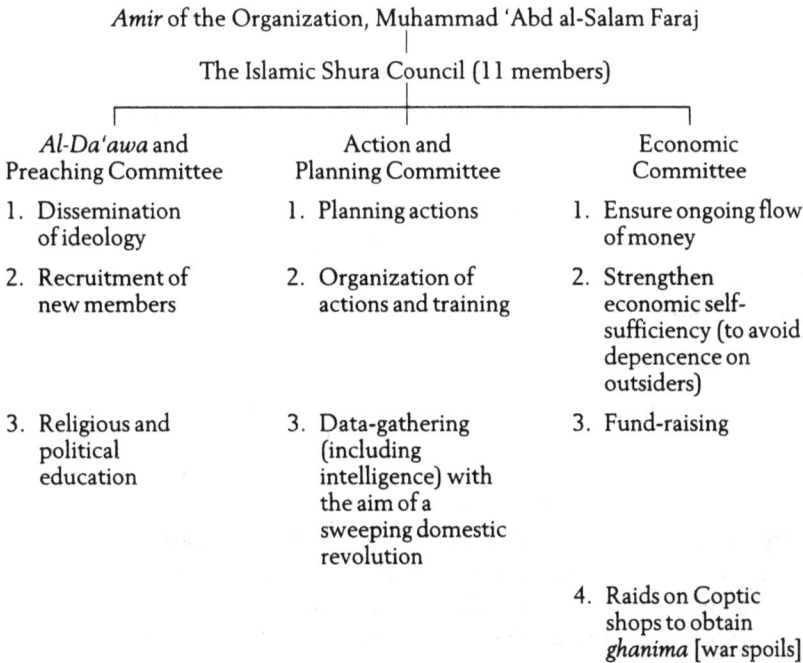

Amir of the Organization, Muhammad 'Abd al-Salam Faraj

The Islamic Shura Council (11 members)

Al-Da'awa and Preaching Committee	Action and Planning Committee	Economic Committee
1. Dissemination of ideology	1. Planning actions	1. Ensure ongoing flow of money
2. Recruitment of new members	2. Organization of actions and training	2. Strengthen economic self-sufficiency (to avoid depencence on outsiders)
3. Religious and political education	3. Data-gathering (including intelligence) with the aim of a sweeping domestic revolution	3. Fund-raising
		4. Raids on Coptic shops to obtain *ghanima* [war spoils]

Before the assassination of Sadat, the Jihad Organization carried out many actions and raids. The methods of operation of the Jihad commanders were very similar to those of the organization of Dr Salih Siriyya. After the assassination of Sadat, there were innuendoes in the Egyptian media about the possibility of a conspiracy between the two organizations. Both advocate a jihad and both advocate the need to eliminate 'corrupt' leaders (rather than to eliminate society or to conquer it after a migration or retreat in order to learn pure Islamic ideology, to solidify into an Islamic unit and then to attack society, as advocated by the organization of Shukri Mustafa, *al-Takfir wal-Hijra*. There is some evidence that Muhammad 'Abd al-Salam Faraj was not a despotic leader. On the contrary, he surrounded himself with strong people who were not intimidated by him, but who respected him. He had unusual powers of persuasion. There is evidence that 'Abbud al-Zumur was the brains behind the organization, as he had been a major in army intelligence, and had designed the strategy for establishing an Islamic caliphate and had passed it on to the leadership of the organization, even though Faraj had conceived the idea of al-jihad and the caliphate in his book *al-Farida al-Gha'iba*. When Khalid al-Islambuli came to Faraj and said that he had been asked to participate in a military parade and that this would be an ideal opportunity to assassinate Sadat and senior government officials, Faraj agreed with al-Islambuli, but he did not give approval before consulting with the other members of the leadership. Only 'Abbud al-Zumur objected to the plan, believing that the organization was not yet ready for this action. He thought there was a good chance that the plan would be discovered and the entire organization exposed. After discussion, however, the plan was approved and 'Abbud al-Zumur withdrew his opposition. In retrospect, 'Abbud al-Zumur was right. On 2 September 1981, about one month before the parade, Sadat gave orders to arrest 1,536 people on suspicion of exploiting previous events in an attempt to bring down the government. Among those arrested were intellectuals, authors, journalists and nine of the eleven members of the Shura Council of the Jihad Organization. 'Abbud al-Zumur believed that at least another two years should pass before any attempt to mount popular revolution to establish the caliphate should be made. Nevertheless, 'Abbud al-Zumur gave his approval and began to carefully make plans, determined to succeed.[27]

Thus, on 6 October 1981, during a military parade in the city of Nasr, near Cairo, Lieutenant Khalid al-Islambuli forced the driver of his vehicle to halt opposite the reviewing stand, lobbed in two hand grenades, only one of which exploded, returned to his car for a machine-gun, and emptied it into the 'who's who' of the government and dignitaries in the stand. Two more officers who were members of the Jihad Organization joined al-Islambuli, opening fire and throwing grenades. A fourth sniper set his sights on Sadat, still standing, who caught a bullet in his neck which proved to be fatal. After the chaos, which lasted no more than 40 seconds, security people who were not wounded began to return fire, capturing three at once and the fourth a few days later.[28]

A central spiritual figure in the Jihad Organization was Shaikh 'Umar 'Abd al-Rahman, born in 1938 in Daqahliyya, who represented the leadership of the movement in Upper Egypt. Shaikh 'Abd al-Rahman became known following a *fatwa* that he issued in the late 1970s which was interpreted as giving license to kill Sadat since he is 'not a ruler of what was commanded by Allah'. This *fatwa* was given in the context of 'Abd al-Rahman's exegesis of the verses from the Quran, 'Whoso judgeth not by that which Allah hath revealed: such are disbelievers'; and 'Whoso judgeth not by that which Allah hath revealed: such are wrong-doers' ('The Table Spread': verses 44–5).

Shaikh 'Abd al-Rahman quoted many interpretations of these verses from the Quran and rejected the claim that they were said only about *ahl al-Kitab*, especially the Jews, saying that when a Jew was caught committing adultery, other Jews complained to Muhammad that the Jewish leaders refrained from stoning him according to the Torah. Relying on these exegeses, Shaikh 'Abd al-Rahman asserted that the intention was both general and absolute. In other words, he who does not rule according to the Quran and the Hadith is an infidel, exploiter and adulterer, and this was clearly meant to include Sadat. 'Abd Al-Rahman was tried in a military court which charged him with being the *Amir* of the Jihad Organization, but the court released him for insufficient evidence. During the trial, testimony was given that he was offered the position of *amirate*, but that he turned it down because of his blindness. Nevertheless, he continued to maintain contact with the members of the organization.[29]

✳

An examination of the composition in terms of geographical origin, age, and professional qualifications of those captured in Cairo and its environs and in the other districts reveals that about half were from Cairo, approximately 40 per cent from Upper Egypt, and the remainder from the northern and southern tips of Egypt. Forty-five per cent of those captured in Cairo and the environs were students, 24 per cent were white collar workers, and 14 per cent were laborers, with the rest being military men, policemen or farmers. Just over half were younger than 24 years, 34 per cent were aged 25–29, and the remainder (a small minority) were above the age of 30.[30]

The Egyptian political sociologist Saad Eddin Ibrahim noted in 1988:

> At present, the anti-society Islamic groupings in Egypt are small. Its membership tends to have the same sociological profile as the member-ship of the anti-regime Islamic tendency: young, educated, high achievers, from rural or small lower-middle-class backgrounds. They represent the raw nerve not only of the Islamic Movement but also of Egyptian society at large. Three decades earlier their counterparts of similar background responded readily to Nasir's Arab Nationalism and Arab Socialism. And six decades ago, the youth of Egypt also responded readily to Sa'd Zaghlul's anti-colonial liberal democratic call.[31]

Most scholars hold Sadat himself responsible for the state of affairs. In the early 1970s, especially after the October War, Sadat assumed the image of liberator of his country from the defeat of June 1967 through the campaign of crossing the Suez Canal and destroying the Bar-Lev Line. He gave freedom, albeit guarded, to the press and to various political factions by creating *manabir* [forums] within the socialist party, with one from the right, one from the center and one from the left; these became political parties in the 1970s. He changed the economic, social and political orientation by economic and political openness toward the West and abandonment of Nasir's radical line; in particular, he sought to foster ties with radical religious groups, hoping that they would help implement his policies. Although at a certain stage they gave him cautious support, this was only an effort to strengthen their hold on society and the government. When their influence increased and the balance was tipped in their favor, Sadat retreated and tried to repress them.[32] The image of the believing president gave way to the policy of separating religion from state. In the eyes of the masses and many intellectuals, his policies were depicted as a jumbled confusion: socialism, liberalism, religious faith, economic *laissez-faire* which benefited a few while the masses sank into a morass of inflation and poverty, oppression of liberals charged with left-wing views, subsequent repression of religious elements after exploiting them against liberals and scorn for the clergy.[33] In the chapter of his book, *Autumn of the Anger*, entitled 'Ceasefire with the Devils', Muhammad Hasanain Haikal writes, 'The genie had already escaped from the bottle and no one had the power to recapture it, even with charms and amulets'.[34]

NOTES

1. Adil Hamuda, *Al-Hijra ila al-'Unf* [The *hijra* to violence] (Cairo, 1987), pp. 171–2; see also Kepel, pp. 73–6.
2. Hamuda, pp. 171–2.
3. Hasan Al-Hudaibi, *Du'at la Qudat* [Preachers not judges] (World Islamic Association of Student Organizations, 1977). According to Kepel (p. 61), the book was written in 1969 in the format of a study of religious commandments in which the author reacts explicitly to the theology of al-Mawdudi and to Islamic extremists, including Sayyid Qutb, though without mentioning him by name. In the book he rejects the claim that it is not enough for a Muslim to pronounce the two testimonies, and asserts that from the moment he utters them there is no doubt about a Muslim's Islam. He also forbids the killing of a Muslim as such. Although God alone rules, God left it to us to organize our lives according to the needs of the generation and the times. Here there is some overlap with the claims of the intellectuals. See the following chapters.
4. Hamuda, *Al-Hijra*, ibid.
5. Nabil 'Abd Al-Fattah, *Al-Mushaf wal-Saif* [The book and the sword] (Cairo, 1987), pp. 39–40.
6. Rajab Madgur (ed. Dr 'Ali Grisha), *Al-Takfir wal-Hijra* (Cairo, May 1985). The author was a member of this organization, but left it in late 1981 (p. 272) and wrote this book in which he discusses each element in the thought of Shukri Mustafa. The original book by Mustafa, *Kitab al-Khilafa* [The book of the caliphate], held by the author in manuscript form was not accessible to me; see also Liwaa Hasan Sadiq, pp. 333–95. The author was head of the Supreme Military Court which tried Shukri Mustafa and his comrades, captured after the assassination of Shaikh al-Dahabi. In the chapter 'The Trial', he presents detailed information about the organization which does not appear in other books; see also Hamuda, *al-Hijra*, pp. 171–202.
7. Hamuda, pp. 228–31.
8. Ibid., pp. 232–47.
9. Saad Eddin Ibrahim, 'Anatomy of Egypt's Militant Islamic Groups: Methodological Note and Preliminary Findings', *International Journal of Middle East Studies*, Vol. 12, 1980, pp. 423–53.
10. Saad Eddin Ibrahim, 'Egypt's Islamic Activism in the 1980s', *Third World Quarterly*, April 1988, pp. 632–57.
11. Hamuda, p. 32.
12. Hamuda relates that Siriyya met with al-Hudaibi (who died in 1973), with Shaikh Muhammad al-Ghazali, with Zainab al-Ghazali (who was closely connected with Sayyid Qutb and was one of the few women in the movement of Muslim Brothers), and with others. After the abortive attempt, all those who had been in contact with him denied any connection. Zainab al-Ghazali even issued a manifesto in which she wrote, 'Zainab al-Ghazali would not agree to meet with a person known to her to be against Anwar al-Sadat. I declare that Anwar al-Sadat is a believer and the son of a believer, and I know his father and his piety.' Shaikh Muhammad al-Ghazali wrote, 'My sole means for disseminating Islam is to serve Islam through thought and open persuasion. I am not a person who will plot against the believing president Muhammad Anwar al-Sadat or who will deny his good deeds.' Ibid., pp. 33–53. However the scholar Rif'at Sayyid Ahmad specifically states that Salih Siriyya was in close contact with al-Hudaibi and with Zainab al-Ghazali (see his book, *Al-Islambuli: Ruya Jadida Li-Tanzim al-Jihad* [Islambuli:

a new view of the Jihad Organization] (Cairo, 1987), p. 67.

13. Details about Siriyya are based on: Yisrael Altman, *Islamic Opposition Groups During the Sadat Regime* (Tel Aviv, Shiloah Institute, 1978), p. 18; and Adil Hamuda, *Al-Hijra*, p. 32. Hamuda asserts that the organization of *Shabab Muhammad* and the Islamic Liberation Party in Egypt were one and the same. The name *Shabab Muhammad* was used as a cover, since the Islamic Liberation Party was known and would not have been attractive to young people. Altman claims that these were two separate organizations. Actually, the name *Shabab Muhammad* appeared in the 1940s as a group that broke away from the Muslim Brothers movement and advocated violence, but it disappeared (see Rif'at Sayyid Ahmad, *Al-Islambuli*, p. 16).

14. Hamuda, p. 38.

15. Ibid., pp. 40–41; Sayyid Ahmad, *Al-Islambuli*, pp. 70–72.

16. Sayyid Ahmad, *Al-Islambuli*, p. 69 and footnote 4.

17. Ibid., pp. 69–70; also Hamuda, p. 46.

18. Haikal, *Autumn of the Anger*, p. 297.

19. Sayyid Ahmad, *Al-Islambuli*, p. 73.

20. Gunaina Ni'mat-Allah, *Tanzim al-Jihad* [The jihad organization] (Cairo, 1988), p. 101.

21. The reference is to the commandment of the jihad. A summary of the book appears later in this chapter.

22. Sayyid Ahmad, *Al-Islambuli*, p. 74.

23. Ibid., pp. 75–77.

24. 'Repentance', verse 14.

25. 'The Table Spread', verse 44.

26. Sayyid Ahmad, *Al-Islambuli*, pp. 77–8.

27. Gunaina Ni'mat-Allah, *Tanzim al-Jihad*, pp. 105–8.

28. Many books contain the full details of this assassination. Among them are: Adil Hamuda, *Qanabil wa-Masahit, Qissat Tanzim al-Jihad* [Grenades and holy books: the story of the al-Jihad Organization] (Cairo, 1986); Liwaa Hasan Sadiq *Judhur al-fitna* [The roots of strife]; G. Ni'mat-Allah, *Tanzim al-Jihad*; G. Kepel, *The Prophet and Pharaoh*.

29. 'Umar 'Abd al-Rahman, *Kalimat Haqq* [A word of truth] (Cairo, 1987), pp. 41–64; and also Sayyid Ahmad, *Al-Islambuli*, pp. 86–7. See the epilogue to this book for a description of the activities of Shaikh 'Abd al-Rahman after his release, of 'Abbud al-Zumur in prison, and of the other Islamic groups, as well as the struggle of the government against these groups.

30. Sayyid Ahmad, *Al-Islambuli*, pp. 96–7, and also Ni'mat-Allah, *Tanzim al-Jihad*, pp. 142–3.

31. Saad Eddin Ibrahim, 'Egypt's Islamic Activism', *Third World Quarterly*, April 1988, p. 654.

32. The Egyptian author and winner of the Nobel Prize in literature, Naguib Mahfouz, captures this confusion in the words (p. 65) of a protagonist in his novel, *Yawma Qutila al-Za'im* [the day the leader was assassinated]: 'What's the meaning of this decision, buddy! You declare a revolution of the 15th of May and then you end it on the 15th of September? All the Egyptians will be sent to prison – Muslims, Copts, party people and philosophers? No one will be left in the field of freedom except the opportunists. God have mercy on you, Egypt!'

33. Sadat publicly mocked the important clergyman Shaikh al-Malawi whom he imprisoned with the words, 'He's been thrown into prison like a dog'. He also publicly scorned the Islamic dress of religious women. Both these incidents evoked great anger among both religious and non-religious in Egypt.

34. Haikal, *Autumn of the Anger*, pp. 301–4.

4   Conclusion to Part I

Militant Islam did not develop *ex nihilo*. There is common ground
between the Muslim Brothers, believed by many Egyptian intellectuals and foreign scholars to be a relatively moderate movement,
and the Islamic jihad movements. All believe that the only solution
to the problems of Egypt and the Muslim world is the establishment
of an Islamic *Shari'a* state to be headed by a caliph who will run the
affairs of state in the spirit of the Quran, the Sunna, and early Islam.
All these movements – the Muslim Brothers and the militant jihad
organizations – totally reject the idea of any other form of rule. The
governments that currently exist – those which gained power by
democratic means and those, following a *coup d'état* or revolution
– are, in their view, the governments of infidels and should be
replaced by an Islamic *Shari'a* state. The only question asked by
both the Muslim Brothers and the militant organizations that
demand an Islamic state **at once**, is how to go about changing the
government.

The question of violent methods was discussed by Shaikh Hasan
al-Banna, the founder and Supreme Guide of the Muslim Brothers,
at great length and in depth from the time of the fifth conference in
1938, as noted, until his death. Al-Banna left behind a complete
legacy of organized codes which were disseminated in the Muslim
Brothers' publications and are followed to this day. They are codified
under the title *'Aqidatuna* [our faith] which has seven sections and
dozens of subsections in which the emphasis is that 'Islam is the
complete constitution of the world, and it should order life in this
world and in the world to come'. This codex orders the life of the
Muslim as an individual and also as an integral part of his family and
the society in which he lives. It dictates that he must belong to no
party, organization, movement or other body except the Muslim
Brothers movement; if he does so he will be considered a traitor to
Islam and an infidel. He must refrain from sending his children

to any school that does not preach the Islamic faith and Islamic behavior. He must avoid any publication, newspaper, book, club, social or political group or other group which acts in opposition to the teachings of Islam. It is incumbent upon every Muslim to believe that the flag of Islam will fly over all humanity, and he must undertake the jihad to carry out this mission, and be willing to sacrifice everything that is dear to him, including property and people.

At the same important fifth conference, Hasan al-Banna posed three fundamental questions:

1. Do the Muslim Brothers intend to use power to achieve their goals?
2. Are the Brothers planning a revolution against the political government and the social order in Egypt?
3. Are the Brothers planning to establish an Islamic regime or to forcefully demand power, and by what means?

Al-Banna responded to the first question in the following words:

> As for power, this is the slogan of Islam in all its regimes and in its legislation. The Muslim Brothers must be strong and must attain power. Power will come gradually. First there will be the power of faith, then the spirit of unity and solidarity among members of the movement, and later the power of force and arms. The movement is not complete without these components.

As regards the second question, the Muslim Brothers do not believe in the efficacy of a revolution, although they speak openly with every government in office and every new government, advising them that if those in authority do not find a speedy solution to the problems, this will necessitate a revolution, not to be carried out by the Muslim Brothers, but by force of circumstance. Al-Banna hinted, of course, that they would take part in the revolution against the current government 'by force of circumstance'. And at the opportune moment after the death of al-Banna, they did send in weapons and army-trained personnel to assist in the Free Officers Revolution in June 1952, when they believed that the Free Officers would share power with them.

As for the third question, al-Banna clearly stated that the Islam in which the Muslim Brothers believe asserts that an Islamic regime is the fundamental basis, and the Prophet Muhammad declared that political rule is the cornerstone. The reluctance of Islamic reformers to demand power is a crime against Islam that cannot be pardoned 'except by rescuing the government from those who do not agree to Islamic law'.[1]

Thus the view commonly held among intellectuals and scholars that the Muslim Brothers movement is moderate and does not advocate force or is not planning to use force or weapons in order to establish a *Shari'a* state is fundamentally in error. Power is an internal function of the ideology of this movement. It is true that in 1928, at the outset of his career, some ten years before the fifth conference and when the movement was just being founded, Hasan al-Banna advocated preaching only as a way to return others to the pure Islamic sources; at this time he did not know how much power his movement would achieve. After great numbers joined the movement in Cairo and in many provincial towns, al-Banna realized that he could move on to the next stage of advancing his ideas, and he did not conceal this. In the 1940s, he even campaigned to enter political life, with some prominent associates running for election to Parliament, so that they could operate from inside the system. This was in blatant contradiction of his own preaching at the fifth conference and even before. During his life, the Muslim Brothers carried out several murders and attempted assassinations of those outsiders who vehemently opposed the movement; there were also executions of internal traitors. Some two or three years after Nasir came to power, the Muslim Brothers movement was outlawed, as noted in Chapters 2 and 3, although the ideology gained growing support in the underground and in the prisons.

The Muslim Brothers ideology is widespread in most parts of the Islamic world and in Islamic societies, such as Pakistan, for example. In Pakistan, which ceded from India and gained independence from Britain in 1948, the soil was already fertile for the growth of extremism, and Abu al-A'la al-Mawdudi, who founded a branch and a publication of the Muslim Brothers in Pakistan, was not operating in a vacuum. In view of the fact that in the 1940s the Muslims in Pakistan were a minority among a Hindu majority the views of Al-Mawdudi served only to radicalize the Pakistanis. These radical views were brought back to Egypt, the source of the Muslim Brothers movement, to supplement the ideology embodied in the four principles that were noted in previous chapters, and in which the slogan of the new *jahiliyya* was coined. This ideology was disseminated in Egypt more vigorously after the confrontation between Nasir and the Muslim Brothers. When the Brothers were thrown into prison by Nasir, their underground ideology became even more extremist, only partially under the influence of the works of al-Mawdudi.

Sayyid Qutb, Shuqri Mustafa, Salih Siriyya, 'Abd al-Salam Muhammad Faraj and the great majority of the al-jihad activists who were in the underground during Nasir's rule, as well as those who were in the underground and also active openly at the time of Sadat, were all 'graduates' of the Muslim Brothers movement, and drew their beliefs and their preaching from this source. Their role was to develop the already existing ideology and to add more militant preaching to it, their aspiration being to take over the government *at once*. The books and preaching of al-Mawdudi were a catalyst, but not the guiding principle. Sayyid Qutb and his comrades did not have to draw ideas from al-Mawdudi about the new *jahiliyya*; they could have arrived at this or a similar concept by themselves. The distance between the preaching of Hasan al-Banna in the late 1930s and 1940s and the extremist and violent jihad movements in the 1970s and 1980s is not great. Sadat, who wanted to be a democrat, within reason and on certain conditions, released most of the leadership of the Muslim Brothers from prison, but they returned the favor by founding the Jihad Now movement, and even published a *fatwa* that Sadat is a traitor to Islam and declared him to be fair game. The tragic end is well known. The terrorism of the Islamic jihad groups in the 1980s and the early 1990s, and to this very day, has risen to disturbing levels, and presents the government of Mubarak with the challenge of 'to be or not to be'.

In Parts II and III we shall examine the reactions of liberal intellectuals to the issues raised by members of the militant jihad movements. We shall also examine the problems with which the government of Mubarak must grapple in order to face the rising tide of extremism which could endanger not only the government in Egypt, but governments in neighboring countries as well.

NOTES

1. A great deal of research into the legacy and the ideology of al-Banna has been carried out. His speeches and sermons continue to be disseminated by the Muslim Brothers' publications. The major aspects of his ideology are set out in the important book by Dr 'Ali 'Abd al-Halim, one of the *'ulama* at al-Azhar: 'Ali 'Abd al-Halim Mahmud, *Wasail al-Tarbiya 'Ind al-Ikhwan al-Muslimin – Dirasa Tahliliya Tarikhiyya* [Educational methods of the Muslim Brothers – an analytical-historical study] (Cairo, 1989).

Part II
Intellectuals and their Response to Islamic Fundamentalism

5 Profiles of Egyptian Intellectuals

In previous chapters, we reviewed the evolution of the demand to impose the *Shari'a*, to establish an Islamic state, to replace the rule of man with the rule of God and to designate a caliph who will undertake this mission. A great many individuals and organizations were willing to risk their lives, to imperil themselves and to suffer starvation and imprisonment for the sake of founding an Islamic state. Liberal Egyptian intellectuals responded to these demands, warning of the dangers they posed to the future of Egypt as a liberal state based on a system of law and order for all its citizens. Their responses will be presented in the following chapters under the themes, the rule of God, an Islamic state and the rule of *Shari'a*; the caliphate; jihad; attitudes toward Jews and Christians. But before reviewing the counterclaims of the intellectuals, it is necessary to provide profiles of and pertinent information about the intellectuals themselves.

NABIL 'ABD AL-FATTAH

A lawyer by training, 'Abd al-Fattah is a researcher at the Center for Policy and Strategic Studies and writes regularly in *Al-Ahram*. He has written books and many articles in various journals in the Arab world on the subjects of nationalism, religion, Israel-Arab relations and the culture of Egypt. His book *al-Mushaf wal-Saif* [The book (Quran) and the sword] (1984) is considered a major sociological-historical analysis of the phenomenon of religious extremism in Egypt, particularly from the 1960s through the early 1980s.

DR AHMAD KAMAL ABU AL-MAJD

Author, journalist and scholar, he has a regular column in *Al-Ahram* and writes on social issues in various journals and newspapers. Al-Majd is a moderate in religion: he calls for the creation of an Islamic state, but rejects terrorism and extremism. He endorses progress when the values of religion are safeguarded. Al-Majd's most important work is *Hiwar la Muwajaha* [dialogue, not confrontation] (1988) in which he calls upon Islamic organizations to abandon terrorism and to conduct a dialogue with both the government and the secularists.

MAKRAM MUHAMMAD AHMAD

Born in 1935, Ahmad is chairman of the board of the al-Hilal publishing house, and editor of the journal *Al-Hilal* and the prominent weekly *Al-Muswwar*. Ahmad has had a rich journalistic career as a military correspondent, in Yemen, in Gaza (June 1967) and in the October War. He was appointed to his present position in June 1981. Ahmad is considered a follower of Muhammad Hasanain Haikal and held moderate left-wing, Nasirist tendencies during the Sadat regime. He supported the peace process with Israel, had a relatively moderate approach to Israel, but with his assumption of the editorship of *Al-Musawwar*, he expressed reservations about Israel and Israelis. He is close to President Mubarak, and has good sources of information: his weekly articles are generally a reliable source of information about political developments in Egypt and in the region. He condemned the extremist Islamic organizations following the attempted assassination of the two former Interior Ministers (Hasan Abu Basha and Nabawi Isma'il) in 1987. These organizations responded by an attempted assassination of Ahmad that same year, but he continues to censure their activities. He has served as chairman of the Association of Journalists and has written one book, *The Revolution in the Southern Arabian Peninsula (Aden and Yemen)*.

HUSAIN AHMAD AMIN

Son of Ahmad Amin, the well-known author and journalist, Husain Ahmad Amin was born in 1932 in Cairo, and studied law in Cairo and English literature in England. He worked as a lawyer, radio announcer and diplomat, serving as Egyptian ambassador to Algeria until his retirement in 1992. Amin has written books, articles, and essays about society and Islam. His two major works are *Dalil al-Muslim al-Hazin* [Guide for the sad Muslim] (1987), which includes also another book, *Hawla al-Da'awa ila-Tatbiq al-Shari'a al-Islamiyya*

[About the call for applying the *Shari'a*]; and *Al-Islam fi 'Alam Mutaghayyir* [Islam in a changing world] (1988). His most recent works are *Risala Tahta al-Maa* [Message under the water] (Cairo, 1992); and *Al-Ijtihad fi al-Islam* [Judgment in Islam] (Cairo, 1993).

JUSTICE MUHAMMAD SA'ID AL-ASHMAWI

Born in Cairo in 1932, Ashmawi graduated in law from Cairo University in 1954 and studied law at Harvard University in the United States. Today, he serves as Chief Justice of the Supreme Court and Chairman of the High Court of State Security. Ashmawi is an expert in Islamic law and has written many books on controversial issues in Egypt and the Muslim world, such as *Jawhar al-Islam* [The essence of Islam] (1984); *Usul al-Shari'a al-Islamiyya* [The roots of Islamic law] (1979); *Al-Shari'a al-Islamiyya wal-Qanun al-Islami* [Islamic law and Egyptian law] (1988); *Al-Islam al-Siyasi* [Political Islam] (1987); *Al-Riba wal-Faida fi al-Islam* [Usury and benefit in Islam] (1988); *Ruh al-'Adala* [The spirit of justice] (1986); *Ma'alim al-Islam* [Milestones of Islam] (1989); and *Al-Khilafa al-Islamiyya* [The Islamic caliphate] (1990). Ashmawi was chief justice at the trial of the Jihad Organization in 1981, and also at the trial of the Nasirists. He is about to publish a new book called *Al-Islam al-Mustanir* [Enlightened Islam]. He participates in many conferences and writes extensively in the Egyptian press, primarily on matters of Islam, in which he vigorously attacks extremism and terrorism. The government is attentive to Ashmawi's words concerning religious extremism. He supports peace with Israel, but takes exception to Israel's position *vis-à-vis* the Palestinians.

AHMAD BAHAA AL-DIN

Born in Alexandria in 1927, Bahaa al-Din holds a master's degree in law, and was in practice until 1951, when he gave it up for a prolific career as a journalist and writer. Bahaa al-Din wrote for the weekly *Rose al-Yusuf*, and in 1956 he founded the journal *Sabah al-Khair* [Good morning]. He was editor of *Al-Akhbar* in 1959 at the time of Nasir, editor of *Al-Hilal* in 1964, and editor of the daily *Al-Ahram* in 1974 at the time of Sadat. In 1976, Bahaa al-Din served as chairman of the Egyptian Journalists Association, and he served four years as deputy chairman of the International Association of Journalists. He is considered one of the outstanding writers in the Egyptian and Arabic press, and his articles carry considerable influence. When Bahaa al-Din quarreled with Sadat over his policies, he emigrated to Kuwait, where he managed the well-known journal *Al-Arabi*. Bahaa al-Din returned to Egypt at about the time of the assassination of Sadat. Until recently, he wrote a regular column in *Al-Ahram* called 'Yawmiyyat' [Diary], in which he frequently criticized Israel's policies in the occupied territories. He has also raised money in Saudi Arabia and other oil states on behalf of the *intifadah* in the territories. He is considered a moderate leftist and opposes Islamic extremism.

Bahaa al-Din wrote about his debates with Sadat in *Muhawarati Ma'a al-Sadat* [My dialogues with Sadat] (Cairo, 1987). He also wrote *Ayyam Laha Tarikh* [Days packed with history] (Dar al-Shuruq, Cairo and Beirut, 1977, second edition 1985) His other significant works are *A Month in Russia; A Proposal for a Palestinian State; The Legitimacy of Rule in the Arab Homeland; Israi'liyyat, King Farouq; Dimensions of the Arab-Israeli Conflict* (two volumes); and *Contemporary Views*. He has participated in many delegations and conferences in Egypt, other Arab countries, Africa and Asia. Bahaa al-Din was twice awarded Egypt's highest Order of Merit, in 1964 during Nasir's regime, and in 1988, under Mubarak.

TARIQ AL-BISHRI

Born in Cairo in 1933, al-Bishri is a lawyer by training and considered the ideologue of modern Arab nationalism. He was a member of various governments under Nasir and belongs to various nationalist organizations. Al-Bishri has written many books, the most important of which are *Al-Siasa fi Misr 1945–1952* [Politics in Egypt 1945–1952]; *Al-Muslimun wal-Aqbat* [The Muslims and the Copts]; *Al-Dimoqratiyya wa-Nizam 23 July* [Democracy and the July 23rd regime]; *Baina al-Islam wal-Uruba* [Between Islam and pan-Arabism]; and *Sa'd Zaghlul Yufawidu al-Isti'mar* [Sa'd Zaghlul negotiates with imperialism]. He writes for many journals in Egypt and the Arab world.

DR FARAJ FUDA

Born in 1945 in Dumyat in the al-Zarqa district, Fuda earned a doctorate in agricultural economics. He was a politician and a member of the New Wafd Party, but quit over political differences. In 1986, Fuda unsuccessfully sought election to the Egyptian National

Council. He tried to found an independent political party called *Al-Istiqlal* [Independence], whose key platform was economic and social liberalism. He wrote books and many articles, primarily in reaction to religious extremism which he viewed as an existential danger to Egypt and to its culture. He supported peace with Israel. Among his major works are *Qabl al-Suqut* [Before the fall] (Cairo, 1985); *Al-Haqiqa al-Gha'iba* [The absent truth] (1986); *Hiwar Hawla al-'Ilmaniyya* [Dialogue on secularism]; *Al-Taifiyya ila Ayn?* [Whither sectarianism?] (1987) (in collaboration with others); *Al-Mal'ub* [The swindled – the story of the investment companies] (1988); *Al-Irhab* [The terror] (1988); *Al-Nadir* [The warning] (1989); *Nakoun aw la Nakoun* [To be or not to be] (Cairo, 1992); and *Hatta la Yakoun Kalaman fi al-Hawaa* [So it won't be just talk], published posthumously in 1992 in Cairo. Fuda also had a regular column in the weekly *Mayo*. Because of his vehement stand against religious extremism, Fuda was killed by members of the Islamic Jihad Organization on 8 June 1992. The day before his death, he had written a particularly fierce article against the *Amirs* of the Islamic groups, accusing them of sexual deviance. Some say that this article is what incited the Jihad Organization to assassinate him. Fuda's funeral was attended by large numbers, including many intellectuals, and was virtually a demonstration against religious extremism. His death was a turning-point in the conciliatory attitude of the government towards the terrorists, and it launched the campaign against extremism, manifested in the publication of books extolling the beautiful side of Islam and condemning extremism, and the execution of terrorists who had engaged in acts of murder.

FATHI GHANIM

Born in 1924 in Cairo, Ghanim graduated from the law faculty of Cairo University. He was editor of the journal *Sabah al-Khair* (1959), head of the Middle East Press Agency (1965–6), editor of the newspaper *Al-Jumhurriyya* (1966–71), and creative writer and journalist on the weekly *Rose al-Yusuf* (1973–7) until his retirement. Ghanim began his literary career writing short stories, and to date has published about a dozen novels, three collections of short stories, one play, and one book of criticism. Among the best known are: *Attempt at Love; Al-Jabal* [The mountain] (Cairo, 1965); *Whence the Hot and the Cold*; the tetralogy, *The Man Who Lost His Shadow* (1962); *The Idiot; Zaynab and the Throne; The Film* (Cairo, 1981); *Girl from Shubra [a neighborhood]; The Sea*; and others.

GUNAINA NI'MAT-ALLAH

Ni'mat-Allah studied for a doctorate in sociology at the American University in Cairo under Professor Saad Eddin Ibrahim. Under his supervision, she carried out extensive interviews with imprisoned members of the Jihad Organization. The findings of her study appeared in *Tanzim al-Jihad – Hal Huwa al-Badil fi Misr* [The Jihad – is it an alternative in Egypt?] (Cairo, 1988). Ni'mat-Allah is now a member of the editorial board of *Civil Society*, published by the Ibn Khaldoun Institute of the American University of Cairo.

MUHAMMAD HASANAIN HAIKAL

Born in Cairo in 1923 and a graduate of Cairo University, Haikal was the foremost journalist at the time of Nasir. Throughout the 1950s and 1960s and until Nasir's death, Haikal was Nasir's close advisor on matters of politics and the media. Haikal was editor of many newspapers, including the important *Al-Ahram*, where he wrote a weekly column 'Bisaraha' [Frankly] in which he openly expounded Nasir's policies of a centralized government, and was quoted throughout the Arab world. Haikal was Minister of Information for a short period, but returned to journalism. With the death of Nasir, Haikal initially supported Sadat against his opponents, but relations soured soon after the October War when Sadat sought peace with Israel. Haikal is a vehement opponent of peace with Israel and is considered a leftist and anti-fundamentalist. He has written many books about Egypt's policies under both Nasir and Sadat. In his major work, *Kharif al-Ghadah* [Autumn of the anger] (Beirut, 1986), he harshly censures Sadat's policies. Among his other works are: *Crisis of the Intellectuals* (1961); *What Happened in Syria* (1962); *Suez Hideout*; *We and America*; *The Withdrawal of the U.S.S.R. in the Middle East*; *Ayat Allah Khumaini*; *A New Visit to History*; and *The Years of Agitation*. Haikal was awarded the Order of Merit in 1960 during Nasir's regime.

TAWFIQ AL-HAKIM

Born in 1898 in Alexandria to a Turkish mother and a propertied Egyptian father, al-Hakim was sent to Cairo as a child to continue his schooling. He studied law in Cairo and began to write plays after the Revolution of 1919. Although sent to Paris to continue his law studies, al-Hakim preferred the study of Western, especially French, literature, and began to write stories and plays. He became an ardent student of western culture, although he did not conceal his displeasure with its 'materialist' side, especially during the Nazi rise to power and the Second World War Al-Hakim advocated returning to the spirituality of the east. In addition to plays, novels and many short stories, he was involved in current affairs, including religion, and wrote copiously about these matters. Al-Hakim was considered one of the most creative writers in Egypt and the Arab world. Indeed, Naguib Mahfouz himself asserted that al-Hakim was more entitled to the Nobel Prize for Literature than he was. Al-Hakim referred to himself as a good Muslim. He is thought to have predicted the coup d'état of July 1952 in his book *'Awdat al-Ruh* [Return of the spirit]. Nasir awarded him the Order of Merit, but al-Hakim became disenchanted with Nasir's cruel policies and published scathing criticism after Nasir's death in his book *'Awdat al-Waay* [Return of recognition] which appeared in 1975. Al-Hakim favored Sadat's peace initiative with Israel. Although he was open to all religions including Judaism, al-Hakim was not averse to criticizing Israel's policies regarding the Palestinian issue. He strongly opposed religious extremism, manifested not only in extremist factions, but also in the religious establishment. Many of his books were translated into other languages. He died in 1987.

ADIL HAMUDA

An author and journalist now in his fifties, Hamuda has intensively studied the extremist Islamic movements. His major works are: *Qissat Tanzim al-Jihad* [The story of the Jihad movement] (Cairo, 1985); *Ightiyal Rais* [Assassination of a president] (Cairo, 1985); *Sayyid Qutb* (1987); and *Al-hijra ila al-'Unf* [The *hijra* to extremism] (Cairo, 1987). He is considered a liberal. Although he condemns extremist religious organizations, he has tried with considerable success to survey them objectively. Hamuda advocates technological progress and is anti-Israel, but there is no evidence that he objects to peace with Israel.

SAAD EDDIN IBRAHIM

Professor of anthropology and sociology and Chairman of the Ibn Khaldoun Institute for Sociological Studies at the American University of Cairo, Ibrahim is considered one of the foremost scholars of modern Islam. He lectures frequently on the social situation in Egypt at conferences and international gatherings. He is editor of the journal *Civil Society*, which appears in English and Arabic. He has written many articles in international journals about Egypt, in particular about religion and society. Ibrahim edited an important book in Arabic, *Egypt Over 25 Years: 1952–1977* (Beirut, 1981), to which the foremost Egyptian analysts of social, economic, and religious issues in Egypt contributed. He also collaborated in the writing of a book in English, *The Middle East: Ten Years After Camp David*, edited by William B. Quandt (Washington, 1988).

Ibrahim was vehemently opposed to Sadat's policies regarding economic issues and peace with Israel until recently, years when he published a revised perspective in his book, *Radd I'tibar al-Sadat* [Rehabilitation of Sadat], where he admits that Sadat has been right and he, wrong. He has also written *Taammulat fi Masalat al-Aqalliyyat* [Thoughts about minorities] (Cairo, 1992).

YUSUF IDRIS

Born in 1927 in the village of Bairum in the Nile Delta (Sharqiyya district), Idris earned a diploma in psychology and completed his medical studies in 1952. Idris began his literary career writing short stories while a student. When he had completed his studies, Idris started writing for *Al-Ahram*, marking the beginning of a prolific literary career in many genres. Idris was chairman of the Association of Authors and Theater Critics. He was considered the founder of a new school of theater, with his plots drawn from modern life and the national heritage. He headed the theater sector in Egypt and was appointed cultural consultant to *Al-Ahram*. Idris was regarded as the best short-story writer of Egypt, but he also wrote novellas, novels, plays, and many articles on social and policy matters. His works have been translated into 24 languages. He wrote nine works for the theater, including *Jumhuriyyat Farhat* and *al-Baklawan*. He published 11 collections of short stories, including *Arkhas Layali* [The cheapest nights] and *Ayyuaha al-Rijal* [Oh, men], as well as ten novels, including *Al-Haram* [The sin] and *Al-Bayda* [The white (woman)]. He wrote 15 books in various other genres, including essays, travel, and others.

Considered a leftist, Idris forcefully opposed Sadat and peace with Israel. He was an enthusiastic supporter of Arab nationalism and Nasir's ideology, although he also expressed criticism about these matters. In matters of Islam and the *Shari'a*, Idris took a nationalist-Arab point of view, which characterized his views of domestic politics. From the 1970s, like Muhammad Hasanain Haikal, Idris acknowledged some of Nasir's mistakes, but he remained loyal to the Nasirist ideology. Thus, his religious views must be placed in a context of Arab nationalism, support for Nasir and censure of Sadat.

Idris received the 'Abd al-Nasir Prize for Literature in 1964 and the Saddam Hussein Prize in 1988. Idris was incensed when, in 1988, he was passed over for the Nobel Prize for Literature in favor of Naguib Mahfouz. He attributed this to his political views, as he explained in an article in the newspaper *Al-Wafd*. Yusuf Idris died in July 1991 in London, after a prolonged illness.

KHALID MUHAMMAD KHALID

Born in 1919 in the village of 'Adwa in the al-Sharqiyya district, Khalid was given a broad religious education and was a prominent clergyman in al-Azhar during Nasir's rule. He is considered a scholar not only of Islam, but also in the fields of philosophy, education and culture. Khalid wrote a great many books, the major one being *Min Huna Nabdaa* [From here we shall start], which evoked considerable public notice in Egypt. He generally gives liberal interpretations of the Quran and is considered part of the left wing of Islam. Khalid has published in all the Islamic and secular journals and newspapers, and has taken a more radical approach in recent years. He has written 29 books. Among his more recent ones are: *Al-din lil-Sha'ab* [Religion is for the people]; *Ma'a al-Tariq* [With the way]; *Azmat al-Hurriyya fi 'Alamina* [The crisis of liberty in our world]; *'An al-Dimoqritiyya* [About democracy]; *Muhammad*; *Muhammad wal-Masih* [Muhammad and Christ]; *Rijal Hawla al-Masih* [Men around Christ]; and *Ana al-Insan* [I the human].

ZAKI NAJIB MAHMUD

Born in the Dumyat district in 1905, Mahmud graduated from the Teachers' Seminary in Cairo and completed a doctorate in philosophy from London University. He has served as guest lecturer in various American universities and was cultural attaché of the Egyptian Embassy in the United States (1954–55). Mahmud is considered one of the foremost Egyptian thinkers of his time, having written many books of philosophy, ideas, literature and current affairs. He writes often in *Al-Ahram* and other Egyptian dailies, and founded the intellectual journal *Al-Fikr* [Thought]. On the subject of Islam, he wrote *Ruaya Islamiyya* [An Islamic viewpoint] (Beirut, 1984); and *Qiyam min al-Turath* [Values from the heritage] (Beirut, 1989). He has won many prizes in literature and philosophy as well as the Order of Merit in 1975. Mahmud supports peace with Israel and has written prolifically in favor of Sadat and the peace initiative.

ANIS MANSUR

Born in al-Mansura in 1930, Mansur holds a master's degree in philosophy, and briefly taught this subject at Cairo University. Mansur is a prolific author and translator (with about 140 titles to his name) and a prominent and veteran journalist. During Nasir's rule, he wrote in *Al-Ahram*, but after being dismissed on Nasir's orders, he became his most fervent opponent. With Nasir's death, Mansur became Sadat's closest adviser. It was Mansur who conducted Sadat's information campaign, as Haikal did during Nasir's regime. After the October War, Mansur became editor of the important journal *October*, in which he outlined Sadat's policies. He accompanied Sadat on most of his state visits, including those to Israel. He often represented Sadat at state affairs abroad, including some in Israel. He remained an adviser to Mubarak until recently, although he was not as close to the latter as he had been to Sadat. He left the editorship of *October* and was editor of *Mayo* [May], the weekly journal of the party in power, until a short time ago. During Nasir's rule, Mansur strongly opposed Israel. When Sadat took over, he became and remained a supporter of peace policies. He frequently and openly welcomes Israeli journalists and attacks extremism at every opportunity.

DR HUSAIN FAWZI AL-NAJJAR

Born in 1918 in the village of Akrash in the Sharqiyya district, al-Najjar earned a doctorate in journalism from Cairo University (1957) and a post-doctoral fellowship degree in political science from Harvard University. Al-Najjar was an officer in the Egyptian Army who participated in the Second World War and the 1948 war against Israel, for which he was decorated. He served as a teacher in the Egyptian Ministry of Education, and later lectured at the Egyptian Military College in national history (1943) and strategy and policy studies (1953). Al-Najjar took an active role in the 1952 *coup d'état*, was media director of the Arab League and later adviser to the Egyptian Ministry of Education. He worked for the Arab League in New York, Washington, San Francisco, Bonn, and Geneva (1954–60). He has taught at al-Azhar University in Asyut, was a research fellow in political science at the University of California, chairman of a sociology journal, a member of the Writers' Association, and a member of the Supreme Council for Islam (Culture Committee). He retired in 1973.

Al-Najjar has written 40 books of biography and political thought, including the subject of Arabic and Islamic nationalism. His two major works about Islam are *Al-Islam wal-Siyasa* [Islam and politics] (Cairo, 1977); and *Al-dawla wal-Hukm fi al-Islam* [State and rule in Islam] (Cairo, 1985). His other major works include *Policy and Strategy in the Middle East* (Cairo, 1952); *The Arab Nation* (Cairo, 1961); *The Unity of Arab History* (Cairo, 1962); and *Lutfi al-Sayyid and the Egyptian Personality* (Cairo, 1993). He has been awarded many prizes for his writing and his activities.

DR 'ABD AL-'AZIM RAMADAN

Born in 1925 in Giza, Ramadan took his doctorate at Cairo University in 1970. He has taught in many universities and was the Dean of the Faculty of Education at Al-Minufiyya University in 1984. He is currently professor of modern history at 'Ayn Shams University and in Alexandria. Considered a moderate leftist, Ramadan is an ardent supporter of peace with Israel. He has written many books about Egyptian history, and is considered the foremost native expert. He is chairman of the Scientific Committee that oversees the Institute for Documentation of the History of Modern Egypt and a member of the Heritage Committee of the National Council for Culture, Art and Communication. He also chairs the Editors' Council preparing a series of books about the history of famous figures in Egypt. Ramadan writes for a large number of newspapers, including *Al-Ahram, October, Al-Jumhuriyya, Al-Wafd* and *Sabah al-Khair*. He also contributes articles to many journals in other Arab countries, as well as in England and France. Ramadan's major work about modern Islam is *Al-Ikhwan al-Muslimun wal-Tanzim al-Sirri* [The Muslim Brothers and the underground organization] (Cairo, 1977). Among his other important works are: *Tahtim al-Aaliha* [Smashing idols] in two volumes (1984); *Tatawwur al-Haraka al-Wataniyya fi Misr 1918–36* [Development of the nationalist movement in Egypt 1918–36] in three volumes (Cairo, 1968); *Misr fi 'Ahd al-Sadat* [Egypt under Sadat], two volumes (1986, 1989); *Al-Sira'a al-Ijtim'i wal-Siyasi fi Misr Mundu Thawrat Julyu Hatta Azmat Mars* [The social and political struggle in Egypt from the July revolution to the March 1954 crisis] (Cairo, 1975); *Al-Muwajaha al-Israiliyya al-Misriyya fi al-Bahr al-Ahmar* [The Israeli-Egyptian confrontation at the Red Sea 1959–79) (Cairo, 1982); and *Mudakkarat Sa'd Zaghlul* [Memoirs of Sa'd Zaghlul], two volumes (Cairo, 1987–88).

DR GHALI SHUKRI

A Copt born in 1935 in the town of Minuf in the Minufiyya district, Shukri received his doctorate in social sciences from the Sorbonne in Paris and became a teacher in the Ministry of Education (1956–60). In 1964, he became editor of the journal *al-Shi'r*, the literary critic of *Al-Ahram* and editor of the literary supplement to the journal *al-Tali'ah* [The young generation]. In the period 1966–73, Shukri held a senior position in the newspaper *al-Balagh*, and then in the newspaper *al-Muharrir* (1973–6). He was lecturer at the Sorbonne in the years 1976–80. In 1980–1, Shukri served as professor of social sciences in Lebanon University in Beirut, and then (1982–6) as professor of social sciences for cultural affairs in the Institute of Journalism and News at the University of Tunis. Shukri wrote for *Al-Ahram* in 1987, and has served as adviser to the newspaper *Al-Watan al-Arabi*, published in Paris, since 1976. He is a member of the Writers' Association, the Journalists' Association, and the Association of Egyptian Writers and Artists. Shukri was a founder of the National Council for Arabic Culture, and a member of the Board of the Arab Association for Social Sciences. Among his books are: *Salama Musa and the Crisis of Arab Conscience* (1962); *The Revolt of the Loner* (1966); *Whither Modern Poetry* (1968); *The Literature of Resistance* (1970); *The Heritage and the Revolution* (1973); *The Rise and Fall of Modern Egyptian Thought* (1978); *The Sociology of Modern Arabic Criticism* (1981); *The Dictatorship of Egyptian Backwardness* (1986); *Al-Aqbat fi Watan Mutaghayyir* (1991); and others. He has also written many books in English and French.

'ABD AL-SATTAR AL-TAWILA

Born in 1928, al-Tawila is a journalist and deputy editor of the weekly *Rose al-Yusuf*. He writes regularly for this journal and has written for many years for the newspaper *Al-Wafd*. Al-Tawila is a leftist and began his political activity as a communist, participating in many left-wing and nationalist demonstrations. In 1947, together with other Egyptian communists, he demonstrated in favor of the partition of Palestine and the establishment of a Jewish and an Arab state there, a stance rare among Egyptian public figures. After the peace agreement between Egypt and Israel, he visited Israel many times. He wrote many books, including Azmat al-Yasar al-Misri [The crisis of the Egyptian left] (Cairo, 1987); *Al-Sadat fi Israil* [Sadat in Israel] (Cairo, 1978); *Israil fi 'Uyun Misriyya [Israel in Egyptian eyes] (Acre, Israel, 1987); Afghanistan – al Haqiqa wal-Mustaqbal* [Afghanistan: the truth and the future]; and *Sharikat Tawdif al-Amwal* [Investment companies] (Cairo, 1988). In recent years, Al-Tawila has written many articles and a book *Umaraa al-Irhab* [The *amirs* of terrorism] (Cairo, 1992), in the context of the Egyptian campaign against fundamentalist terrorism and assassination attempts against intellectuals and tourist centers in Cairo and Upper Egypt.

DR FUAD ZAKARIYYA

Born in Port Sa'id in 1927, Zakariyya completed his doctorate in philosophy from 'Ayn Shams University in 1956, and has taught philosophy there. In the period 1957–62, he taught in New York, and subsequently served as head of the philosophy department of Kuwait University. One of Zakariyya's most important works in philosophy is *Nietzsche and Spinoza*. His major works about Islam are *Al-Haqiqa wal-Wahm fi al-Haraka al-Islamiyya al-Mu'asira* [Truth and fantasy in the contemporary Islamic movement] (1986) and *Al-Sahwa al-Islamiyya fi Mizan al-'Aql* [The Islamic awakening in the scales of mind]. He has written many articles about philosophy, Islam, and current affairs and is considered a leftist in his views. In addition to his writing, Zakariyya participates in symposia on current affairs, is a member of UNESCO's Committee on Arab Education, and has won many prizes in Egypt, Kuwait and other countries. In late 1993, Zakariyya returned to Egypt.

6 Perspectives on the Application of the *Shari'a*, the Rule of God, and the Islamic State

Bernard Lewis has written that Islam from its inception has been a religion of power:

> In the Muslim world view it is right and proper that power should be wielded by Muslims and Muslims alone. Others may receive the tolerance, even the benevolence, of the Muslim state, provided that they clearly recognize Muslim supremacy. That Muslims should rule over non-Muslims is right and normal. That non-Muslims should rule over Muslims is an offense against the laws of God and nature, and this is true whether in Kashmir, Palestine, Lebanon, or Cyprus.

Lewis goes on to point out that Islam is seen not as a religion in the Western sense but

> as a community, a loyalty, and a way of life . . . the Islamic community is still recovering from the traumatic era when Muslim governments and empires were overthrown and Muslim peoples forcibly subjected to alien, infidel rule. Both the Saturday people [Jews] and the Sunday people [Christians] are now suffering the consequences.[1]

P.J. Vatikiotis takes up the same issue in his *Islam and the State* and remarks:

> True knowledge is that of God and His Law, which embraces all human activity. This is an important ingredient in Islamic thinking from the start, which later became more explicit in countering heresy and enthroning orthodoxy. Truth was to be sought only in divine revelation.[2]

Finally, in *Islamic Liberalism*, Leonard Binder comments:

> For Islamic traditionalists, the language of the Quran is the basis for absolute knowledge of the world. For Islamic liberals, the language of the Quran is coordinate with the essence of revelation, but the content and meaning of revelation is not essentially verbal. Since the words of the Quran do not exhaust the meaning of revelation, there is a need for an effort at understanding which is based on the words, but which goes beyond them, seeking that which is represented or revealed by language.[3]

This is, perhaps, the essence of the outlook of different orthodox Islamic groups. The passages above show a great deal of commonality between 'moderates' and 'extremists'. Islam is the highest religion given by God. It is appropriate for every time and every place. Its rule is necessary for the transformation to a world of peace which is a world of Islam – by means of establishing an Islamic state under the 'rule of God' and headed by a caliph who will govern according to the *Shari'a* of Allah, which is the law of the Quran and the Hadith. It is the caliph's duty to uphold this law and the state's duty to fight the infidels in a jihad. As for the adherents of those religions which preceded Islam, Jews and Christians, their own true belief ostensibly obligates them to accept Islam. For it is 'written' in their Torah and in their sacred Scriptures that Muhammad is destined to appear, the last of the prophets, the bearer of the final and elect godly faith. Nevertheless, they are permitted to uphold their own 'distorted' faith in accordance with the conditions dictated by the Quran. In practice, this means accepting the rule of the Islamic state and paying a tax in return for its protection.

The recent past, and in particular the last two decades, have seen a surge of radical Islamic currents. Resurgent Islam is gradually imposing itself on Egyptian society and becoming the dominant force in the country. It is competing with democratic, liberal, socialist and even nationalistic political trends. Nor is the Islamic revival confined exclusively to Egypt; it embraces the entire Muslim world, from Morocco to Indonesia.[4] But Egypt is the core. Should religious extremists gain control in Egypt and establish a *Shari'a* regime like Iran's – the considerable differences between the religious approaches in the two places notwithstanding – it would trigger a chain reaction in many other Arab Islamic states.

To neighboring states, Egypt has always been a model to emulate. Developments there have a far-reaching impact, and many Egyptian intellectuals, aware of this, are voicing increasing concern over the rise of radical Islam in their country. Were an extremist regime to be established in Egypt, life would, they fear, regress hundreds of years. They do not accept all the assertions voiced by the proponents of an Islamic awakening, or the interpretations of the literal-minded commentators from Ibn Hanbal, Ibn Taymiyya, the Wahhabiyya, Jamal al-din al-Afghani, to Rashid Rida, Hasan al-Banna, Sayyid Qutb, Salih Siriyya, Shukri Mustafa, Muhammad 'Abd al-Salam Faraj and many al-Azhar staff and preachers, who differ from Islamic extremists in their readiness to wait until conditions are ripe for the establishment of an Islamic *Shari'a* state. In all other essentials, however, their outlooks are identical. Some liberal intellectuals[5] are willing to take their life in their hands, jeopardize their livelihood and risk boycott, ostracism and threats by publicly condemning the radical preaching of the religious fanatics. This chapter, then, considers the intellectuals' responses to the concepts of an Islamic state, *Shari'a*, and the rule of God.

JUDGE MUHAMMAD SA'ID AL-ASHMAWI

Judge Ashmawi is strongly at odds with the proponents of the slogans calling for the application of *Shari'a*, the rule of God, and the establishment of an Islamic state. He contends – notably in his two books, *Jawhar al-Islam* and *Al-Islam al-Siyasi* – that the word *Shari'a* appears only once in the Quran,[6] and three times it is derived from the root *shar'a*.[7] The four forms derived from the word *shar'a* in four Quranic verses refer to a scheme, path or way. God transmitted to His prophets and His messengers a single faith, namely belief in Him and devotion to Him. For Allah, then, religion is unitary, but the *Shari'a* [the Way] differs among the messengers and the prophets. Each of them has a *Shari'a*: ('To each of you have we given a path and a scheme'). The *Shari'a* of Moses was justice; of Jesus, peace and love; and of Muhammad, compassion. This is the meaning of the difference between the *Shari'as* of the various faiths.

The principles of the Islamic *Shari'a* were handed down to Muhammad as a result of events which required judgment to resolve. Therefore the correct application of the principles of *Shari'a* involves linking them to events which took place. With the exception of the first suras at the outset of Islam, these verses were handed down only in connection with a specific reason. It follows that the correct application of the principles of *Shari'a* entails knowing the reasons for each principle and the essence of the event for which it was handed down, and understanding the verses that annul *nasikh* the annulled verses [*mansukh*] and the principle which can be learned from them.[8] The *Shari'a* did not lay down a defined and unchanging governing regimen. However, since *Shari'a* correctly understood means a scheme, it must perforce adapt itself to every instance of progress or development. The correct Islamic regime is one that stems from the good society, from the will of its members, and from the conditions and character of the period.[9]

Islam as a religion and a state in its pure sense existed only in the time of Muhammad, which was the period of 'Umar Ibn al-Khattab and of 'Umar Ibn 'Abd al-Aziz, an Umayyad who is considered a God-fearing believer by most Islamic sects even though he belonged to the Umayyad dynasty, viewed by many Islamic streams with disfavor. Ashmawi maintains that 'Abd al-Aziz held power for only two years.[10] According to Ashmawi, then, a state-religion regime in Islam, in the purely religious sense, existed for no more than two or three decades. Following al-Khattab's death, he asserts, the situation of the Islamic nation reverted to its previous state, that is, to its condition in the period of the pre-Islamic *jahiliyya*. Thus were the tables turned. Earthly life resumed its former course and politics again foisted itself on religion. From this time Islamic religious history takes on a bloody political hue and *Shari'a* assumes a sectarian form akin to the state of the Arabs in the *jahiliyya* period. As Islam sank into a political morass, Islamic history became a struggle between different tribes, different groups (in Andalusia, for example) and different sects and between the Arab and Persian peoples. Religious content and political action became hopelessly intertwined, and so every dispute and every disagreement flared up, drawing emotional resonance from the faith and intense passion of the *Shari'a*.[11]

Islam is not a religion of *tashri'* [legislation] like Judaism, claims Judge Ashmawi; it is a religion of mercy, compassion and morality. Of the Quran's 6,000 verses, 700 are devoted to matters of general religious law and only 200 to matrimonial laws, inheritance laws, precepts of behavior and punishments. In other words, only one-thirtieth of the Quran's verses are considered laws; and some of these were annulled by *nasikh*, leaving only 80 verses, or one-seventy-fifth of the total. Islamic thought followed in the footsteps of Judaism but without taking note of the difference between the essence of Moses's mission and the essence of Muhammad's mission. Ashmawi asserts that the Quranic term *hukm* refers to a judgment or ruling in a dispute between individuals, or to a trial just in its wisdom. It should not be understood in its modern sense of governing, which is designated by the term *imara*; it is for this reason that 'Umar Ibn al-Khattab and the caliphs who followed were known as *amir al-muminin*, rather than *hakim al-muminin*. However, those who espouse the faith's political orientation seize on this distorted interpretation and thus take various Quranic verses to mean that religion and state are intertwined and that government must be the rule of God. But as government is in human hands, the slogan of the rule of God is false.[12]

In *Shari'a*, a civilian government rules in the name of the people, and not a religious government with pretensions to being the rule of God; for only the Messenger or the Prophet governs according to the rule of God. After the Prophet, no one may govern according to the rule of God in a manner that will make him beyond questioning or beyond criticism, for the Prophet was questioned before God and the divine inspiration rectified what was in need of adjustment. Whoever claims that this is the rule of God does so in order to imbue his rule with sanctity and vest his opinion with *'isma* [immunity from sin]. A religious government, invested with sanctity and wholly infallible, is alien to an understanding of Islam. A government cannot be religious simply because its members are religious, because in matters of religion Islam is not based on specific people or a specific stratum of society; its source lies in the tenet that every believer is a cleric. Nor is a government religious because it implements the principles of *Shari'a*, for Islamic society implements the *Shari'a* principles through each of its individual members, and not through the government alone. The individual in Islam can be God-fearing and good, but his words, deeds and behavior will always remain those of a lay person.[13]

DR FARAJ FUDA

In his book, *Before the Fall*, Fuda takes issue with the religious zealots over the question of the Islamic state which existed in the period of Muhammad and the first four caliphs. The utopian state, according to Fuda, has never been realized throughout the entire course of human history, and the same holds true for the whole history of the Islamic caliphate, even in its most flourishing periods. 'Anyone who tells the keen youngsters that the establishment of a religious government might transform the whole society into a paradise on earth is describing a dream that can never become reality, for this is an illusion that has no place in historical reality.' Fuda maintains that there is a major difference between Islam as a religion and Islam as a state, and that criticism of the latter does not mean denial or rebellion against the former. If this is true with respect to the period of the first caliphates, it is all the more true of later periods. Fuda differentiates between Islam as a religion and Islam as a state in order to preserve the former, whereas he condemns the latter as an impractical model for realization. He views the former as a 'divine message' and the latter as concerned with affairs of this world. 'God revealed in His message what is needed to order the affairs of this world in certain chapters, leaving other chapters for humanity but without neglecting anything in His book.' But, according to Fuda, He embraces in His compassion people who are better versed in the affairs of their world than the ancient forefathers.

> Forsake, therefore, political discourse about the Book [the Quran] and about the sword, for the Book is within the heart. As for the sword, one can look to history; indeed, there is nothing like history to relate its story. For the sword has beheaded far more Muslims than infidels . . . Tell them what Sa'ad Ibn Abi Waqqas said when he withdrew from the *fitna* [the dispute]: Show me a sword that knows the difference between truth and falsehood.[14]

Fuda believes that those who, in the course of making comparisons, ignore the conditions of the different periods and the changes that occurred in them, are in fact leading us along a difficult if not impossible path:

> for it is no solution to have a certain group migrate to the caves of the Eastern Desert or to the pathways of Yemen, bearing a faith that has been reduced to its exterior sheen, devoid of content, and thinking that to use toothpicks and to use kohl for the eyes, and to accuse the society of apostasy and to ask themselves the names of the benevolent patriarchs constitute the height of worshipping the Creator. This is not a solution but a clash between Islam and the conditions of the period.[15]

Fuda advocates a separation between religion, politics and matters of government, believing it would be of the greatest benefit to both religion and government, despite what is said by those who advocate their non-separation. He draws a distinction between two issues. The first, which he accepts and whose implementation he urges, is the separation of religion and politics. The second, which he rejects, is the disregarding of religion as a basic element of society. The difference is major, in his view, because religion is needed as one component of society's conscience. He derives his argument from the stories in the history books not only about the later periods of Islamic rule, but about the genesis of Islam, such as what happened at the end of the period of 'Uthman[16] and what caused the insurgents to rise up against him. Among the insurgents were five of the ten to whom paradise was promised: 'Ali Ibn Abi-Talib,[17] 'Abd

al-Rahman Ibn 'Awf,[18] al-Zubair Ibn al-'Awwam,[19] Sa'ad Ibn Abi
Waqqas,[20] and Talha Ibn 'Ubayd-Allah.[21] It was they who accused
'Uthman of appointing his relatives as governors in the conquered
lands. He used Treasury funds without any rules and he persecuted
the companions of the Prophet. 'Ask me whether 'Uthman's actions
were religion or politics', asserts Fuda. The same applies to the
period of 'Ali. It is not, then, a matter of Quran or Sunna, but of
their interpreter. 'For neither you nor I doubt that both disputants
understand the Quran and cling to it and to its true source, the
messenger of God. Nevertheless each of them thought so differently
that they ended up killing one another and the blood flowed like
rivers'.[22]

Writes Fuda:

> 'I hereby affirm that there is no God but Allah and Muhammad is his
> servant and messenger.' This is the testimony of one whom the bad
> climate induced to brandish the slogan of religion as a substitute or to
> give priority to citizenship as proof of what demands neither proof nor
> emphasis. This is an unavoidable preface in the confrontation with [the
> adherents of] a current who at the slightest pretext will accuse a
> Muslim of heresy or fire the arrow of the *ridda* [apostasy] at anyone
> who disagrees with them[23] . . . I am an Egyptian citizen who laments the
> fate of his Egypt which is being dragged, in all good faith, in a direction,
> heaven forbid, which I will call the future.[24] For how far is the future
> from a theocracy which I do not believe the period can sustain, or in
> which the homeland can be sustained without its unity being threat-
> ened and everything cultural in it being crushed?

Fuda believes that the present call to implement the Islamic *Shari'a*
is merely a reaction to an outside influence and, like any reaction, it
takes a violent and hasty form – namely, the 1967 defeat and the
results of Israel's victory. Those who call for the application of the
Islamic *Shari'a* immediately and without delay are making a
seemingly logical statement, a statement which is posed in the form
of a logical question: what frightens you about applying *hudud* [the
punishments stipulated in the Quran]? After all, they will be
applied only against an adulterer or a drunkard or whoever forsakes
Islam or corrupts others. On the face of it this is a convincing
question. The application of the Islamic *Shari'a* inevitably leads to a
theocracy, claims Fuda, and the religious state will lead ineluctably
to the rule of divine truth. The idea of such a state was unknown in
the period of Muhammad. The rule of God can be implemented
only by means of clerics directly or indirectly, Fuda continues, 'and

everything we have said above leads without doubt to the collapse of national unity in Egypt'.[25]

DR FUAD ZAKARIYYA

In his book, *Al-Haqiqa wal-wahm fi al-Haraka al-Islamiyya al-Mu'asira* [truth and fantasy in the contemporary Islamic movement],[26] Zakariyya accuses those who advocate the application of *Shari'a* of constantly making statements which have a powerful emotional effect on the masses. Because of their impact, no one stops to consider these statements, even though they are extraordinarily vague and seriously flawed and thus cannot withstand a rational analytical critique. He cites two examples. The first is: divine rule in parallel to human rule.

> I admit, [he says] that I cannot fathom it. What form will the divine rule, or referring everything to the judgment of divine law, take? . . . Government, from start to finish, is a human activity and referral to the divine texts does not prevent the intervention of human beings in selecting the appropriate texts and interpreting them in a manner which will satisfy the ruling powers, as indeed has been the case throughout history, from ancient times to the present.

Zakariyya asserts that only during the period of the prophets was it permissible to speak of divine rule. Subsequently the appearance of the messengers and prophets ended, and the task of ruling passed into human hands. This will remain the case even if judgment is attributed to God. He warns that even the most sublime legislative principles cannot prevent the emergence of a despotic ruler who will persecute his flock, terrorizing and exploiting them. In the same way the most exalted divine laws do not prevent, and have not prevented, the emergence of tyrannical rulers who play with the ruled as they please. Most important, cardinal, and substantial are 'guarantees' which will dissuade the ruler from deviating. This interpretation of 'guarantees' is a purely human one which has evolved over time and was subject to a style of give and take. What matters most, according to Zakariyya, is that human beings alone are rulers and they are the ones who turn every divine *Shari'a* into something human, which will be right or wrong, in the course of governing – just as in most cases the ruler will apply constitutional principles and interpret them in a manner calculated to serve his goals and interests.[27]

Recent calls for this application undoubtedly have very broad mass support, Zakariyya acknowledges, and proponents cite this as confirmation of the idea's validity, asserting that they are obviously on the right track. 'Certainly, thirty years of repression, of rule by fiat and of a political regime against which argument is impossible bring about a situation in which this mass support is inevitable.' As a result, claims Zakariyya, we have witnessed broad sectors of the public flocking to the religious sects which base themselves on the ceremonial aspects of religion and on prohibitions in sex, clothing and other domains, thinking that the most important aspect of applying the *Shari'a* is to implement the punishments for drinking alcohol, for theft and for prostitution; while at the same time they turn away from economic and political problems.

> This cannot be a sign of health [notes Zakariyya], but an exceptional instance such as Egypt knew only in periods of lengthy one-man rule and in the era when the door was open to the infiltration of the backward thought which emanated from 'oil' societies which used religion as an instrument to preserve their interests domestically and to spread their lackluster ideologies outside.

The truth, continues Zakariyya, is that any population desiring to be genuinely Islamic must give priority not to a return to systems of laws that existed in early periods, but to removing all the qualifications that were attached to these laws during the periods of tyranny.[28]

Zakariyya stresses that it would be a gross injustice to treat the tens of thousands of serious young people who desire reforms as though they were deviants or an erring group which should be fought. 'In my view,' he says, 'their main problem is that they don't exercise their intelligence fully.' Zakariyya believes that hostility or persecution would not be useful in solving this kind of problem. Dialogue which strives to clarify thoughts and stands may solve it and eliminate the obfuscation which results from staring too long at an unchanging fixed point. He believes that a nation that imbues its members with this kind of thinking is leading itself to certain collapse in the near future.

> I believe that the most baseless myth in our life is the assertion, reiterated by many adherents of the Islamic movement, that imperialism in general, and America and Zionism in particular, fear the Islamic awakening and are out to quell it. After all, in Egypt Sadat encouraged the Islamic stream at the same time that he decided on a purely American orientation.

In Saudi Arabia there is a clear alliance between Islamic orthodoxy (which supports the majority of the Islamic movements in the Arab states both materially and morally) and serving American interests.

Zakariyya takes exception to the contention that the *Shari'a* is appropriate for every place and time. 'I doubt whether this is supported directly in any religious precept.' He believes that even a casual perusal of this expression will reveal two major contradictions in it. The first is that because human beings are changeable, it is essential that the principles that organize their life also be amenable to change. According to Zakariyya, those who advocate adapting the *Shari'a* for every place and time in a straightforward, naive interpretation must also recognize another contradictory fact: it was through the intelligence with which God endowed human beings and the knowledge He encouraged them to acquire that the basic fact of changeability, from which no human phenomenon is exempt, was discovered. The second contradiction is closely bound up with the first, as the direct implication of those who advocate adapting the *Shari'a* is to insulate human beings and condemn them to perpetual stagnation. For the straightforward interpretation of their statement is that in a certain period God bestowed on mankind laws which must be followed until the end of time. The contradiction here is that the exponents of this view stress that God bequeathed the earth to man and invested him with honor and exalted him above all else; but can this heritage and honor be reconciled with a situation in which the human path is predetermined? For Zakariyya,

> the question of adaptation for every time and every place obligates a comprehensive and revised interpretation in light of a truth which is today a convention of intelligence and science, namely that in the human domain there is nothing permanent or final. Many have acknowledged this, emphasizing that the general principle is amenable to interpretations from *ijtihad* [judgment] according to the needs of each period.[29]

In an emotional appeal to both state institutions and the media, Zakariyya calls for a dialogue to be conducted with those demanding the application of the *Shari'a*. Its implementation would mean a total change in the life of the individual and the society. It would affect education, culture and communications. It would influence the society, the way of government, the thrust of legislation, the use of the state's resources, and its foreign relations. Large numbers of people indeed sincerely believe in the *da'awa* [message, mission]. The great majority of them are good people who seek personal and social reforms. The ardent supporters of the application of *Shari'a* are usually pictured as upright, very religious youngsters who join Islamic groups and always listen to the sermons in the mosques. For the most part, these youngsters have heard only one opinion; therefore they believe it without argument. They generally have little exposure to modern education, even if they work in professions requiring knowledge in some area of modern science, such as medicine or engineering; this is because they do not allow their area of expertise to affect their view of life and the world. A new style is required to deal with these masses. In Zakariyya's opinion, what they need is for a dialogue to be conducted with them based on respect for their good will and their aspirations for reform, but which will direct their attention to the fatal mistakes of their spiritual guides and mentors. The present time is the most suitable for such a dialogue, as many voices are calling for the immediate application of the *Shari'a* which, ostensibly, contains the final and decisive solution to all problems: 'Attempts have emerged to apply the *Shari'a* in Arab states close to us, and we must analyse them in order to discover whether they have led to positive or negative results and to learn how profound the ramifications would be on society if it were implemented in Egypt.' The problem concerns the entire nation. Hence, it cannot be resolved by administrative fiats or by legal judgments. If it is not decided first and foremost in the minds of the people, it will flare up again and again, and when it erupts in the future, it will be far more dangerous.[30]

HUSAIN AHMAD AMIN

Husain Ahmad Amin addresses the issue at hand in a chapter on 'Call for the Application of the Islamic *Shari'a*'. Amin notes the outcry in Islamic societies to apply the principles of *Shari'a* and the pressure on leaders to understand that they are living in Islamic lands and are governing Muslim majorities. Amin affirms that every nation has the right to be ruled according to its faith:

> This is a truthful assertion which has the goal of truth, despite our feeling that there are governments and groups which are competing amongst themselves over religion and over encouraging the radical streams, or are trying to strengthen their rule in the face of opposition forces (such as the government of Zia al-Haq in Pakistan), or as a means

to expunge the ghost of the Iranian revolution (as in some of the Gulf states), or in order to serve private influences and interests, or to topple regimes from which these groups derive no benefit.

However, Amin also notes that despite the need to apply the *Shari'a*, 'This call is not as simple as most of its proponents deem it to be'. Amin begins by presupposing that the *Shari'a* is fundamentally not amenable to change in the light of social, economic and political developments. He then defines the Islamic *Shari'a* as constituting all the laws promulgated by God for the Muslims to follow in their behavior, their relations toward the Creator and their relations with fellow humans. Amin then asks:

> However, when I look more closely, I find that so immense, in both volume and scope, are the religious writings which interpret the *Shari'a* laws that they define which musical instruments we may and may not use [here follows a list of seemingly absurd examples] Are all these laws and rules truly included in the *Shari'a*? Are they binding? And if so, what is the divine authority for this?

Husain Ahmad Amin, like Judge Ashmawi (both men are jurists), asserts that the percentage of *Shari'a* laws which appear in the Quran, and even in the Hadith, is extremely low relative to the rules and principles which appear in the books of religious practices. In his view, there are no more than 80 verses in the Quran relating to questions of law such as theft, adultery and the rules for last wills and testaments. And the majority of these 80 verses make do with determining general principles which enable different interpretations and applications that can be correlated with the needs and circumstances of the period. Notes Amin:

> With the Prophet's death and the cessation of divine revelation came also the end of the legislation which can be extracted from the Quran and from the Hadith when the need arises. Did we not see how Abu Bakr changed the punishment of the wine drinker from flogging with whips to flogging with shoes? We know how 'Umar Ibn al-Khattab annulled the punishment of cutting off a thief's hand in the year of *al-ramada*[31] and how he prevented *mut'ah* marriages[32] and the pleasure of *al-Qubdhah* ('Two pleasures were customary in the time of the Prophet and I prohibit them in the form of an interdiction and I shall punish them', 'Umar declared), the connection between *Shari'a*.

One effect of the expansion of the Islamic state, according to Amin, was the mingling of the Arab conquerors with the adherents of other faiths, especially Judaism and Christianity, resulting in their increased influence over the Arabs. At the same time, however, the Muslims were meticulous about removing the influence of other faiths from their religion, even though, according to their theoretical belief, Islam is the religion of all the messengers from Adam to Muhammad and the Quran affirms what was stated in the Torah and the New Testament. Therefore there was no reason to fear the possible influences of other sacred faiths other than what they corrupted or distorted. As a result, according to Amin, some Muslims began to refashion what they accepted from the Torah and the New Testament in the form of traditions which they ascribed to the Prophet of Islam, and they began to interpret the Quran in the spirit of those same alien influences in order to reassure the Muslim public that their source was purely Islamic. This state of affairs facilitated the efforts of the governments of Islamic states, beginning in the nineteenth century, to revise their civil, criminal, commercial and administrative legislation according to western codes; to expand and emulate Western laws and abandon the Islamic *Shari'a*, with the exception of matrimonial laws, without feeling the need to offer an excuse for the change.

If we take into account that the majority of the *Shari'a* laws in Islam derive their authority from the *ijma'* [consensus of the *'ulama*], and that there are key aspects of the Islamic *Shari'a*, such as the caliphate theory, which are determined exclusively on the basis of *ijma'*, how then, asks Husain Ahmad Amin, is it possible to say that one must adhere to *Shari'a* laws which change with the times, when they are laid down by human beings like ourselves, and when we are just as capable as they of seeing and of exercising thought which one generation accepts as *Sunna*, another generation rejects as *bid'a* [innovation], and which a third generation may once again accept as *Sunna*? How is it possible to say that these laws are permanent and valid for every time and place and that if governments do not accept them they must be accused of heresy and deposed?

One of the flaws which vitiates Islamic thought and the Muslims' perception of their religion, asserts Amin, is the disregard for and inability to accept an historical perspective and the concept of 'development'. For this reason the Muslims long ignored the true worth of Ibn Khaldun,[33] the only Islamic thinker who subscribed to the concept of development. The overwhelming majority imagine that the *Shari'a* laws, as they have reached them, derive from the Quran and the Hadith, whereas every historian of Islam knows that the *Shariʻa* is a vast edifice in which most layers were added by people, one by one, over hundreds of years, in light of the development and needs of the Islamic society. Even though this great majority have read neither the history of Islam nor the basic books of the *Shariʻa* and religious law, the stringent among them very confidently attack anyone who deviates one iota from the letter of the texts. Amin's view is that the time has come to abandon this frozen, naive interpretation in order to grasp the truth about the stages by which the *Shariʻa* was built.[34]

YUSUF IDRIS

Arab nationalism is the issue in domestic politics that most interested Yusuf Idris, and that interest colored his attitude toward matters related to Islam or the *Shariʻa*. Like Muhammad Hasanain Haikal, he had, since the 1970s, admitted some of Nasir's mistakes, but remained loyal to the Nasirist ideology. As a result, it is impossible to consider Idris's ideas on religion without linking them to his Arab-nationalist outlook and his support for Nasir and attacks on Sadat.

In an article entitled 'Does Islam Object to Nationalism?' which appears in his book *Intibaʻat Mustafizza* [provocative impressions], Idris wrote:

> There is a surprising fear *vis-à-vis* Islam and *vis-à-vis* the Muslims, and a passionate outcry for a return to the correct Islam, to the period when the Muslims were rulers and subjects at the outset of Islam – as though we had long been heretics or as though the one and only solution to all our psychological, social, economic and political problems is the immediate application of the Islamic *Shariʻa*, or, more accurately, by applying Islam's criminal law, by hiding women in their houses as though they were a satanic instrument meant to seduce men and divert their attention from religion and their daily affairs.

Idris asserts that the phenomenon of fear is surprising because 'we were and still are Muslims. The illiterate Egyptian fellah knows his Creator well and conducts his prayers at the proper times.' Idris refers back to the period of the British occupation in Egypt when the call of the Muslim Brothers began to be heard, of which the harbinger was Shaikh Hasan al-Banna. He recalls that al-Banna's call enjoyed great success, particularly among the young people, and that it was only natural that the Muslim Brothers, as a vast assemblage of Islamic youth, should take part – men and women

alike – in the national movement. 'When we were [students] at
university we worked together – Muslim Brothers, Wafd members,
left-wingers and plain patriots – in full coordination and without
altercations.' The flourishing of the Muslim Brothers and the close
relations among its members, according to Idris, made it a prime
front for struggle. During the July Revolution, when the people
began to object to the rule of the military, the Brothers also opposed
it. Jamal 'Abd al-Nasir, concerned about their growing strength, the
more so when he realized they had gone underground and become
a fighting military group, moved to liquidate them on a massive
scale. He was unable to eliminate the entire Brothers movement
because they had scattered among the Arab states and elsewhere,
awaiting a more propitious time. Inside, a new radical Islamic
movement had already begun to organize. With Sadat's assumption
of power and the well-known stand he took toward the Nasirists
and left-wingers as the preface to his joining the American camp, he
saw that his only backing, inside and outside, came from these
'Muslims'. Under these conditions, according to Idris, the underground organizations multiplied and flourished on completely new
foundations. These were no longer political groups, like the Muslim
Brothers; they had become a radical organization which bared its
teeth and nails. This was sufficient to create a cover under which
Sadat could effect a conciliation with the Jews and 'hand over
Egypt, and then all the Arabs, to America and Israel'. The Khomeini
revolution proved to all those who were urging it that it was indeed
possible to establish an Islamic state led by shaikhs, preachers and
amirs of the underground Islamic groups. In the absence of a
nationalist leader following President Nasir's death, the imperialist
circles began to think about replacing 'Arab nationalism' with the
'Islamic idea', but things did not work out as America and Israel
wished. For the underground and open Islamic groups sprang from
young Arabs who were searching for their identity. They found the
greater part of that identity in Islam, and it was essential to round it
off with a patriotic national identity. 'They are, then, patriotic
youngsters, as we were in the 1950s and 1960s', declares Idris. 'They
joined the Islamic movements in good faith, pure and untainted,
battle-ready, with a powerful craving to brandish the banner of the
Islamic nation and of religion'.[35]

There is an urgent need for a genuine creative dialogue, not only
regarding the application of the Islamic *Shari'a* in a democratic or

totalitarian manner, but as regards all areas of our lives, with everyone listening to everyone else and everyone speaking out, so that the failure to listen to others does not become a revolt of the deaf against the speakers.

Idris urged a dialogue, particularly concerning the application of the *Shariʻa*, because the issue of applying the *Shariʻa* and Islamic rule had become the main topic in the establishment and opposition press alike, particularly in the opposition papers.

I have read a great deal about the opinions of respected clerics on this question and on the need to implement the Islamic *Shariʻa* immediately and without delay. I asked myself: What kind of Islamic government do they wish to establish? Is it the Islamic rule of Khomeini, that is, to turn clerics into governors as was done for Ayat-Allah? Or would it be a Wahhabi government, as in Saudi Arabia and the Gulf states? Or a Qadhafi-style Islamic government of the kind that exists in Libya? Or the kind of government Zia al-Haq has set up in Pakistan, or a Numairi-type rule [as] in Sudan? Will it apply the religious doctrines of the *Imam* al-Shafiʻi or of Ibn Taymiyya or the school of Ibn Hanbal? How shall we go about implementing whichever school it is, once we have made the choice? Are we to consider all the innovations in our lives since the death of those great *imams* and the closing of the gates of *ijtihad*, such as modern dress, radios, watches, televisions, cinema, theater, music and so forth . . . as a revolt against the *Shariʻa* simply by virtue of the fact that they were not mentioned in the Hadith or in the *ijtihad*, and then do away with all of them and go back to living in tents or clay dwellings? . . . I personally have no objection to our being ruled by a cleric, I even dream of it, provided this religious ruler has the broad horizons of Muhammad ʻAbduh, the purity of Shaikh al-Ghazali, the openness of Khalid Muhammad Khalid, the aggressiveness of Shaikh Kishk ʻin his confrontation against the enemies alone and not in his curses against female television announcers', and the gentleness of ʻUmar al-Talmasani.

In an impassioned appeal to the left-wing Islamic ideologue Khalid Muhammad Khalid, Yusuf Idris argues that the reaction of every person 'with an iota of common sense' to the discussion in the press about applying the *Shariʻa* can only be that the Prophet Muhammad delivered his message of reason while he still had a limited number of believers and fought the enemies of Islam and the Message. It was not the concern of the Messenger that one Muslim stole or fornicated; rather, he was concerned that the Muslims should first vanquish the enemies of God and their enemies. In order to adopt the *Shariʻa*, argues Idris, the first step is to protect Islam against its external enemies who have an interest in sowing divisiveness among its adherents.

> If this is not the first action of those who advocate application of the *Shari'a*, what, then, is? Cutting off the hands of two hundred thieves as was done in Sudan? Flogging twenty adulteresses and adulterers, while in Iran and Iraq and Lebanon hundreds of innocent Muslims die who were forsaken by their rulers only because they were busy with a more important problem: applying the *Shari'a* to the enemies of Islam within Islam itself – women who do not cover their hair and female television announcers who do not appear in modest *Shari'a* dress?[36]

Yusuf Idris, one of Egypt's great writers, a leftist, a liberal, a Nasirist and a champion of Arab unity, thus did not attach particular importance to the application of *Shari'a* law. His primary concern was the situation of the Arabs today and in Egypt, in particular. Like other Egyptian liberals, he viewed the gravest danger to be the revival of Islamic fundamentalist extremism, which he believed would cause further deterioration in the state of the Arab nation and Egypt.

DR 'ABD AL-'AZIM RAMADAN

In an article published in the weekly *October* (December 1988) entitled 'Between the Islamic *Shari'a* and Egyptian Law', Ramadan writes: 'I believe that the principal problem of Islam in this country is dramatized, from start to finish, in the ignorance of most people concerning religious matters.' Ramadan explains that religion is known to be part of the superstructure of society, that is, the cultural edifice that provides a faithful reflection of production relations and especially of property relations. If property relations are feudal in character, he notes, this is reflected in religion to the same degree that it is reflected in all spheres of thought and culture. The situation changes with the change of attitude toward capitalism and so forth. Many people do not understand what this means and they are upset when someone raises the issue. Ramadan contends that in the various periods since the sun of Islam rose, vast amounts of exegesis, *ijtihadath*, have been formulated and differences between the schools of thought induce those who exploit religion in their political preaching to achieve power, to attract large audiences among those who do not know or are unfamiliar with religion, in an effort to solicit support for their speechifying. Hence we now witness religious movements which attract young people whose knowledge is limited, and which try to foist their views on society by the use of dazzling slogans such as 'application of the Islamic *Shari'a*'. In some cases, these movements push the young people to kill in the name of religion. On countless occasions, notes Ramadan, 'we have pointed out that this slogan is of no relevance to the actual situation, since civil law is consistent with the *Shari'a*'. Ramadan believes that the difference centers on the view of the criminal law to the *hudud* [punishments in Muslim religious law], theft, slander, prostitution, highway robbery, wine drinking and forsaking of Islam. In meting out these punishments, the ruler has the prerogative of *ta'zir* [mitigating the penalty]. Says Ramadan:

> My opinion here is based on al-Hudaibi, the former head of the Muslim Brothers, and not on Marx or Lenin. Nevertheless, I have faced a flood of accusations, such as that I am a Marxist or a Communist or a heretic, from those who exploit religion to further their own political interests, and from their deceived supporters.[37]

Under the title, 'The Society of Beneficiaries of the Application of the Islamic *Shari'a*', Ramadan notes that many people, especially the younger generation, think that the present demand in Egypt for the application of the Islamic *Shari'a*, as reflected in the passage of the law in the National Assembly prohibiting wine drinking, is something new. In truth, asserts Ramadan, this is an old view, one that periodically renewed, sometimes strongly, at other times more moderately. Ramadan asks a complex question that he believes may be bothering many people, namely: How did it come about that we follow non-religious laws in our judgments, whereas our forefathers were accustomed to judge according to the Islamic *Shari'a*? Ramadan replies with a brief historical survey: It is known that Islamic legislation was created in the period of the Messenger and was based on the Quran and the Hadith. It developed further in the period of the first caliphs and the followers of Muhammad, when Islam spread east and west, north and south, and at which time legislation was founded on the *ijtihad* which is essential for understanding the book of God and the tradition of His Messenger. At the same time, the laws and traditions of the lands which became part of the Islamic empire began affecting the religious law and legislation. As a result, two trends emerged in religious law and the *Shari'a*: the trend of those who adhered to the Hadith, whose center was the Hijaz, and which later gave rise to the Maliki, Hanbali and Shafi'i schools; and the *ahl al-ray* [men of opinion] trend whose center was in Iraq. The doctrine of the Shafi'i school was intermediate between the two trends. Islamic legislation entered a period of maturation following the establishment of the Abbasid state in which the four major schools of Islam crystallized (Maliki, Hanbali, Shafi'i and Hanafi). However, Islamic legislation came to an end with these four great schools of law which at that time could provide all the solutions and related judgments for economic and social problems. Now, alleges Ramadan, some shortsighted people think that social life cannot advance beyond that limit. Societies, though, evolve continuously and are in constant movement, so that when the Islamic thinkers could go no further, having encountered the limits of the *ijtihad* of the four *imams*, what befell the Islamic societies was inevitable, particularly in the period of decline and stagnation. As a result, they began to supplement their legislation by borrowing Western laws. As for Egypt, the shift from Islamic *Shari'a* to non-religious laws involved a series of developments under Western influence. In the meantime many Islamic organiza-tions began to call for application of the Islamic *Shari'a*, particularly after the appearance of the Muslim Brothers and the *Misr al-Fatat* [Young Egypt] group, the latter attracting many Islamic groups which sought to escape the suffering caused by imperialism and exploitation. According to Ramadan, the self-interested among the reactionaries took advantage of the ratification of the 1936 alliance to start harping on religious fervor in order to appropriate government from the people and place it in the hands of the palace. They began brandishing the slogan of religion and the implementation of an Islamic regime and came up with the idea of placing Farouq on the throne in a religious ceremony at al-Qalah [Muhammad 'Ali's strong-hold], with Shaikh al-Azhar handing him the sword of his grand-father, Muhammad 'Ali, following which the masses would flock to him as to an *imam*, and the *Shari'a* rules would be published in his name. Al-Azhar supported this idea ardently, backed by the Muslim Brothers and Young Egypt. The members of these organizations streamed to the palace in order to grant him a *bay'a* [a religious appointment for life according to the Islamic *Shari'a*] in accordance with the book of God and the Hadith. Thus arose the idea of reviving the Islamic caliphate and appointing the semi-illiterate boy Farouq as caliph over the Muslims, a dream which was thwarted by the outbreak of World War II. The call for the application of the Islamic *Shari'a* died down until in our own time it has increased again. What always raises doubts concerning the application of the Islamic *Shari'a*, in the eyes of Ramadan, is that its proponents forget that it is a totality whose economic foundations and political, judicial and ideological edifice are indivisible. Therefore they demand that only the judicial structure be utilized.

> I do not think that there is a liberal force in this homeland which would refuse to apply the Islamic *Shari'a* in its economic and judicial foundations together. As for its application on a non-Islamic economic basis, this would adversely affect Islam and Muslims. For it would mean that Egyptian capitalism wishes to protect its property by subjecting the poor to the cruel punishments of Islam but at the same time not wishing to subject property to a just Islamic distribution! It does so at a time when its profits are piling up in an unprecedented manner but is refusing to divert these gigantic profits for the benefit of the country.

Thus, Ramadan maintains that while the pillars of Egyptian capitalism are calling for the application of the cruel Islamic punishments in order to preserve their property, they ignore the fact that Islam laid down punishments only after determining an economic base that rejects any justification of violations. Ramadan asks why those who call for application of the Islamic *Shari'a* do not say a word about the Islamic economic base. It is, he says, because this Islamic economic base is not consistent with their interests. For all these reasons one does not find among those urging the application of the *Shari'a* anyone advocating the implementation of the proper economic edifice, as this would entail a great upheaval that would shake the country's economic and social foundations. It would be more violent than what ensued in the wake of the decisions on nationalization and agrarian reform, believes Ramadan, hence the call for the application of the *Shari'a* assumes an exterior form only. Thus, concludes Ramadan, 'We, like you, and like all progressive forces, demand the application of the Islamic *Shari'a*, but we demand its entire implementation on an economic base before the judicial aspect. Thus we shall prove that we are more Muslim than you and have a deeper understanding of the faith.'[38]

Ramadan is not alone in this last declaration. Other liberal intellectuals, Judge Ashmawi among them, have also claimed to be 'more Muslim' rather than less so in their opposition to a fundamentalist understanding of Islam.

TAWFIQ AL-HAKIM

In an article entitled 'The Principles of Islam which Transform the Individual into a Human Being and a Muslim', Tawfiq al-Hakim writes:

There is no doubt that every Muslim is delighted at this activity by the state and by religious bodies for 'Islamic preaching', but the question is what purpose it serves. Is the intention to provide knowledge about Islam, which has already existed for fourteen hundred years? Or is this a new perception of the meaning and goals of Islam to make this religion shine upon the world as it moves toward the year 2000? If this religion is meant for the whole world, have we endeavored to disseminate its content and goals by translating the Quran and the Hadith? Otherwise, what kind of preaching or call will there be?[39]

In the words of al-Hakim:

I am not satisfied with reports, definitions and statements handed down to us from our childhood, like canned preserves of rote learning, and because I must follow my own instincts and analyze and think about the conceptual and intellectual nourishment I receive, I peruse the books of religion in this way and I emerged with beautiful, sublime foundations of Islam which transformed me into a human being and a Muslim: compassion, knowledge and humanity. But before all else and above all else, naturally, is the affirmation: 'There is no God but Allah and Muhammad is the messenger of God.'

Al-Hakim quotes dozens of verses from the Quran and from the words of the Prophet on these three foundations, and then asserts that most energy has been expended on formal matters – ceremonies and rituals – and that people have turned to extremism to such an extent that they have forgotten what is said of Islam, that it is 'a deep religion and therefore dive into it gently'. Al-Hakim attests that the meaning and purpose of Islam have not been studied freely and in depth in a manner sufficient to show that it is indeed appropriate for every time and every place. He notes:

We concentrated on its past, and we almost began to be convinced that it was suitable only for the period in which it sprang up. We are now on the threshold of the year 2000 as we begin the 'call or the preaching to Islam', and the question that arises is: 'What does Islam have to offer for the year 2000?'[40]

With my last remaining strength [pleads al-Hakim] I call for the renewal of Islamic thought, because Islam today faces a danger in that its believers have deviated from its essence in their thinking, being content with an interest in formal matters, externals and materialism. I noticed this when a respected cleric visited me in my office with some of his associates. I asked him about the meaning of 'Say that I am only flesh and blood like you . . .' and what was meant by flesh and blood. He replied: 'That he eats, drinks and sleeps' like everyone else. I did not want to argue with my guest, but I started wondering about his reply, for how was it that a learned man like him did not notice that an animal too, and not only a human being, possesses these same attributes – an animal, after all, also eats, drinks and sleeps. God, all praise to Him, made man unique through the attribute of knowledge. That is why this word is mentioned so frequently in the Quran. And, as the Messenger of God said: 'Shall the Quran be of any use without knowledge or science?'[41]

Now that the enactment of Islamic religious law is being considered so that the *Shari'a* will become the source of legislation, al-Hakim calls for study of the source of the *Shari'a* in the society in which it first emerged, and the path on which the *Shari'a* principles advanced. He asks if these principles have remained complete in society, or if something of them is still left. What is consistent with the *Shari'a* in civil law? What are the differences? Al-Hakim advocates that the clerics familiarize the people with the broad horizons shown by the Prophet of Islam when he accepted unflinchingly what had been customary before Islam, as he accepted the punishment of cutting off a thief's hand which was the custom in the *jahiliyya* period, following which the Quran prescribed the same punishment. The same holds for the punishment of stoning which was practised in the Torah. This proves that there is nothing to prevent Islam from accepting what was not engendered within Islam itself. In the words of al-Hakim, 'This is what the Prophet meant when he said, "Seek knowledge even in China". There is thus nothing to prevent Islam from accepting what will benefit Muslims, but the clerics in our time lack the boldness to do what the Prophet himself did.' Al-Hakim urges that the foundation be in the daily acts of life which are beneficial to people, and not only in the ancient ceremonies. Therefore Islamic philosophy should be founded upon a stable edifice which the Islamic thinkers erected, just as philosophy is constructed like a building: brick by brick, effort by effort. The edifice of Islamic philosophy must be grounded in the foundation of life in two worlds: this one and the next. The clerics must delve deeply into the issues relating to this world, that is, they must have intimate knowledge of this world alongside their expertise in knowledge of the next world. By effecting a balance between the two types of life, Islamic and Arab philosophy will grow. 'All this', concludes al-Hakim, 'in the spirit in which Islam has excelled, namely moderation and an absence of exaggeration, extremism and bombast.'[42]

DR AHMAD KAMAL ABU AL-MAJD

In his article, 'Those Who Fear Islam and Those Fearful for It', Abu al-Majd writes:

> Across the length and breadth of the Islamic world, from the ends of the East to the ends of the West, a passionate debate is under way over one phenomenon which has nearly shunted aside all the other problems and concerns of the Arabs and the Muslims. Some accept this phenomenon with satisfaction, and therefore sometimes term it Islamic expansion or an Islamic awakening. Others view it with outrage and concern and therefore call it 'religious extremism' or religious terror.

What is strange in this whole phenomenon, in Abu al-Majd's view, is that many who take part in the debate do not truly reveal what they want, yet they are entrenched in their stands. They 'hide behind masks' to conceal their intentions and thus leave readers and listeners bewildered. But the solution to the problem is not advanced by even one iota. Abu al-Majd believes that what is needed is a quiet discussion about the legitimate fears of those who are appalled at the mistakes of some preachers and the excesses of many young people who terrorize people in the name of Islam and fill public life with calls for the application of the *Shari'a*, the reform of the faith and the 'Islamization' of society. Abu al-Majd believes that there are four reasons for these concerns:

1. The desire to exhume the past, to restore the experiences of the fathers of Islam and to ignore the facts of the present and the changes of the future. This fear is justified because many adherents of the contemporary Islamic streams view 'the nation's past' as a period of pristine purity and privilege which purges the ills of the cultures which are set apart from Islam. They believe that attachment to this past is a sure guarantee against the 'cultural invasion' which afflicts nations in their periods of weakness. This yearning for the insularity of the past is sometimes called *salafiyya* [return to the era of the forefathers] and sometimes emulation, and it is politically and socially reactionary.

2. The tendency to follow slavishly to the letter of the religious texts and eliminate the role of intelligence in activity intended to alter society. This fear is also justified because many preachers from the Islamic groups have one fixation in their writing, that *ittiba'* [adherence] is the proper Islamic way and that *ibtida'* [creating innovations] is a deviation and an error and that

obedience to the Creator requires strict adherence to the letter of the texts. The call to use one's intelligence is considered to be either non-Islamic or the kind of preaching associated with Islamic sects such as the Mu'tazilites, which go beyond the logic of the followers of the *salafiyya*, the path of the Sunnis. Therefore they curse them. This fear is reinforced by the perception of many advocates of 'applying the *Shari'a*' that the *Shari'a* is, ostensibly, a whole and complete building which, if only society were to bring it into play at the proper historical juncture, would lead to the reform of the entire society and the disappearance of all its corruptions; this without taking note of the social consequences entailed in the application of these texts and without paying heed to the demands of social development which oblige religious law to evolve in order to provide a response to the changing needs of Islamic societies in different periods and different places.

3. The aspiration for the establishment of an autocratic religious political regime in which the ruler could govern as a cleric to the point where, ultimately, he would create a regime of absolute despotism without taking into consideration the rights of his subjects. There is no justification for the fears relating to the first element in the establishment of such a regime; the concern is that religious ardor and the desire to expedite the application of the *Shari'a* are liable to tempt those of good will to accept the ruler's tyranny, his discrimination against those who differ with him, contempt for the Shura and the undermining of rights and freedoms – as long as he continues to work for the application of the Islamic *Shari'a*. There are many examples of such views at this time and close at hand. The need to warn people against being taken in is urgent.

4. The utilization of violence, undermining the laws (with the assent of those who advocate application of the *Shari'a*), and abrogation of non-Muslim rights in Islamic societies.[43]

NABIL 'ABD AL-FATTAH

In his book, *Al-Mushaf wal-Saif* [the book and the sword], 'Abd al-Fattah writes that the original framework for building the Islamic model based on rejection of the western heritage and the presentation of Islam as a perfect model for life in Islamic societies is given expression by the *salafiyya* stream, which draws its inspiration from the historical model. This, notes 'Abd al-Fattah, means that the structure of the *salafiyya* stream and its foundations, and even analysis, began with the theory of Sayyid Qutb and al-Mawdudi in connection with the *jahiliyya* of the society, and extends all the way to the path that avoids this *jahili* situation. The latter situation should indeed be rejected and discarded, and replaced by a new order in life. 'This is the order of the first stage of the [Islamic] call.' In fact, states 'Abd al-Fattah, this model is based on the external roots of the past. The salafite conception of society is a recurring model because all that was left, after achieving the Muslim ideal in the period of the Messenger of God and his companions, was the recurring preoccupation with and reactivation of the same ideal by emulation and rote learning. In our time it is bound up with religious perceptions and the rewards of the next world and beyond, through an effective modern revolutionary dynamic. This consolidates the process of emulation and envelops it in an aura of sanctity and devotion. Man stands in the shadow of this model in a quantitative, not a qualitative posture. His life is predetermined, politically and intellectually, and he must act according to precepts of permission and prohibition – that is, the salafite, which consolidates these parameters – thus dramatizing the fact that the salafite stream is suffering from a true crisis in its intellectual development and in its disregard of creative social ramifications. In the words of 'Abd al-Fattah:

> What is beyond doubt is that any attempt to find a formula for a cultural or developmental model is independent of the West; it is a generations-long effort which cannot ignore the fact that Islam is one of the primary components of Egyptian national identity which is being trampled by the burden of Westernization, by the lure of the sources, culture and economy of the imperialist West.[44]

DR HUSAIN FAWZI AL-NAJJAR

'Islam did not propound a theory of the state, although it did determine a foundation for government based primarily on the needs of society.' The state, according to al-Najjar, was not a goal of Islam nor was it set forth in the *Shari'a*; nothing was mentioned which points to the establishment of a state or a ruling regime and its characteristics. The ancient world witnessed the emergence of what in modern terminology is known as the nation-state: Egypt was the earliest. However, the Islamic *Shari'a* did not require the establishment of a state or a government, but determined clearly and in a manner that brooks no argument the existence of *umma Islamiyya*. The term *umma* as it appears in the Quran denotes a large group of people, greater than *sha'b* [a people], *qawm* [ethnic group] or *qabila* [tribe]. Al-Najjar cites numerous verses confirming his interpretation of the term *umma*. Thus, the Islamic *umma* is the nation of Islam and of the Muslims, incorporating all their peoples, ethnic groups and races. The land of the Muslims is the world which contains them, for Islam came for all peoples. But the *bala'gh* [message] has not been completed to this day. Notes al-Najjar, 'When the whole world becomes a single Islamic nation, the world-state which Islam seeks to produce will come into being.'[45]

✳

In this survey of the thought of liberal intellectuals, an effort has been made not to repeat ideas. Naturally, many more figures could have been included. Nor did we consider the predominantly Islamic thinkers who demand in no uncertain terms the establishment of an Islamic state, the application of the *Shari'a* and so forth, such as Muhammad al-Ghazali, Fahmi Huwaidi, Dr Muhammad 'Amara, Dr Husain Hanafi and others. Perhaps a passage from a book by Dr Fahmi al-Shinnawi, *Nahwa Islam Siyasi* [toward a political Islam], may be quoted to demonstrate the intellectual thrust of all the Islamic preachers in our time including those mentioned above:

> Islam is today shackled and enclosed within the mosque. All that is needed is the undoing of its shackles and its release into the street . . . The attempt to release the bonds of Islam from within the mosque, and in Egypt in particular, is an historic task and an historic turning point . . . In short, Islam is fundamentally political, and the Islamic cleric is fundamentally political. The situation of the Muslims throughout the world requires an urgent change, otherwise [Islam] is doomed to extinction. This change begins with a return to political Islam. The Islamic movement must embrace the Islamic nation, not [just] on a local or national scale. It must fight every national or nationalist conception for the good of the unity of the Islamic nation. The goal of unifying the Islamic nation must be the object of every Muslim everywhere on this earth, which has today become a single village.[46]

This, then, is what concerns the liberal intellectuals, but their voices are fading as they fear for their lives. Those who nevertheless are bold enough to express themselves do so out of concern for

Islam, ostensibly, and they begin by demonstrating their faith and 'Islamicism', as we have seen. But this enhances their credibility neither in the eyes of the reader nor in the eyes of the preachers of Islam.

NOTES

1. Bernard Lewis, *Alei Hahistoriya* [leaves of history] – a collection of research articles (Jerusalem, Yad Ben Zvi, 1987–88), p. 292 (Hebrew editor, Rachel Simon). Taken from an article that first appeared in *Commentary*, Jan. 1976, pp. 39–49, entitled 'The Return of Islam'.
2. P.J. Vatikiotis, *Islam and the State* (1987), p. 21.
3. Leonard Binder, *Islamic Liberalism* (1988), p. 4.
4. Saad Eddin Ibrahim, 'Egypt's Islamic Activism in the 1980s', *Third World Quarterly*, April 1988, pp. 632–57.
5. For the purposes of this discussion, 'intellectual' will be defined as any philosopher, author, thinker, historian, researcher or journalist who writes about social affairs and the government in Egypt, including matters of religion. 'Liberal' will be defined as any intellectual who believes in the separation of religion and state in the sense accepted in the West, even if he himself is religious, and is open to the opinions of others, even if he is sometimes opposed to those opinions, and is willing to relate with some under-standing and sympathy to others and to other religions. Most of these liberal intellectuals are thoroughly versed in western culture and open to its methods.
6. 'Crouching', verse 44:18.
7. 'Counsel', verse 42:13; 'The Table Spread', verse 4:48; 'Counsel', verse 42:21.
8. Muhammad Sa'id al-Ashmawi, *Jawhar al-Islam* [The essence of Islam] (Cairo, 1984, pp. 12–28.
9. Ibid., p. 52.
10. Muhammad Sa'id al-Ashmawi, *Al-Islam al-Siyasi* [Political Islam] (Cairo, 1987), p. 10. 'Umar Ibn 'Abd al-Aziz was active in the years 717–20.
11. Ibid., p. 15.
12. Ibid., pp. 34–6.
13. Al-Ashmawi, *Jawhar al-Islam*, pp. 53–5. For additional details about Ashmawi, see David Sagiv, 'Judge Ashmawi and Militant Islam', *Middle Eastern Studies*, Vol. 28, No. 31 (July 1992); David Sagiv, 'Egypt – A War of Religion and State', *Davar* (Israel), 26 June, 1992; and Shulamit Hareven, and David Sagiv, 'An Interview with Muhammad Sa'id al-Ashmawi', *Hotam*, 10 Nov. 1989.
14. Faraj Fuda, *Qabl al-Suqut: Hiwar Hawla Tatbiq al-Shari'a al-Islamiyya* [Before the fall: a dialogue on applying the Islamic *Shari'a*] (Cairo, 1985), pp. 18–33. For details about Fuda and his views, see David Sagiv, 'The Small Jihad and the Big Jihad', *Davar*, 19 June, 1992 (ten days after his assassination).
15. Fuda, *Qabl al-Suqut*, pp. 51–3.
16. 'Uthman Ibn Affan, the third caliph (643–56), killed by the son of the first caliph, Abu Bakr.
17. The fourth caliph, cousin of Muhammad (656–61), killed by a Khawariji.
18. One of the first to convert to Islam (580–652).
19. One of the first to convert to Islam (593–656).
20. A military commander who conquered Iraq in the Battle of al-Qadisiyya and then con-quered Persia (595–675).
21. One of the first to convert to Islam. He was killed in the Battle of Al-Jamal at the side of Aisha, who fought 'Ali in 656.

22. Faraj Fuda, *Al-Haqiqa al-Ghaiba* [The absent truth] (Cairo and Paris, 1986), p. 14.
23. Fuda, *Qabl al-Suqut*, p. 51.
24. Ibid.
25. Ibid., pp. 51–2.
26. Fuad Zakariyya *Al-Haqiqa wal-wahm fi al-Haraka al-Islamiyya al-Mu'asira* [Truth and fantasy in the contemporary Islamic movement] (Cairo, 1986).
27. Ibid., pp. 5–10.
28. Ibid., pp. 10–16.
29. Ibid., pp. 16–20.
30. Ibid., pp. 119–23.
31. The year of *al-Ramada* is the 'year of death' in which many people died because of a prolonged drought at the time of Umar.
32. *Mut'ah* – marriage that was for a set period; this was annulled by the Sunnis, but remained in force for the Shi'ites.
33. Ibn Khaldun (1333–78), well known for the sociological preface to his book, *Kitab al-'Ibar* [The book of admonitions].
34. Husain Ahmad Amin, *Dalil al-Muslim al-Hazin* [Guide for the sad Muslim] (Cairo, 3rd edition 1987), pp. 185–98.
35. Yusuf Idris, *Intiba'at Mustafizza* [Provocative impressions] (Cairo, 1986), pp. 80–4.
36. Ibid., pp. 103–8.
37. 'Abd al-'Azim Ramadan, 'Between the Islamic *Shari'a* and Egyptian Law', *October* (journal), No. 635, 25 Dec. 1988.
38. 'Abd al-'Azim Ramadan, *Misr fi 'Ahd al-Sadat* [Egypt during Sadat], Vol. 1 (Cairo, 1986), pp. 293–303.
39. See summary in David Sagiv, 'Dialogue with God: The Debate Between Tawfiq al-Hakim and Religious Zealots', *Apiryon* (journal), special issue: *The View Toward Egypt* (ed. Erez Biton) (Ramat Gan, 1989).
40. Tawfiq Al-Hakim, *Fi al-Waqt al-dai'* [In lost time] (Cairo, 1987), pp. 145–57.
41. Ibid., pp. 158–9.
42. Tawfiq al-Hakim, *al-Ta'aduliyya ma' al-Islam* [The equilibrium with Islam] (Cairo, 1983), pp. 163–7.
43. Ahmad Kamal Abu al-Majd, *Al-Khaifun min al-Islam wal-Khaifun 'Alayhi* [Those who fear Islam and those fearful for it], *Al-Hilal*, July 1987, pp. 8–16.
44. Nabil 'Abd al-Fattah, *Al-Mushaf wal-Saif* [The book and the sword: the struggle between religion and state] (Cairo, 1984), pp. 47–8.
45. Husain Fawzi Al-Najjar *Al-dawla wal-Hukm fi al-Islam* [State and rule in Islam] (Cairo, 1985), pp. 9–116.
46. Fahmi Al-Shinnawi, *Nahwa Islam Siyasi* [Toward a political Islam] (Cairo, 1985), pp. 5–8.

7   Attitudes to the Caliphate and the Imamate

In Chapter 1 we noted the controversy touched off by Shaikh ʿAli Abd al-Raziq with his book *al-Islam wa Usul al-Hukm* [Islam and the basis of rule] in which he spoke out against the institution of the caliphate in Islam. We also noted how he was castigated for this view, especially by Shaikh Muhammad Bakhit. First we shall briefly review the development of the caliphate in the history of Islam.

The caliphate came about following the death of the Prophet Muhammad, with the ceremony of *bay'a* – formal acknowledgement of a new caliph – in the year 632. After a stormy argument between the followers of al-Ansar, who chose Saʿd Ibn ʿAbada as the caliph, and the followers of Abu Bakr, led by ʿUmar Ibn al-Khattab. Abu Bakr was declared *khalifat rasul Allah* [successor of the Messenger of Allah] by the oath of those disciples of Muhammad who had gathered in a place called *al-Saqifa* [the hut] in the city of Medina. From that moment, Abu Bakr was successor to the Prophet and caliph of the Muslims. Abu Bakr was given the opportunity to pass on the caliphate, and when he died in 634, the *bay'a* was immediately held for ʿUmar Ibn al-Khattab. The oath of the *bay'a* was given only by those present in Medina, and there were Muslims throughout Saudi Arabia who challenged the selection of ʿUmar. Before his assassination, ʿUmar had decided to allow the six heads of the Muslims to choose the caliph from among themselves, including ʿUthman Ibn ʿAffan and ʿAli Ibn Abi-Talib. The *bay'a* was held for ʿUthman. It can thus be seen that there was no single method designated for choosing a caliph. The first was chosen by those gathered in *al-Saqifa*, the second was declared caliph by his predecessor, and the third was elected by the six heads of the Muslims.

The caliph was also considered the *imam*; he was expected to lead the *haj* pilgrimage; it is his right to declare jihad; and it is his lifelong responsibility to preserve the Quranic message and *al-Sunna* [the tradition of Muhammad]. The *imam* often ruled at his discretion within the context of these two elements – the Quran and the *Sunna*. 'Uthman was assassinated because he apportioned the wealth of the state to those close to him, and appointed governors from among his family. When asked to give up the caliphate because of his corruption, 'Uthman refused and was assassinated in 656. After his death, 'Ali was elected caliph. However, Mu'awiya Ibn Abi Sufian challenged the leadership of 'Ali who was killed in a violent quarrel within his own camp, and thus the road was paved for the rule of Mu'awiya, who appointed himself caliph. Mu'awiya passed on the caliphate within his dynasty, the Umayyads, based in Damascus. The rule of the Umayyad dynasty came to an end in 750 following bitter conflict and the caliphate was 'returned' to Muhammad's family by way of the descendants of 'Abbas, based in Baghdad. However, the Abbasids adopted from the Umayyads the system of passing on the caliphate within their own dynasty. Caliph al-Mansur went so far as to claim that he represented 'the rule of God on earth', and was not merely a caliph successor to Muhammad. In Spain (Andalusia), a caliphate was established in parallel to the caliphate in Baghdad. In Egypt, a Shi'ite caliphate was set up by the Fatimids who ruled Egypt, Syria and Palestine (909–1171), which threatened the caliph in Baghdad. The Mongols put an end to the Abbasid caliphate when they assassinated Caliph al-Mu'tasim in 1258. Later, the Mamelukes renewed the Abbasid caliphate which was bereft of all real power and faded away with the Ottoman conquest in 1517. The Ottoman sultans did not refer to themselves as caliphs until the late 1700s. In 1922, following the revolt of the Young Turks led by Mustafa Kamal Ataturk, the caliph in Ankara became only a symbol and in 1924 the caliphate was completely abolished. Many, including the Shaikhs of al-Azhar, mourned the abolition of the caliphate; we have noted how King Farouq attempted, unsuccessfully, to declare himself the caliph with the support of al-Azhar and the Muslim Brothers.[1]

JUSTICE MUHAMMAD SAID AL-ASHMAWI

At the beginning of the mission (610), the Prophet was one who prophesied and warned. He was not a ruler. After the *hijra* to Medina (Yathrib) in the year 622, his rule began and lasted for ten years . . . After the death of the Prophet, his companion Abu Bakr became the first caliph. The term *khalifa* has two meanings: one who succeeds someone legally or actually; or one who succeeds someone chronologically.

With reference to Abu Bakr, the first generation of Muslims meant by *khalifa* the second meaning, that is, that he came after him chrono-logically, especially since prophecy is not handed down. Prophecy is not inheritable. And there is no caliphate for the prophet in his regime, as this rule is unique to him. However these two meanings became obscured in the Islamic approach, and people began to treat the caliphs as if they were successors to the Prophet, in particular inheriting some of his prophetic powers. One generation after the death of the Prophet, the Islamic state turned into an empire and the caliphate was passed on across generations (660). The caliph actually became an emperor. The caliphs and their exegetes focussed on the point of view which says, if only by implication, that the caliph is one who inherits the Prophet's rights [without his obligations]. Islamic political law began to center on the caliph and his rights as a ruler who does not give attention to the rights of the ruled and the nation, except marginally.[2]

For the Shi'ites, Ashmawi continues, religious and secular leader-ship are vested in the imamate. The *imam* must issue from the loins of the Prophet Muhammad, specifically from the offspring of his daughter Fatima and her husband 'Ali Ibn abi-Talib, the cousin of the Prophet. And because the *imam* of our times has not yet appeared, according to the belief of the twelfth school of the imamate, which is the largest Shi'ite school of thought, every ruler will be merely the successor of the *imam* (as in Iran today). The Shi'ite considers the imamate to be the sixth principle of faith (in addition to the five Islamic principles of the Sunni). Thus, in their view (as opposed to the Sunni view), the *imam* or the ruler is a religious power. In the Shi'ite view, the *imam* is chosen by Allah (or Allah denotes him) and he possesses the holy light, and therefore he is considered *ma'sum* [infallible] in his words and deeds, even though the Quran itself did not refer to the Prophet as infallible. According to Sunni belief, in contrast with Shi'ite views, the caliphate is not a religious power, although in actuality it has become religious; and there are explanations in theory that this is required 'in order to keep the religion and leadership of the world', which has made the caliph infallible, in effect, in his words and deeds.

In order to furnish the caliphs with religious justification for their foreign policy, the exegetes divided the world into two parts: the world of peace (or the world of Islam) in which all the territory under the caliphate and most of the inhabitants are Muslims; and the world of war, which is elsewhere. This division is not grounded in the Quran or in the words of the Prophet, but is a product of the exegetes. The time has come to renounce this division in order to discover the true face of Islam with respect to tolerance, equality, and peace and to erase the terrible impression derived from behavior connected with Islam.[3]

Ashmawi stresses that Islam does not endorse or dictate any particular form of rule. It does not set the regime of the government. And it is absolutely against what is called a theocracy which gives rulers immunity or holiness in any form whatsoever or under any name whatsoever, with the result that they act against the interests of the people and against freedom and justice, while exploiting the titles they bear, or else they distort religion or reality.[4]

FARAJ FUDA

Obviously the most important criteria for a ruler – and you might think that these criteria are lenient – must reflect that he is a Muslim who is sane and has the utmost integrity. But you encounter a strange criterion quoted in many books of exegesis, that he [the ruler] must be a descendant of the Quraysh tribe. You might be amazed that some people advocate this criterion in the name of Islam, in which all creatures are equal before it [Islam] 'like the teeth of a comb', where an Arab is not superior to an *a'jami* [non-Arab] except in piety. A strange thought might occur to you, which would be correct, that this criterion was set in order to justify the rule of the Umayyad or the Abbasid dynasties, all descendants of the Quraysh tribe. You might even have associations with what you read in recent history about King Farouq at the beginning of his rule, when the politicos of Egypt presented him in the image of the good king, appearing in pictures with his beard and beads and half-closed eyes, with ambitious religious leaders competing among themselves to declare him king and *imam* of the Muslims. The clever ones among them tried to prove his lineage to the Messenger of Allah, and the media quickly emphasized this lineage (even though his patrilinear grandfather was Mohammed 'Ali Basha the Albanian, and his matrilinear grandfather was Suleiman Basha of France), in order to fulfill one condition of the *imam*. One cannot but recall the gathering at *Saqifa* of the tribe of Sa'ida in Medina in which al-Ansar's followers chose Sa'd Ibn 'Abada, but Abu Bakr, 'Umar, and Abu 'Ubayd al-Jarrah quickly approached them and suggested Abu Bakr. A long argument ensued between the two sides which ended in the election of Abu Bakr. When you review this debate, you will not find the slightest mention of the Prophet's words noted above, since if they were true, Sa'd Ibn 'Abada, head of the al-Khazarj tribe, would not dared to have offered himself . . . Suffice it to say that Sa'd Ibn 'Abada consistently refused the *bay'a* of Abu Bakr until the day of his death. The Messenger of Allah did not address the matter [of the caliphate] either directly or indirectly. Otherwise, the dispute would not have arisen in the meeting of *al-Saqifa*, and 'Ali would not have objected to the appointment of Abu Bakr, despite the difference between the versions [of events], the weaker one claiming that he refused to appoint him for several days, while the common version is that he refused to appoint him until the death of Fatima. On the contrary, if the *al-Saqifa* method of selection had been the best, Abu Bakr would have used it and left the choice of his successor to Muslims or to those in power among them, but he did not. In fact he recommended appointing 'Umar in a signed missive, according to which the Muslims appointed 'Umar before Abu Bakr's death, without knowing the content of the missive. Even 'Umar acted according to a different method by limiting the decision to six known people, namely 'Ali, 'Uthman, Talha Ibn al-Zubair, Ibn 'Awf, and Sa'd. Also, the method of choosing 'Ali was different as it gave him the *bay'a* in some of the regions, while in others, Mu'awiya took it by sword and Yazid, by inheritance. Hence we see six different methods for choosing the ruler, and the orthodox refuse to circumvent them, but differ about which they prefer; while the liberals conclude that the only meaning can be that there is no norm, and that a tolerant and just Islam does not reject a system of election by direct or indirect vote, which I don't believe ever was a basis of general agreement among the advocates of a religious state. One additional obstacle exists to all the methods cited above, which is that the ruler, in every case, is appointed for life: it is meaningless to say that the *bay'a* is conferred on the basis of adherence to the book of Allah and the Hadith, and there are those who say that a ruler should be overthrown if he violates them. How many cases of violations have there been when the ruler was not deposed, and not even reprimanded for his past or present deeds[?] I believe the reader will notice that I emphasized the previous sentences in order to solicit inspiration from the thought of those who advocate an Islamic state, and a logical answer about how the *shura* is a guarantee of the prevention of violence by the ruler and protection of the rights of the citizens. But I wish to remind them that even this leads to a new obstacle, which is the dispute with regard to the nature of the *shura*: does the *shura* obligate the ruler, which is the minority opinion, or not obligate him, which is the majority opinion; this distinguishes between whether or not the ruler is obliged to consult with them or is not obliged to act according to their opinion, even if all or some of them are united against him.[5]

HUSAIN AHMAD AMIN

In Chapter 1, we cited Shaikh 'Ali 'Abd al-Raziq's work, *Al-Islam wa Usul al-Hukm*, which raised such bitter controversy at the time of its publication. Ahmad Amin, reflecting on this date (1925), contends that the main motivation for its appearance was to obstruct some religious leaders from declaring King Fuad the caliph, and this aroused the ire of the king, who instructed the sages of al-Azhar and others to censure 'Abd al-Raziq and declare him an infidel. This is because the book actually succeeded in abolishing the concept and thwarting the desire of King Fuad.

> Although the book appeared in the form of pure scientific research, behind it was a defined practical aim: preventing the appointment of a caliph for the Muslims. Therefore all the aims and arguments of the book were biased toward explicating the idea that Islamic religion has no connection with the caliphate that is familiar to the Muslims. The caliphate does not belong to religious plans, but purely to political plans, and the interest of the Sultans was to disseminate the fallacy among the people so as to use religion to protect their positions and to deflect those who come out against them.

'Ali 'Abd al-Raziq was the first to focus attention on the fact that adoption of the rule of the caliphate as a *Shari'a* belief and declaring it to be one of the precepts of religion has no source whatsoever in the book of Allah or the Hadith. Since the days of Abu Bakr, rule had been based on power, domination and compliance. Many who followed him saw this rule as the best excuse for their tyranny. 'Abd al-Raziq was the first person in the history of Islam to suggest that Allah's rites and religious manifestations are not based on the type of rule called the caliphate by the exegetes, nor on those called caliphs by the people. 'Thus the caliphate was and is a tragedy to Islam and to Muslims, and the source of wickedness and corruption.' He contended that the rule of the prophets is spiritual, but the rule of sultans and *amirs* is not. For 'Ali 'Abd al-Raziq, the most powerful sources of evidence for his opinion were the verses from the Quran which emphasize that the Prophet has no connection to political rule, such as: 'There is no coercion in religion'. However, it should be noted that the Quranic verses that 'Ali 'Abd al-Raziq cited as evidence for his claim are verses from the period in Mecca, before the Prophet migrated to Medina, and before He set up a regime there that had political and the religious features, and before He received verses such as: 'The Prophet is superior to the other believers'. But, to our astonishment, the author ignored these references. They can be considered to provide strong support for those who say that the Prophet did indeed found a state, and that His leadership over his *umma* was not, as 'Ali 'Abd al-Raziq had claimed, purely spiritual, like that of his fellow prophets. It did not occur to

them to found a state or to organize a regime. The problem, if it is a
problem, is the reconciliation between the group of Mecca verses
on which 'Ali 'Abd al-Raziq relies and the group of Medina verses
on which we have relied, since a government and a monarchy did
exist at Medina. 'I am not claiming that the spirit of the earlier
verses contradicts the content of the later verses. The entire matter
can be summarized in that there was a development of the criteria
and circumstances in which the verses were given.'[6] Husain Ahmad
Amin concludes that while most Muslims accept the concept of
development with regard to some verses, they refuse to accept it in
other cases, and in the matter of the caliphate, too, the principle of
development should be accepted, that is, it could be applied or not.

LIWAA HASAN SADIQ

In his book *Judur al-Fitna*, mentioned in previous chapters, Liwaa
Hasan Sadiq reacts to Shukri Mustafa's book *Kitab al-Khilafa* as
follows: 'Shukri's claim that the *bay'a* is one of the fundamental
principles of Islam, without which Islam is incomplete, is a web of
lies and falsehood.' In Sadiq's view, the *bay'a* to which Shukri
referred was only unquestioned devotion to him, so that no one
would disagree with him about anything or oppose any of his deeds.
Shukri had explained that as soon as the *imam* is given the *bay'a*,
the individual has no choice but unquestioned acceptance, because
the *imam* takes precedence. In other words, he completely nullified
his personality in deference to the personality of the *imam*. Thus he
could command the husband to divorce his wife and his followers
to kill those who opposed him. It can therefore be seen that he
exploited the *bay'a* as a shelter for action and for every crime that
he wanted to commit without having to be accountable to others,
on the grounds that he is the only caliph of the Messenger of Allah,
and Islam started out being alienated and will return to being
alienated. Shukri sees that the constitution is null and void since it
does not derive from the Islamic *Shari'a*, and because most of its
sources are foreign laws. Proof that it is invalid is the fact that the
nation is the source of authority while 'All affairs are given over to
Allah'. And when Shukri was told that the purpose of having democratic rule, a constitution, and a People's Council is to prevent the
ruler from being a tyrant to the people, he responded that this
meaning is not realized, that the *umma* is not given rule over a ruler,
but that the ruler is given rule over the *umma*. According to Sadiq,

Shukri's response is misleading, because it is said explicitly that there are only five principles of Islam, and these are the precepts or fundamental principles of Islam. No one has the right to add anything to them or permission to take anything away from them. Otherwise, whoever has permission to augment will also have permission to subtract.[7]

DR FUAD ZAKARIYYA

'The historic attempts were nothing but a long sequence of failures because tyranny was the basis and exploitation was the core of the connection between the ruler and the ruled.' In Zakariyya's opinion, justice, generosity, the *shura* and the other principles of the *Shari'a* are just words which justify the deeds of the tyrant who disregards everything connected with these lofty principles. There is consensus that the persistence of those who advocated application of the *Shari'a*, whatever their differences concerning the details, in continuously citing quotations about their claim from the period of the early caliphs, especially from the time of 'Umar, is the very proof that they did not find any evidence from the rest of history to show that the regime acted in the name of the *Shari'a*. In other words, the application that continued for 1,300 years was actually a denial of the principles of the *Shari'a* and a rebellion against it. Zakariyya asks:

> Do these honorable preachers not know that 'Umar Ibn al-Khattab was a unique personality, the like of which has not returned and has not been duplicated? Since all attempts throughout hundreds of years, like the attempts in the present period, have failed to bring a ruler who approaches 'Umar Ibn al-Khattab, why then do they amuse their followers with the vain hope that the period of 'Umar Ibn al-Khattab could be restored? And if the paradigm of truth, justice and the good has declined over the centuries and reached the lowest ebb in the contemporary attempts to apply the *Shari'a*, on what basis do they hope that the next attempt, about which they are preaching in Egypt, will be the one to succeed, when all Islamic regimes over the centuries have failed? The important element of their rosy dream is that the application of the *Shari'a* will automatically evaporate all the problems from which we suffer. How? No one knows. Most seem to believe deep within their hearts that divine providence will guard us in the application of the *Shari'a*. Afterwards, the forces of heaven will intervene to solve our problems without anyone making any effort. From within the fragrance emanating from these enchanted sentences, no one is thinking

and asking: Did anything like this happen in the attempt to apply the *Shari'a* in Sudan or in Pakistan or in other countries? Did not the problems of these countries increase in the shadow of regimes which have pretensions of applying only the precepts of Islam?[8]

ABD AL-SATTAR AL-TAWILA

Al-Tawila notes that in recent times, representatives of the political stream of Islam have revealed their hidden intentions regarding rule in Egypt, and have thus returned to the stories of the need for a caliphate. According to al-Tawila, the jurist Maamun al-Hudaibi was so enthusiastic in presenting the issue in the Egyptian People's Council that he exaggeratedly described it as one of the principles of Islam and a condition of acceptance of the Islamic faith, until Dr Rifat al-Mahjub, chairman of the People's Council, set him straight and reminded him that there are five principles of Islam and that the caliphate is not one of them. To the mind of al-Tawila, those who advocate the slogan of the caliphate care nothing for democracy and take no interest in the people ruling themselves. For them the important thing is that the ruler will apply what they call the Islamic *Shari'a*. Al-Hudaibi had said openly in the Parliament that the caliph can be a king or president of the republic; the important thing is the application of the *Shari'a*. Rejection of democracy by the political stream of Islam is not new, as the Muslim Brothers have always objected to political parties and have threatened to revoke them when they are in power. They helped the July Revolution abolish parties and cancel the constitution, and they did not oppose the revolutionary forces in matters of democracy until 'Abd al-Nasir failed to give them a share of power, although no one can deny the role they played in the events of the revolution. As for the extremist wing of the religious trend, they are not satisfied with rejecting democracy, but also condemn it, calling it an invention of the human mind and not a manifestation of divinity like the *Shari'a*. Al-Tawila reminds the reader of what was openly said by the leaders of the groups *al-Takfir wal-Hijra* and *al-Jihad* in their interrogations and trials: that they reject democracy and claim that the British Parliament allows, for example, sexual deviance. Al-Tawila notes that the political religious stream in Egypt does not disguise its solidarity with the regime of murderers and criminals in Iran. This regime represents the height of dictatorship, in al-Tawila's opinion, despite the existence of a governmental cabinet and a house of representatives. The question is how to choose the caliph. Hudaibi does not care if the caliph is king or the president of the republic. As for the Egyptian nation, 'we rejected and defeated the monarchy, as we are not property or an inheritance that can be passed on'. Al-Tawila points out that there is no definitive method or text or decision explaining how to determine the caliph who will rule over the Muslims. Nor is there an instance of election of the caliph by the people in the history or heritage of Islam. During the period of the four Rashid caliphs, *ahl al-Hall wal-Rabt* [people of influence] chose Abu Bakr to succeed the Prophet, and 'Umar Ibn al-Khattab designated six people from the Muslims to choose a caliph from their number. The people of influence were not the Muslim masses. And Mu'awiya Ibn Abu Sufian rejected the selection of 'Ali and led an armed *coup d'etat* against the Muslims and killed all those who opposed him. As for the Ottoman caliphate, notes al-Tawila:

> you can talk endlessly about its crimes, ugliness and backwardness. I can only call the reader's attention to the book by Faraj Fuda, *Al-Haqiqa al-Ghaiba*, which included the real and surprising history of the Umayyad and Abbasid caliphate! What kind of caliphate and caliphs do those of the political religious stream want for us? Is this a conspiracy to arouse a religious and ethnic controversy in the country over nothing?

Al-Tawila calls attention to the seriousness of the matter of establishing the Islamic caliphate in this period. If, for example, an Egyptian is appointed caliph over Muslims in Egypt:

> this means the beginning of a new Crusade on a worldwide scale, as the caliph of the Muslims is their *imam* everywhere – in Pakistan, Indonesia, Sudan, or the islands of the moon, the United States, Finland and the Soviet Union. He will have the responsibility of managing things and liberating, when necessary, from the rule of infidels. And, in the nature of things, the infidel Christian governments of socialist countries are infidel regimes, and Muslims ruled by them must be liberated.

Al-Tawila thus cautions that:

> The call for a caliphate, in addition to its antagonism to democracy and to every cultured constitution, is a futile call of a most serious nature. It bodes evil. So open your eyes wide. Allow us to hold onto our democracy and to expand it in order to save the country from all these destructive views. For it cannot withstand this other view in the broad framework of political freedom in our country.[9]

TAWFIQ AL-HAKIM

Let us mention one issue from among those concerning rule and theory in Egypt. This is the issue raised in *al-Islam wa Usul al-Hukm* by Shaikh 'Ali Abd al-Raziq. This problem arose after abolition of the caliphate by Mustafa Kamal. The Arab kings who were under English rule coveted the inheritance of the caliphate, waiting to claim it. Among them was the King of Egypt Ahmad Fuad who invested great additional efforts to this end. He published a journal called *al-Khilafa* and put in charge of it the well-known Islamic man of religion Rashid Rida, owner of the journal *Al-Manar*. At the same time, in 1925 'Ali Abd al-Raziq published his book *al-Islam wa Usul al-Hukm* in which he opposed the concept of the caliphate. His book totally repudiates the caliphate, as distinct from the principles of Islam. Naturally King Fuad, the English, and the *'ulama* [the representatives of the clerics] of al-Azhar were furious. The King spoke to the Council of *'Ulama* of al-Azhar and incited them to put him on trial, even though he himself was one of the *'ulama* there and a judge in the *Shari'a* court. The Shaikh of al-Azhar told him that 'This entire book errs and leads astray.' 'Ali Abd al-Raziq replied: Everything brought by Islam – the tenets, the norms, the manners and the punishments are religious law for the sanctification of God's name and for religious needs of people and nothing more. As for the purpose of life on earth, Allah has given people freedom to conduct their lives. The leadership of the Prophet was a religious leadership, and by this I mean that it was inspired by a divine message. Thus after the Prophet, there is no religious leadership in this sense, only civil or political leadership, which is the leadership of the government and the Sultan. As far as I'm concerned, in the case of a dispute, the key is why we don't accept, in place of a trial and violence, the words of Allah in his book: 'Call unto the way of thy Lord with wisdom and fair exhortation, and reason with them in the better way.' The verdict issued against Shaikh 'Ali 'Abd al-Raziq was cancelled and he was returned to the position of *'ulam* at the time of Shaikh al-Azhar, who was known as an adherent of freedom of thought, Mustafa al-Maraghi and the other enlightened *'ulama* who wanted to save the reputation of al-Azhar from the effects of the previous order.[10]

DR HUSAIN FAWZI AL-NAJJAR

According to al-Najjar, the *bay'a* is not one of the basic principles of Islam. Islam did not delineate the form of regime and did not designate a successor to the Prophet who would rule the Muslims after him. When the Muslims chose Abu Bakr to be responsible for Muslim affairs, their thoughts did not exceed the limits in which the Islamic group lived during the life of the Prophet, something which Abu Bakr expressed as: 'Muhammad has died and there is no other option for this religion but to choose one who will be responsible for it.' The caliphate was created according to a pure Arab conception which has no trace of imitation of others. Some believe that they chose one who would be responsible for them before they distinguished between the titles that existed among the kings of the time such as caesar or potentate. The title 'caliphate' was derived from its meaning and from their desired intention. Abu Bakr accepted the title, while 'Umar, on the other hand, wanted the title *Amir al-Mu'minin* [head of the faithful]. The *bay'a* exists on the basis of consensus and election. The *Imam* Malik decreed that the oath of compulsion should be abolished. The *bay'a* remained the law for the caliphate of the Muslims after having been the *bay'a* of the Rashidi caliphs; it was not a general *bay'a*, but the caliphs were chosen by men of state and the rest of the Muslims heard and obeyed. Therefore Mu'awiya struggled to receive the *bay'a* for his son Yazid so as not to deviate from the Muslim norm. The *bay'a* became a condition to show willingness for the caliphate even though it originated as coercive, and became distorted for the sake of agreement, turning into a kingdom which *'ududa* [bites] during the Umayyads, and a divine kingdom during the Abbasids and the Ottomans. The Muslims became fragmented into sects and disciples. However, the ultimate desire remained for a ruler and not for a nation, which is fundamentally opposed to the concept of rule in Islam.[11]

DR AHMAD KAMAL ABU AL-MAJD

What is the caliphate? asks Abu al-Majd.

> We do not find in the roots of Islam, the writings and the general consensus of the *mujtahidun* anything that would lead us to cling to the word 'caliphate'. As our *'ulama* say, intentions and interpretations are cardinal, not words and their inflections.

The term 'caliphate', in Abu al-Majd's view, created during the days of Abu Bakr, denoted no more than the appearance of *amirs* of the faithful, one after another, to head the Islamic state after the death of the Prophet. The term did not express a perfect political regime. The proof of this point is that the method for choosing the head of state varied and was not confined to one style during the period of the first four caliphs nor among the *imams* and the caliphs who came after them. No rule can be Islamic, avers Abu al-Majd, unless it is based on the *Shura*, is just and respects the rights and freedom of the people.

> The time has come for the preachers of Islam and those who call for application of its precepts to notice the glaring contradiction in the governmental regime and theories, as if the caliphate is one of the basic principles of Islam, while they violate the other principles which are no less important in Islam. If only all these would sense the absence of the 'rule of law' in the government and its transformation to a rule of those whose will outweighs the will of the law and the will of the people. This is something not compatible with the call for a caliphate, application of the *Shari'a* and rule according to what Allah decreed.

Abu al-Majd declares that the issue is one of two approaches. Islam dictated to the Muslims *Shura*, justice and questioning of the rulers. These principles do not collapse with the fall of the *mujtahidun* in setting the 'forms and formulas' that enable the principles to bear fruit in the context of the social, economic, and political conditions to which Muslims, like other nations, are subject.

> This way, [notes Abu al-Majd] established by the legislator, praise him, is the goal of every creed, the proof of every wisdom, and a gate to mercy. Through it alone Islamic rule will achieve what it desires in good values in the relationship of the shepherd to his flock, and the relationship among the people themselves, and the opening of the gates before the human *ijtihad* to find the 'maximum possible' interests in the shadow of variable and changing conditions. Would that we would notice these large truths through the legislation of Islam. Would that we would conclude this lengthy dispute about Islam and the state so that we could turn our attention to the work and science of building the state, instead of talking about it so much.[12]

AHMAD BAHAA AL-DIN

Bahaa al-Din is a vehement opponent of the concept of the caliphate, and views it as a form of dictatorship which does not suit Egypt or any Arab state. Like Husain Ahmad Amin and other liberal Egyptian writers, Bahaa al-Din extols 'Ali 'Abd al-Raziq's book condemning the caliphate. In an article which appears in his *Ayyam Laha Tarikh*, Bahaa al-Din reviews the book extensively and writes:

> It's clear from the text that he assails not only the caliphate and the religious state, but also monarchist rule. When the book appeared, it evoked a tempest from all directions: The king [Fuad] and his lackeys were indignant because the book contains a general attack on the kings

and a shattering of the shiny dream of the caliphate. Religious leaders were furious because they saw in this logic something that might undermine their authority, thwart their interests in trafficking in religion, and reveal the truth of the corruption and tyranny concealed in their thick turbans. There are also the reactionaries who curry favor with the masses, even aligning themselves with the forces of ignorance and darkness! As for the religious leaders, they have already fired off their shots in articles, research, and books . . .[13]

MAKRAM MUHAMMAD AHMAD

As noted, an attempt was made on the life of Makram Muhammad Ahmad in June 1987. This attempt came in the wake of articles written by this senior journalist condemning the extremist Islamic organizations which had attempted to assassinate two former Ministers of the Interior of Egypt, Hasan abu-Basha and Nabawi Isma'il, as well as, a year earlier, Israeli and American diplomats, this previous attempt resulting in the death of two Israelis and the injury of others. In a dialogue between the editor-in-chief of *al-Musawwar* and the Shaikh Ahmad abu al-Nasr, the current Supreme Guide of the Muslim Brothers, Ahmad notes:

> Perhaps you are looking toward the era of Ottoman rule as the symbol of the Islamic caliphate, but this should not prevent you from saying that Egypt was then in a period of ignorance and decline among the worst in its history; suffice it to say that both our forefathers were slaves whose backs were seared by the whips of the Ottomans . . . When Mustafa al-Mashhur says that he is one of the pillars of the *Jama'a* [group], that he who opposes the Brothers opposes God, are we to accept these statements as venerable or are we to adjust them to the rules of the debate, since the Brothers are, after all, just flesh and blood who might be in error . . . When you bear aloft the slogan 'Islam is the solution', would it be the words of an infidel to Islam to ask what the solution is? What is the content? How would it be applied? What is the guarantee that what took place in Iran would be prevented? Is it not our job to raise all these questions? Or lest it be our role to accept the generality, without seeking details as to the intention of the general slogan? Honorable Supreme Guide: as we have mentioned the matter of extremism, let us be frank among ourselves: Your voice was weak in condemning the waves of violence that swept over society recently in the name of religion. We did not hear even one clear voice emphasizing that these actions are not for the good of the homeland. Permit me to say in all frankness that when one reads your writings about the dialogue with extremist elements, the aim of most of this writing is to justify what is taking place. At best, you give advice to mislead young people

who are trying to expedite the end by engaging in violence prematurely, to pick fruit that is not yet ripe or whose time has not yet come; while we would have expected, since you have already become part of the parliamentary system of rule, that you would defend democracy more clearly, the democracy which brought you seats in the People's Council.[14]

TARIQ AL-BISHRI

As the standard-bearer of Arab nationalism, Tariq al-Bishri does not support the creation of an Islamic state, the application of the *Shari'a*, or the appointment of a caliph as head of state. On the contrary, he argues that this would harm the national unity of Egypt and its aspiration of general Arab unity. He does not deny the contribution of the Copts in Egyptian culture and their role in all aspects, including political, of contemporary Egyptian society. The importance of the Copts is quite significant, especially in Alexandria and in Upper Egypt. The creation of an Islamic state would perforce injure their status as equals in rights and obligations, and would change them into *dimmim* [non-Muslims], at best, who are under the rule of an Islamic regime, and this would harm the national unity of Egypt. Like other liberal intellectuals, al-Bishri comes out against the institution of the caliphate, and he also relies on *Al-Islam wa Usul al-Hukm* by Shaikh 'Ali 'Abd al-Raziq, and on al-Raziq's legal arguments that the caliphate is not drawn from the Quran or the Hadith concerning the form of Islamic rule; both the Quran and the Hadith allow the *umma* to choose the regime suitable for it according to the circumstances.[15]

*

It can be said in summary that all the liberal intellectuals in Egypt explicitly reject the concept of the caliphate, some in moderate language and others more brazenly, as a cruel form of religious dictatorship which is not appropriate in any way for a modern regime. Almost all the liberals who addressed this issue quote 'Ali 'Abd al-Raziq's work as a classic which reviews the history of the caliphate and analyzes the shortcomings of the system. The book, the co-author of which was Shaikh Azhari who was knowledgeable about the mysteries of the Quranic verses and the Hadith, completely repudiates the claim that the caliphate is one of the principles of Islam. Furthermore, even when the institution was accepted in the course of Islamic history, the choice of the caliph was not made according to a single method. The *bay'a* has become coercive, and therefore should not be regarded as a choice made by the *shura*. On this issue, the efforts of the religious extremists to substantiate their claims are weak, and thus it was easy for these liberals to attack the method. The liberal view receives support from moderate or establishment religious leaders whose views on the caliphate are less strict than their views about the application of the *Shari'a*. They regard this matter as not open to compromise.

NOTES

1. The concept of the caliphate has always aroused controversy among Muslims, but many Islamic writers and exegetes, past and present, and throughout the world have discussed it. For example, see *The Encyclopaedia of Islam* (Leiden, E.J. Brill, New Edition, 1977), Vol. IV, pp. 937–53. See also Hava Lazarus-Yafeh (ed.), *Studies in the History of the Arabs and Islam* (Tel Aviv, 9th edition, 1984), pp. 154–202; Muhammad Sa'id Ashmawi, *Al-Khilafa al-Islamiyya* [The Islamic caliphate] (Cairo, 1990).
2. M.S. Ashmawi, *Al-Islam al-Siyasi* [Political Islam] (Cairo, 1987), pp. 84–5; also Ashmawi, *Jawhar al-Islam* [The essence of Islam] (Cairo, 1984), pp. 51–2.
3. *Al-Islam al-Siyasi*, pp. 85–7.
4. Ibid., p. 91.
5. Faraj Fuda, *Al-Haqiqa al-Gha'iba* [The absent truth] (Cairo, 1986), pp. 17–21.
6. Husain Ahmad Amin, *Hawla al-Da'wa ila-Tatbig al-Shari'a al-Islamiyya*, pp. 277–91.
7. Liwaa Hasan Sadiq, *Judur al-Fitna*, pp. 336–62.
8. Dr Fuad Zakariyya, *Al-Haqiqa wal-wahm fi al-Haraka al-Islamiyya al-Mu'asira* [Truth and fantasy in the contemporary Islamic movement], pp. 170–7.
9. 'Abd al-Sattar al-Tawila, *Rose al-Yusuf*, 18 Jan. 1988, pp. 12–13.
10. Tawfiq al-Hakim, *Fi al-Waqt al-Dai* [In lost time], pp. 266–8.
11. Dr Husain Fawzi al-Najjar, *Al-dawla wal-Hukm fi al-Islam* [State and rule in Islam], pp. 165–6.
12. Dr Ahmad Kamal Abu al-Majd, *Hiwar la Muwajaha* [Dialogue, not confrontation] (Cairo and Beirut, 1988), pp. 104–8.
13. Ahmad Bahaa al-Din, *Ayyam Laha Tarikh* [Days packed with history] (Beirut and Cairo, Dar al-Shuruq, 2nd edition 1985), pp. 157–77.
14. Makram Muhammad Ahmad, 'Meeting with the Guide', *Al-Musawwar*, No. 3280, 21 Aug. 1987, pp. 4–6.
15. Tariq al-Bishri, *Al-Muslimun wal-Aqbat* [The Muslims and the Copts in the context of the national society] (Beirut, 1982), pp. 277–307. See also Leonard Binder, *Islamic Liberalism*, pp. 270–80.

8 Perspectives on Jihad

An important slogan that weaves its way through Islamic thought over the generations is the call to jihad. This slogan has powerful psychological and emotional impact on many Muslims throughout the Arab and Muslim world, whenever Muslims are in political confrontation with a non-Islamic state. The word jihad is derived from the verb *jahada* meaning 'to make an effort' or 'to strive' (to spread Islam). In the west, the term acquired the meaning of a holy war, suggesting a war that an Islamic state wages on a non-Islamic state in order to spread Islam or to defend itself against foreigners or foreign influence. This word appears many times in various Quranic verses and the Hadith. During the dawn of Islam in Mecca (610–622), jihad meant to work at spreading the new religion and resisting the infidels of Mecca who rejected it and persecuted the followers of Muhammad until, under his leadership, they emigrated to the city of Yathrib (Medina). After Muhammad's victory at Badr and his conquest of and return to Mecca, the term jihad took on the meaning of a holy war against infidels in general, not just the infidels of Mecca.[1]

JUSTICE MUHAMMAD SAID AL-ASHMAWI

Like other liberal intellectuals in Egypt, Ashmawi grasps the concept of jihad in the spiritual sense, more than the militant sense of war against infidels or Muslims who renounce Islam. He interprets the roots of the term as explained above, noting that the word has derived from the verb *jahada* during the period of the birth of Islam in Mecca. The use of this concept was spiritual, meaning restraint or the struggle of the Muslim for self-control. It is his duty to make a physical effort on behalf of God, religion and the truth in his struggle against the infidel people of Mecca. The Muslim must withstand the pressure that infidels exert upon him to abandon his new religion and must deflect the evil directed at him.[2] Ashmawi quotes many verses from the Quran in this sense, from which we shall quote three: 'But if they strive with thee to make thee ascribe unto Me as partner that of which thou has no knowledge, then obey them not. Consort with them in the world kindly . . .';[3] 'As for those who strive in Us, we surely guide them to Our paths . . .';[4] and 'So obey not the disbelievers, but strive against them herewith with a great endeavor'.[5] Ashmawi stresses that the concept expanded to become a call for material support in addition to the idea of spiritual struggle and support.[6] Two examples of verses in this vein are: 'The (true) believers are only those who believe in Allah and his messenger and afterward doubt not, but strive with their wealth and their lives for the cause of Allah';[7] 'Go forth, light-armed and heavy-armed, and strive with your wealth and your lives in the way of Allah!'[8] For during this period, Muhammad and his followers suffered persecution at the hands of the Meccans, and they were forced to emigrate in order to mobilize material support to withstand them.

A further development in the meaning of the concept jihad took place after the believers waged their first battle with the Meccans at Badr in 624. Muhammad saw that the material meaning of the concept had overridden its spiritual content, and so he stated after the battle, 'We returned from the minor jihad (the battle of Badr) to the major jihad'. In other words, the battle was only a small jihad. The jihad is not a sword to brandish or a war to wage against one's enemy, but rather a concerted effort against man's evil inclinations, such as lust, ignorance and tyranny. This is the major jihad after the victory in battle.[9] Ashmawi quotes many verses in this vein such as: 'But be patient with a patience fair to see';[10] 'Say: (it is) the truth from the Lord of you (all). Then whoever will, let him believe, and whoever will, let him disbelieve';[11] and 'And exhort one another to truth exhort one another to endurance'.[12]

But the people of Mecca continued to persecute the Prophet and his followers, and then the verses were revealed which permitted a declaration of war against them. This, however, is a war in self-defense, as in: 'Sanction is given unto those who fight because they have been wronged; and Allah is indeed able to give them victory. Those who have been driven from their homes unjustly only because they said: Our Lord is Allah';[13] and 'Fight in the way of Allah against those who fight against you, but begin not hostilities. Lo, Allah loveth not aggressors'.[14] Thus, war is not a holy war to be waged on any terms, but a war against those who declare war on the Muslims, that is, a war in self-defense.[15] There are verses directed against the people of the book, Jews and Christians, which were revealed to Muhammad after the second battle at al-Khandaq (the War of the Trench) in 626. The people of Mecca besieged Medina where the Muslims had found refuge and protection, and they almost conquered the city. The Muslims claimed that the Jewish tribe of Banu Quraiza, who resided in Medina at the time, had come to the aid of the Meccans in their battle against the Prophet, and this was considered an act of treachery. The main verse states: 'Fight against such of those who have been given the Scripture as believe not in Allah nor the Last Day, and forbid not that which Allah hath forbidden by His messenger, and follow not the religion of truth, until they pay the tribute readily, being brought low'.[16] In this context, Ashmawi explains that the verse does not refer to all the people of the book, Jews and Christians, for time immemorial, but only to those who do not believe in God or the afterlife, and who do not abstain from that which Allah forbids, and who do not believe in the true faith. In other words, the verse is directed against those who are unfaithful to their own religions – Judaism and Christianity. Furthermore, the war against them must cease the moment they pay the *jizya* tax, which enables them to prove their good intentions.[17]

To complete the picture, Ashmawi engages in a comparison between this verse and the verse against the Meccan infidels which was revealed when Muhammad conquered the city in 630:

> And slay them wherever ye find them, and drive them out of the places whence they drove you out, for persecution is worse than slaughter. And fight not with them at the Inviolable Place of Worship until they first attack you there, but if they attack you (there) then slay them. Such is the reward of disbelievers. But if they desist, then lo! Allah is Forgiving, Merciful. And fight them until persecution is no more, and religion is for Allah. But if they desist, then let there be no hostility except against wrongdoers. The forbidden month for the forbidden month, and forbidden things in retaliation. And one who attacketh you, attack him in like manner as he attacked you. Observe your duty to Allah, and know that Allah is with those who ward off (evil).[18]

In other words, the war ends with the cessation of hostilities and it must be waged measure for measure, no more. A verse after the conquest of Mecca states: 'And wage war on all the idolaters'.[19]

We thus see, according to these quotations, that war against the

Meccan infidels is total, until they convert to Islam, while war against the people of the book is waged only against those who are unfaithful to their own religion. War against them must cease the moment they pay the ransom or the *jizya* tax. From this one can glean the original and primary meaning of the jihad as interpreted by Justice Ashmawi (and by many liberal intellectuals). It is a continuous struggle against one's evil inclination and the ability to endure the travails of life. It is not necessarily a total war against infidels, and today there are no infidels in the sense of idol worshippers. And if war is indeed waged, it must be a war of self-defense only, measure for measure, and no more.[20]

DR FARAJ FUDA

Islam does not have the slightest connection with the fact that the only way the members of the Jihad Organization could find financial support is to attack the jewelry shops of the Copts, to murder them, and to steal their property. I don't want to continue because I don't wish here to put salt on open wounds. But it is connected to a *fatwa* issued by someone to whom we should shout . . . Save Islam . . . Save Islam . . . as Islam has never been a religion of terrorism, and Islam has no part in the killing of a citizen who is sitting securely in his shop, or the orphaning of children, or the destruction of homes for no other reason than that their religion is different from yours, or because an *amir* issued a judgment and erred, which forces an Egyptian citizen to pay the price of this error with his life. A man like me can feel only pain and sorrow in reading this strange sentence of Ahmad 'Umar Hashim:[21] 'The Muslim is not prohibited from conducting business with non-Muslims, but he is prohibited from deep friendship with him and loyalty . . . because a deep friendship is permitted only between a Muslim and his Muslim brother.' No, my dear doctor, a deep friendship will arise between Egyptian and Egyptian, whether Muslim or Copt, regardless. Any other words would sunder the ranks. A man like me can feel only pain and sorrow when the voice of the preacher declares that the Muslim from India is closer to the Muslim from Egypt than the Egyptian Copt is . . . No, I swear, not now and not in the future. Because the Egyptian among us – and I mean all the Egyptians – are distinguished only by the love of their homeland and loyalty to their country. Only God knows who stands behind this wild attack which sows discord, discriminates against groups, and is so disheartening and divisive. Only God knows . . . Are they religious people who won seats in the Parliament while dreaming of a seat in government? . . . Are they the *imams* of the mosques, who have become cassette stars whose recordings compete with those of singing stars, with their severe moralizing, accusations of infidelity, predicting painful torture and ensuring hell to all . . . Are they our honorable neighbors who find it so hard to see Egypt in the heart of the region as an oasis of stability, national unity, and, above all, culture, and thus vow to reverse this by way of temptations from the lives of our forefathers as they dream of rending it [Egypt] asunder by a quarrel, thinking that every illness has its remedy, and the remedy of the illness of civilization is money, be it dollars or rials . . . Only God knows . . . Is it one of the superpowers which believes it to be in their interest that the entire region regress and everything collapse? Progress will be *bid'a* and going astray, and it only has to push Egypt in this direction for everyone to follow because it [the superpower] is the lighthouse and the leader . . . Perhaps it is their desire to drag the entire region into dark places of interethnic strife so that it will not flourish anew until the twenty-second century . . . The only thing I do know – and so does everyone and we must all resist it – is that a religious state ruled by religious leaders either directly or indirectly will open the door directly to ethnic strife, and possibly to the rending asunder of the homeland . . . Dear gentlemen . . . give up the deception. After all, religious rule is not a matter of majority and minority, but of general consensus.[22]

DR HUSAIN FAWZI AL-NAJJAR

Al-Najjar does not talk about Muslim wars as a jihad in the religious sense, but about a war that, in his opinion, is an inseparable part of every human society in order to survive against another society. As for war in Islam, he notes:

Islam does not deny war as a social phenomenon, but tries to refine it from all the motivations that are evoked and also the style it takes. War in Islam is a given fact, but its goal is to repel evil, to distance tragedy, and to raise truth above falsehood. Hence the grounds for war in Islam are self-defense, defense of the faith, and the freedom of the call – preaching – and not for the sake of aggression or tyranny. Islam harshly condemns aggression in the Quran: 'Begin not hostilities. Lo, Allah loveth not aggressors.' The Muslims warred first with the members of the Quraish tribe until their defeat, and then with the Meccans until they did away with idol worship. These battles came after they were prepared for them, by way of permission from Allah (*Al-Hajj*, 22:39–41) for them to battle those who exploited them and threw them out of their homes. Hence, this is a war to end exploitation and aggression . . . War is an obligation when it is just . . . and that is the meaning of jihad in the Quran. Thus, the jihad is a war against tyranny, exploitation, and aggression until the Muslims are secure and the freedom to preach their faith is assured. It is not what evil-intentioned people claim when they interpret the jihad to be the spread of Islam by the sword or coercing people to convert by force of arms. War is one form of jihad, but not its entirety. For the jihad in Islam is not only war and not a war with others on behalf of the truth only, but the battle of man to overcome his evil inclinations. [The writer then supports this exposition with many verses from the Quran in the same way as Ashmawi and others do.] [23]

ADIL HAMUDA

In the name of Islamic jihad, members of the [Jihad] Organization carried out the worst crimes . . . theft . . . murder . . . and assault of others. They accused the entire society of apostasy . . . Everyone in this society had become an infidel, and thus they were declared fair game and their blood was cheaper than water, their souls cheaper than the dust of the earth, their lives cheaper than a train ticket. Even if there was justification for the theft, there was no justification for murder . . . And even if there was justification for theft, there was certainly no point in passing the stolen goods or some of them to the sister of the head of the organization. Violence was the general character of the organization, power was the most conspicuous phenomenon, terror was its hallmark from birth until the day of its burial. [24]

LIWAA HASAN SADIQ

Jihad for Allah is cited in the Quran and the Sunna follow this. That is beyond doubt. But what is jihad? Linguistically, its root is struggle, hard work . . . According to Islamic law, there is jihad in war and jihad in peace. The former is the struggle against the polytheists and the latter is a struggle against one's inclinations and Satan. According to tradition: 'We returned from the minor jihad to the major jihad, which is the jihad against the evil inclination.' Hence the jihad is not limited either linguistically or theologically to warfare, but the struggle against infidels can be waged by hand, wealth, words, or the heart. All these are the ways to call to God in the path outlined in the Quran, walked by His Messenger when he said, 'Call for God with wisdom and good preaching, and debate with them in the better "way"'. Is the jihad a *fardh 'ain* [commandment to an individual] which obligates every Muslim? Those well-versed in religion and its commandments say that the jihad by warfare was a commandment in the days of the Prophet. Thereafter it is a *fardh kifaya* [commandment to the community] if a need for it arises. It will be a commandment to every Muslim man and woman in any period when Muslim lands are conquered: 'Fight against the infidels with your wealth, your hands, and your words.' As for the *jihad al-nafs* [struggle against inclinations], this is a commandment to every Muslim man and woman in every period of time, as the Prophet said: '*Al-mujahid* is someone who struggles with himself to obey God, may he be praised.' But there is another saying of the Prophet: 'I was sent by the sword against time.' This is a true saying, but what does it mean? Should we accept its words in their simplicity without noting the other traditions? What appears in the booklet [the book by 'Abd al-Salam Faraj] is exactly what the Orientalists say who condemn Islam as [a religion] spread by the sword. Both are wrong. For the Quran resolved the matter by saying, 'There is no coercion in religion.' Hasan Sadiq brings many verses from the Quran and sayings of the Prophet which prove that jihad is not a war in all periods, but only when the Muslim state is attacked, and that the Muslim is not considered an infidel for not following all the religious precepts, unless he formally repudiates Islam.[25]

KHALID MUHAMMAD KHALID

On the matter of the jihad, Khalid writes:

Islam does not condone murder except in war, i.e., a war between Islam and its enemies. That's the first point. Second, Islam does not condone war or an aggressive war, as the jihad in Islam is only in cases of self-defense. The Messenger of Allah never set out with an army to attack or to wage war throughout his blessed life except in self-defense and for repelling the aggression of polytheists. This is true from the first invasion, the battle of Badr, through the last invasion, the battle of Tabuk. Hence assault in the name of religion or nationalism is absolutely forbidden and is contemptible to religion and to nationalism both.[26]

*

From the above and from the early chapters, we can see that the issue of jihad has evoked great controversy in Islam through the ages. The numerous verses in the Quran and the Hadith, sometimes contradicting each other, only increased the confusion and the controversy. The most stringent view jihad as an ongoing command-ment until Islam rules the entire world, a world of war until all come under the banner of Islam. The moderates – not just the liberals but also clearly religious people – stress that jihad will not be declared except in periods of real danger to the state or Islamic states, that is, in times of war or self-defense against external aggres-sion. War should not be waged other than to retaliate against or to repel aggression. Both groups of thinking cite substantial evidence in support of their position. The liberals, who yearn for progress, are not eager to invest the efforts of Egypt and other Muslim countries in wars that will drain their resources and display them as states engaged in terrorism and violence against other countries. In either case, the concept of jihad arouses deep-seated feelings in the average Muslim, because of the fact that during Muhammad's time

and for several decades afterwards, Islam ruled considerable territory from China to North Africa and Western Europe. Every Muslim
would like to return to that glory and, for many, only the jihad
enables attainment of that goal.

NOTES

1. *The Encyclopaedia of Islam* (New Edition, Vol. 2, reprinted 1965), 'Djihad', pp. 538–40.
2. Ashmawi, *Al-Islam al-Siyasi* [Political Islam], pp. 95–6.
3. *Luqman*, verse 31:15.
4. *Al-'Ankabut* [The Spider], verse 29:69.
5. *Al-Furqan* [The Criterion], verse 25:52.
6. Ashmawi, *Al-Islam al-Siyasi*, pp. 97–8.
7. *Al-Hujurat* [The Private Apartments], verse 49:15.
8. *Al-Taubah* [Repentance], verse 9:41.
9. Ashmawi, *Al-Islam al-Siyasi*, p. 97.
10. *Al-Ma'arij* [The Ascending Stairways], verse 70:5.
11. *Al-Kahf* [The Cave], verse 18:29.
12. *Al-'Asr* [The Declining Day], verse 103:5.
13. *Al-Hajj* [The Pilgrimage], verse 22:39–40.
14. *Al-Baqarah* [The Cow], verse 2:190.
15. Ashmawi, *Al-Islam al-Siyasi*, pp. 98–9.
16. *Al-Taubah* [Repentance], verse 9:29.
17. Ashmawi, *Al-Islam al-Siyasi*, p. 99.
18. *Al-Baqarah* [The Cow], verse 2:191–4.
19. *Al-Taubah* [Repentance], verse 9:36.
20. Ashmawi, *Al-Islam al-Siyasi*, pp. 99–100.
21. A regular writer in the journal *Al-Liwaa al-Islami*. The reference is to issue no. 153.
22. Dr Faraj Fuda, *Qabl al-Suqut* [Before the Fall] (Cairo, 1985), pp. 82–4.
23. Dr Husain Fawzi Al-Najjar, *Al-Islam wal-Siyasa* [Islam and politics] (Cairo, 1977), pp. 269–88.
24. Adil Hamuda, *Qissat Tanzim al-Jihad* [The story of the al-Jihad Organization], p. 75.
25. Liwaa Hasan Sadiq, *Judhur al-Fitna*, pp. 413–19.
26. Khalid Muhammad Khalid, 'Sayartadd al-'Unf 'ala al-Mutarrifin' [Violence will be a boomerang to the extremists], *Al-Musawwar*, Issue no. 3272, 26 June 1987, pp. 26–7.

9 Attitudes to Judaism, Christianity, the West and Modern Science

Many Egyptian liberal intellectuals fear that Islamic extremists will discriminate between Muslims and non-Muslims (primarily Christians, since there are practically no Jewish citizens of Egypt; there are about 10 million Copts in Egypt today, but what follows holds true for Jews as well). Such discrimination would create tension between Muslims and Christians, making the latter second-class citizens not just in theory, but in fact. The intellectuals hold that such a position must not be tolerated in an era of equal rights, accelerated modernization and world culture.

Relations between the Muslims and the Copts of Egypt are as poor as they have ever been. The Copts, especially in Upper Egypt, have become the target of unbridled attack by religious extremists. Islamic Jihad groups assault the Copts, loot their stores, prevent them from constructing or repairing churches, obstruct the establishment of Coptic charitable organizations, and even from time to time attack their churches and monasteries. It has recently been reported that Islamic groups regularly collect 'hush money' from Coptic organizations – similar to the head tax on *dimmim* [Jews and Christians] common in early Islamic states – and they force Coptic women to appear in 'modest' dress. The Jihad organizations set up their own quasi-government in Dairut, a town heavily populated by Copts, with an '*amir*' who is head of state and ministers for foreign affairs, security, internal affairs, and welfare.

The battle waged by the security forces against these organizations is no longer effective. *Al-fitna al-taifiyya* [ethnic strife] has become a central theme in the Egyptian press which had ignored this issue for years, and many recent studies and monographs have appeared on the subject, many by Coptic writers, some by Muslims.

For several centuries, the Muslims treated the Copts with friendship and by and large did not force them to convert to Islam. They did not restrict their construction of churches or monasteries and, in fact, the first Christian monastic order was in Egypt. In the eighth century, Arabic became the official language of Egypt, but only in the eleventh century did it become the language of the entire nation. Both Greek (a vestige of the Greek conquest) and Coptic retreated to be the languages of prayer in churches and rituals.

Dr Ghali Shukri, a Coptic intellectual and literary critic with left-wing views who had long denied the Coptic problem, recently published a book, *al-Aqbat fi Watan Mutaghayyir* ['The Copts in a changing homeland'],[1] in which he protests at 'the gaps in collective consciousness, the rents in the national memory' manifested by 'the absence of a Coptic period in the history of Egypt'. According to Shukri:

> It's amazing that the departments of philosophy and history in our universities take an interest in Christian history and the history of the church in Europe, but Coptic Egypt has completely dropped out of sight, except for the Coptic Museum and the Coptic religious institutions. Our school system, our national broadcasting, our literature and newspapers, our national holidays – and one hears only about Pharaonic Egypt, Greek-Roman Egypt, Islamic Egypt. It is astonishing that we do not recognize a Coptic Egypt, that is, a Christian Egypt, an Egyptian Egypt. This is even more astonishing in light of the fact that what have survived from Pharaonic Egypt are monumental sites, and what has survived from Greece and Rome are remnants, while what has survived [from] Coptic Egypt, alongside these sites, are people who live among us like an authentic scarlet thread in the weave of the Egyptian nation . . . As if the Islamic conquest was the beginning of the history of Egypt, and the non-Muslims are the uninvited guests of this history.[2]

Most Coptic intellectuals write in a similar vein that the Copts are the source of Egypt and an integral part of Egyptian people and nationalism. In the past there was cooperation between the Muslims and the Copts, when the latter held key positions in political parties, the government, the media, literature and the administration. With the rise of Islamic fundamentalism in Egypt, however, and the appearance in 1928 of the Muslim Brothers movement, the Copts began to worry about their standing. They claim that they were the pioneers of Nasir's Arab nationalism, and that earlier they were the moving spirit in the 1919 rebellion against the British conquest led by Egyptian leader Sa'd Zaghlul.

In 1934, the Egyptian Ministry of the Interior publicized a decision with ten conditions concerning the construction and repair of churches. The Copts viewed this as a serious restriction of their needs. They protested in conferences and newspaper articles, but relations between the communities did not deteriorate to open conflict. Later the Copts enthusiastically supported Nasir's concept of Arab nationalism, they served in his wars against Israel and Yemen and they praised his policies, even though there were occasional reservations about his pan-Islamic policies.

With the growth in population of the Copts, especially in Upper Egypt – the authorities estimate the Copt population at 5–6 million, while the Copt estimate is over 12 million – the Copts began to ignore the ten conditions. They built new churches and established welfare bodies, schools and community institutions. Muslim extremists reacted at once by constructing mosques on the same locations, sometimes even before the churches were constructed.

In 1970, two Muslim young men in Alexandria converted to Christianity, presumably for economic reasons. The news spread among the Muslims, and the *imams* condemned 'the phenomenon of missionizing'. The Egyptian Ministry of Religious Affairs warned against the serious results that could ensue from this 'phenomenon', even though there had been only one case. During this period, Sadat capitulated to Muslim pressure and amended the Egyptian constitution to say that 'the *Shari'a* is the source of Egyptian legislation'.

In late 1971, the Patriarch Shnuda was elected Chief Bishop of the Copts. Shnuda asked that the court judgment be nullified which had permitted the Copts bigamy or divorce, similar to what the Muslims were permitted. He also demanded that the clerical college of the Alexandrian church be opened and returned to its international standing. Following the escalation of hostility between the two communities, Sadat convened the Conference of 'Socialist Union' – the only party at that period – in which he declared that attempts were being made by Copts outside Egypt, especially in the United States, to disrupt the unity of Egypt.

Mobs reacted in September 1972 with an attack on the Association of Orthodox Renewal in the town of Sanhur. On 6 November during the 'Id al-Fitr holiday, a Muslim mob set fire to the building of the Association of Holy Books, a Coptic religious-spiritual center in the town of al-Khanka near Cairo. A week later, a delegation of Coptic priests and believers marched to the building which had been burned and held prayers there. That evening, mobs of Muslims gathered in the nearby Mosque of Sultan al-Ashraf and held a counter-march. During this march, a rumor spread that a Copt had opened fire over the heads of the Muslim demonstrators. The impassioned crowd made its way to the home of this Copt and to other Coptic homes and set them on fire.

On 17 November 1977, a Coptic conference of priests and representatives of the community was held in Alexandria to discuss their demands: freedom of religious worship, protection of family life and marriage and condemnation of bigamy, equal opportunities for Copts, proper representation of Christians in parliamentary bodies, a halt to religious extremist trends and freedom of expression and of the press.

Acts of incitement of Islamic groups against Copts in the first four months of 1980 caused serious incidents in the universities of Alexandria, Asyut and Minya. There were some killings as security forces fired into crowds of rioters. In response, the Coptic leadership took unprecedented measures: On 30 March 1980, just as Sadat was about to depart for a visit to the United States, they announced the cancellation of official ceremonies for Easter, in strong protest against the government's lenient attitude toward the Muslim extremists. They also protested at the words of the Egyptian Minister for Religious Affairs, 'Abd al-Mun'im al-Nimr, who was quoted as having declared publicly that the Copts are infidels. The Coptic leadership felt that government leniency toward the fundamentalists was directed against the Coptic community.

In a dramatic address to the People's Council on 14 May 1980, Sadat vehemently attacked the Coptic leadership and blamed them for the escalation, declaring Egypt to be an Islamic state and its president a Muslim ruler. Although he also attacked the fundamentalists and forbade their activities, the speech focused on criticism of the Coptic protest activities and not on their underlying causes. This fed the sense of security felt by the Muslim extremists, and the prohibitions against them did not take effect until September 1981, a month before Sadat was assassinated by members of the Islamic Jihad. In this same speech, Sadat accused the Copts of attempting to establish a Coptic state whose capital would be Asyut (which has a large Coptic minority). He dismissed the Chief Bishop, Shnuda, exiled him to the al-Natrun Monastery, and replaced him with a clerical council appointed to administer the affairs of the Coptic community.[3]

With Mubarak's rise to power, Shnuda was reinstated in his previous position in an effort to appease the Copts. But Muslim extremism had already gained great momentum and continued to put a stranglehold on the Copts, particularly in Alexandria and Cairo, while stepping up efforts against the Mubarak administration.

The following are the views of some liberal intellectuals on the subject of non-Muslims, the west and modern science.

TAWFIQ AL-HAKIM

Al-Hakim raises an important question concerning the essence of religion in general and the attitude of Islam to other religions, especially to Judaism and Christianity. He notes that religion is an instrument of man necessary to sustain his existence and survival in the universe created by God according to His ability. Religion was created, therefore, for the benefit of those who worship God, and not for the benefit of the Creator, who has no need for it.[4] Al-Hakim asks:

> What is the wisdom of the two faiths that preceded Islam – Judaism and Christianity; did the coming of Muhammad nullify Moses and Jesus? Of course not, otherwise the Quran would not relate to them with the respect that they deserve. The Quran clearly states, 'Say: O People of the Scripture! Ye have naught (of guidance) till ye observe the Torah and the Gospel and that which was revealed unto you from your Lord'.[5]

Al-Hakim asserts that God loves the Muslim religious sages who study another holy scripture. And if Muslims refrain from studying it, claiming that it distorts Islamic religious writing, their duty is to locate the specific distortion and to draw attention to it. 'However it is possible that the rulers and their friends among the religious sages are responsible for this division into extremism and hatred'.[6]

In Chapter 6 we noted al-Hakim's attraction to science and the use of reason. He raises this motif to the pinnacle of human achievement, and does not consider science, thought or skepticism to be opposed to faith. On the contrary. God gave man intelligence so that he would think. But intelligence stimulates a variety of opinions and ideas, and we must bear responsibility for them. Al-Hakim, like any normal Muslim, acknowledges the superiority of Islam over other faiths. However, on the basis of the exegesis of al-Qurtubi as cited by al-Mawradi, al-Hakim asserts that religions are relative because humanity in essence is relative, and that God seems to have hinted in the Quranic verse from the sura *Al-Mursalat* [The Emissaries] what scientists would discover hundreds of years later in the person of Einstein. The fascination with science and skepticism is not necessarily apostasy.[7] Al-Hakim writes:

It seems to me that the way to You [God] in the future will pass through practical and empirical science, since the discovery of galaxies distant from us by thousands of light years was achieved by the scientists only recently through new optical equipment . . . God is the creator of these galaxies, and science is the only way to reach the galaxies that he has created. How is it possible, then, not to seek knowledge in our times and in all periods and in every place?[8]

Even the Quran says, 'The erudite among His bondmen fear Allah alone'.[9]

But those who are lazy among the religious sages keep silent because of their ignorance concerning the progress of human science, and this seems to prove that Islam is compatible with only one period, the early years [i.e., the period of the birth of Islam], even though it is appropriate for all times and all places by keeping up with science and its progress.[10]

Furthermore, there is no better proof of the acknowledgement and worship of God than the words of Einstein, who said, 'I bow my head with awe and reverence to this wonderful ability that reveals itself in each and every cell of the universe'; and Koestler, who says: 'The more I study the composition of matter, I am doubly convinced that we have no knowledge of it [matter] . . . for part will remain incomprehensible as it is concealed from us. Concealed in what? Concealed in the one fundamental essence: God'.[11]

Thus the quest of science and the scientists today. Al-Hakim predicts that future religious leaders will come from the scientists in order to approach Him through creativity and not only through verbal expression.[12]

JUSTICE MUHAMMAD SA'ID AL-ASHMAWI

We have already noted that in *Al-Islam al-Siyasi*, Ashmawi says there are Quranic verses directed against the people of the book following the battle of al-Khandaq. The people of Mecca besieged the city of Medina where the Muslims had sought refuge, and almost conquered it. The Muslims then claimed that the Jewish tribe of Banu Quraiza, who resided in Medina at the time, aided the Meccans in their war against the Prophet, and this was regarded as treachery. The main verse states: 'Fight against such of those who have been given the Scripture as believe not in Allah nor the Last

Day, and forbid not that which Allah hath forbidden by His messenger, and follow not the religion of truth, until they pay the tribute readily, being brought low.'[13] We have already noted that, in this context, Ashmawi explains that the intention is not to fight all people of the book in all times, but only those who do not believe in Allah and in the afterlife. In other words, the verse is directed against those who are unfaithful to their own religions. Furthermore, the war against them must cease the moment they pay the *jizya* tax.[14] Ashmawi cites many other verses in this same context to emphasize that war against them must be measure for measure and must also cease when the aggression ends.[15] In keeping with these Quranic verses, he asserts that war against the infidel Meccans is total until they convert to Islam, while war against the people of the book is directed only against those who were unfaithful to their own scriptures. War must be solely for self-defense, and not for aggression. In his book, Ashmawi raises another important point:

> Culture in the western world is not entirely evil. Western culture also has lofty values such as organization, hygiene, credibility, precision, innovation, planning, cooperation, and service to the other. These values constitute part of the conceptual world of the spirit. It [western culture] is not necessarily only materialistic. Thus it follows that no one man or group has the right to be patronizing. Patronizing all people nationally or internationally would create a fascist tyranny in the name of religion, which is the worst kind of all.[16]

Ashmawi pleads that 'Islam faces a danger that borders on tragedy and Egypt is in terrible peril'. He warns against the trend to politicize religion. Egypt must sound the alarm, educate, and do everything in its power to restore spiritual Islam to its role as a humanist, universalist, and cultured religion, not extremist, and free of the racist and tribal competition that had characterized the pre-Islamic period of *jahiliyya*.[17]

DR FARAJ FUDA

> The question is, do those who preach the establishment of an Islamic state know that this is the prelude to a religious state, whose most dangerous features are illustrated in an article by Dr 'Abd al-Rahman al-Rajihi in the journal *Al-Liwaa al-Islami*, which asserts: 'The three evils in human thought have Jewish sources – Communism was the offspring of Karl Marx, writer of *Das Kapital*, and Karl Marx was a flesh and blood Jew. This system of governance is a product of Zionism and

Judaism. The second evil is the so-called Freud who said that the origin of human instincts is the sex instinct, and you know the meaning of the sex instinct, which means animal lust, and thus he reduced human perfection to a deep pit. The third is Darwin, who said that the origin of man is the ape. This is the third of the filthy trio, and this trio is connected by a Jewish thread: Karl Marx was a Jew, Freud was a Jew, and Darwin was a Jew' [here Fuda expresses his amazement, pointing out that Darwin was a Christian, not a Jew]. The danger in a statement like this is judging someone's thought on the basis, primarily, of religious differences. This is a perilous path. The writer summarized the thought of each one in words that I do not permit myself to comment upon because they are cloaked in ignorance, but I will say in sanitized language that the ignorance is great and the distance is great from the veracity of the thought. I say unequivocally that he did not read one line of the principles of these three theories. And more ominously, he described these three great men in the history of human thought, regardless of whether or not we agree with their views, as a filthy trio. How would matters be if we took refuge in the religious state as envisioned by Dr al-Rajihi and his sort. I do not have the slightest doubt that the writings of Karl Marx would be banned, the theories of Freud would be forbidden to students of psychology, and the theories of Darwin would be extirpated from the curriculum. Furthermore, I am certain that following this 'filthy' trio, there would be a long list of 'filth' that people like al-Rajihi would do with as they see fit.[18]

Oh to those who plead, 'Woe to Islam, woe to Islam', save your pleas. Islam is fine. The danger to Islam comes only from your prodding of fresh young ones to abandon the universities at an early age just because their sciences are secular. You fill their heads with superstitions of which the most moderate is that thunder is the flatulence of a large Satan, the woman is the gate to sin and evil, and all society is *jahiliyya*. God only knows that you are the most ignorant of all Muslims in matters of Islam, as Islam was, is, and will remain a religion of science and sanity. It would be better for Islam and the Muslims to study the sciences of biology, nature, and chemistry rather than the religious law pertaining to the locations for bloodletting, etc.[19]

We all believe that religion is the fundamental basis of society. Indeed, it is the conscience of society itself. However we want to be elevated by religion above political strife and the ambitions of the cassette stars from the pulpits . . . to attend mosques and churches to hear religious sermons that do not arouse controversy. And to go to the People's Council to haggle and quarrel with each other without concern or limitation. We need a change in the distribution of labor – for religious leaders to talk about religion and statesmen to talk about politics. That religious leaders not terrorize by waving political slogans and politicians not polarize by waving religious slogans. That is the danger that we must all be wary of.[20]

ZAKI NAJIB MAHMUD

Under the title 'Yes . . . Islam is enough, but how?', Zaki Mahmud responds to a question asked by one of his readers: 'Isn't Islam sufficient for us to forego the West and everything in it?' His reply is:

I don't know how to reassure the reader before I continue writing that I am a Muslim Arab Egyptian. That I am an Egyptian who wants the good of his country, and I am an Arab who exists only in the bosom of his Arabness, and I am a Muslim who would not sell a grain of his faith for the entire universe and its contents . . . I was not surprised when this question arrived, because I know the intellectual climate in which we have lived for so long, and which will probably remain with us for many more years . . . I can only briefly review the stages in our intellectual development from the beginning of this century and the end of the previous century, which led to the second stage through which we are currently passing. I had wanted or hoped that, presto, there would be a third stage, after the stage in which the cultural and civilizing elements that we desire will be complete . . . The second stage now at hand is the antithesis of the first stage. In each there is a positive element that we cling to and, in each, a shortcoming that we pray we can recover from. The positive element of the first stage was our fierce pursuit of the West in all its innovations, hoping we might be able to participate in that enterprise. The positive element of the present stage is our fierce pursuit of the true connections with our sources. But the shortcoming of both stages is the hollow boasting that is satisfied with the given, and rejection of the other. The first stage excelled in comparison with this stage in that its people combined the innovation of the West with the heritage of the past, while people at this stage want to hear only one voice and turn a deaf ear to other voices. The greatest lie in the present cultural stage is the false claim propagated that one must choose either Islam or this age with all its arts and sciences. That if a Muslim wants the true Islam, he must abandon this age and everything in it. If we see someone inclined toward the age and its values, we consider him an infidel to Islam. And I say that the true Muslim cannot acquire what is distinctive about this age through Islam alone. My question is, does something in Islam drive you to acquire knowledge and science, or does something in it repel you from them? When I began writing this response, I looked into the concordance to see how many times the word 'science' appears in Quranic verses, and I found numerous pages with citations of words referring to 'science' or its forms. Thus we have before us a book [the Quran] that accorded science and thought a status that you will not find with respect to any other concept. What is in Islam that would deprive Muslims of the culture of our period in all its aspects? And where is the devil who whispered to us that spiritual life is limited to a reading stripped of action? As to the discoveries of science, they remain in the hands of cursed materialists. Ask me again if

Islam is not enough for us to forego the West and everything in it. I will reply that Islam is indeed enough if we live the life of Muslims, lives which do not reject any basis of the present culture, but will add bases on top of those which exist from previous cultures.[21]

DR FUAD ZAKARIYYA

Zakariyya observes that the Islamic resurgence in its present form appears to be a manifestation of the backwardness of the Muslim and the Arab world, particularly in the 1970s. The resurgence is a direct reflection of the defeats and frustrations felt by people and not a 'response' to them or an attempt to avoid them. The escape to formal rituals, to disregard of the real problems of life, to absolute obedience and denial of the critical intellect, and to the past are themselves but a reflection of the sense of defeat and general frustration among people. In Zakariyya's view, this phenomenon is not the product of the anger of the younger generation about their situation and their failure to achieve power, as is believed by researchers such as Saad Eddin Ibrahim, for example, since all these elements existed previously. Until the mid-1970s, the young people held left-wing views. Rather, Zakariyya contends that the phenomenon is a direct expression of intellectual deterioration reaching a nadir:

The same intellectual atmosphere that turned Tharwat 'Abada into an author of official Egypt, and Mustafa Mahmud into one of the most important thinkers and philosophers, and Ahmad 'Adawiyya into the most popular artist, is exactly what turned religious extremism into the prevalent trend among the younger generation.

He further claims that:

it is only the youth within these extremist groups who seem to have accomplished something, disregarding the motives of this achievement, as they cured the paralysis which seemed to be permanent and likely to continue for years. In contrast, neither the progressives, the democrats, nor the seculars had a role in this sudden movement of events, but rather, the surprise seems to have happened just as they had reached a dead end. Thus the political scientist confronts a real problem that is hard to resolve. Our country, it seems, is facing two options, both of which are terrible: either make do with progressive, enlightened thought which can understand, criticize and analyse, but does not have the ability to act. Or heed a regressive voice, which lacks the ability to comprehend, criticize, and analyze, but can alone motivate to action.

The real dead end for Egypt as it aspires toward the future is the need to make a choice between thought without action or action without thought. I believe that we shall have no salvation until thinkers reach a level that enables them to apply their thought to the field of effective action, or men of action reach a level that enables them to perceive the value of enlightened reason and development of the intellect.[22]

Dr Zakariyya incisively responds to Shaikh Muhammad Mutawalli Sha'rawi who condemned the achievements of science, writing as follows:

For whose sake are these things said in a country struggling to catch up with the train of science and technology and in a race against time to establish a place for itself in a world where scientific control increases day by day? What will the impact of these words be on the younger generations . . . Doesn't our Shaikh know that our future is dependent upon the ability of science to discover energy sources to replace depleted oil reserves, to find new methods of creating food so that we can be autonomous and protect ourselves from hunger, and to have economic systems that will enable us to build homes, pave roads and renew cities? The attack on human reason and accusations of impotence have become the most conspicuous signs of Islamic preaching in our day.[23]

TARIQ AL-BISHRI

In *Al-Muslimun wal-Aqbat*, al-Bishri argues with great naiveté on behalf of unity in Egyptian society for Muslims and Copts. He writes *inter alia*:

Self-control is the bulwark of security and the tool for every con-frontation. It is the real sense of belonging to society. Therefore great care should be taken to unify a society in difficult times. He who is greedy well understands that his security cannot come from his tools or equipment, but from fragmenting society and undermining its foundation, that is, by destroying the sense of belonging, through eradicating it and evoking a sense of belonging that is antithetical or secondary . . . We have a magnificent and admirable example of strengthening ties among Egyptians and unity among them in their confrontation with the British occupation in 1919.[24]

Throughout his book, al-Bishri surveys developments in Egypt from both the Muslim and the Coptic side, seeking to prove that without unity between them, Egyptian society will face the danger of extinction.

KHALID MUHAMMAD KHALID

In an interview in the journal *al-Muasawwar* about assassination attempts against Makram Muhammad Ahmad, Hasan Abu Basha, Nabawi Isma'il and others, Khalid Muhammad Khalid responds as follows:

Islam does not accept killing by assassination, which is classified among the worst crimes, not just for Muslim citizens but also for Christians. What is more . . . the injury and not just the murder is not at all acceptable in Islam. When we follow the Quranic verses and the instructions of the Messenger, we must not distort this truth. Note how the Messenger forbids passing a group of people with one's sword unsheathed. Here prevention is preferable to treatment . . . Take note of it in his saying that he who harms a *dimmi* or an ally is no longer protected by Allah or Muhammad. If even a wound, just a wound, that you inflict on a Muslim or a Christian is a sin and a crime in Islam, how much more so killing or assassination, the spread of terror and anarchy among people . . . Did you know that Mu'awiya denied rightful ownership of the caliphate to one who deserved it, the *Imam* 'Ali, by refusing to accept his authority, which caused a civil war.[25]

NOTES

1. Dr Ghali Shukri, *Al-Aqbat fi Watan Mutaghayyir* [The Copts in a changing homeland] (Cairo, 1991).
2. Ibid., p. 7.
3. Jamal Badawi, *Al-fitna al-Taifiyya fi Misr* [Communal strife in Egypt] (Cairo, 1992), pp. 21–5. See also David Sagiv, 'Who Owns Egypt? Muslim-Copt Relations', *Davar*, 7 May 1993.
4. Tawfiq al-Hakim, *Al-Ahadith al-Araba'a*, p. 36.
5. *Al-Ma'idah* [The Table Spread], verse 5:68.
6. *Al-Ahadith*, pp. 45–6.
7. Ibid., p. 50.
8. Ibid., p. 50.
9. *Al-Fatir* [The Angels], verse 35:28.
10. *Al-Ahadith*, p. 53.
11. Ibid., p. 30. I did not verify these quotes. They appear here as presented by al-Hakim.
12. Ibid., p. 32. The term 'verbal expression' refers to utterance of the two testimonies in Islam.
13. *Al-Taubah* [Repentance], verse 9:29.
14. *Al-Islam al-Siyasi*, p. 36.
15. Ibid., pp. 99–100.
16. Ibid., p. 68.
17. Ibid., p. 152.
18. Faraj Fuda, *Qabl al-Suqut*, pp. 59–60.
19. Ibid., p. 82.
20. Ibid., pp. 111–12.

21. Dr Zaki Najib Mahmud, *Qiyam min al-Turath* [Values from the heritage] (Beirut and Cairo, 2nd edition, 1989), pp. 133–42.
22. Fuad Zakariyya, *Al-Haqiqa wal-wahm*, pp. 115–16.
23. Ibid., pp. 31–2.
24. Tariq al-Bishri, *Al-Muslimun wal-Aqbat*, pp. 5–8.
25. Khalid Muhammad Khalid, in 'Sayartadd al-'Unf ila al-Mutatarrifin' [Violence will be a boomerang to the extremists], *Al-Musawwar*, 26 June 1987, pp. 26–7.

10 Conclusion to Part II

In the five chapters of Part II, we looked in detail at the views of liberal intellectuals who oppose religious extremism in Egypt. These individuals were not selected at random. Senior government officials, such as prime ministers or ministers, were not included. Rather, we chose a representative sample of a broad range of Egyptian thinkers and researchers. All are people of public stature, and all are major figures in their fields of interest. The great majority regularly write or have written against militant fundamentalism. More could have been presented of their writing, of course, but that would extend this study unnecessarily.

The individuals included are of varied backgrounds. There are authors such as Tawfiq al-Hakim, Yusuf Idris, Fathi Ghanim and Anis Mansur, who is also a well-known journalist. There are jurists such as Justice Muhammad Sa'id al-Ashmawi and Husain Ahmad Amin; prominent journalists like Muhammad Hasanain Haikal, Ahmad Bahaa al-Din, Makram Muhammad Ahmad, 'Abd al-Sattar al-Tawila and Adil Hamuda — most of these have also become author-scholars; philosophers and thinkers such as Fuad Zakariyya, Zaki Najib Mahmud and Faraj Fuda; historians such as 'Abd al-'Azim Ramadan, Dr Husain Fawzi al-Najjar and Liwaa Hasan Sadiq (the latter two are also army officers); sociologists such as Saad Eddin Ibrahim and Nemat Guenena; scholars such as Dr Ahmad Kamal Abu al-Majd, Dr Ghali Shukri, Tariq al-Bishri and Nabil 'Abd al-Fattah; and people of religion such as Khalid Muhammad Khalid and Fahmi Huwaidi, who are also scholars and authors. The range of political views is also broad. Some are socialists and left-wingers who carry considerable influence, such as Yusuf Idris, Fuad Zakariyya, 'Abd al-Sattar al-Tawila and 'Abd al-'Azim Ramadan; proud nationalists who write of pan-Arabism such as Tariq al-Bishri; Nasirists such as Muhammad Hasanain Haikal, Yusuf Idris and Khalid Muhammad Khalid; and liberals such as Justice Muhammad

Sa'id al-Ashmawi, Faraj Fuda and Zaki Najib Mahmud. And the range is sufficiently wide to enable conclusions to be drawn about the attitudes of the intellectuals toward religious extremism which leads to terrorism.

In many cases, the words of these intellectuals have been presented without embellishment. Their views have been presented thematically, in reaction to the subjects and slogans of the extremist fundamentalists, so that they could be compared with each other, to clarify and sharpen the picture. The claim is often heard among intellectuals, and certainly among fundamentalists, that Western Orientalists and scholars distort their words. Blind hatred is then directed against these Westerners. We have tried to present accurate summaries of their beliefs and quotations from their thoughts in an effort to prevent the accusation of distortion. Although not a single word has been appended to the original material, we do not harbor the illusion that we can avoid this accusation. However, we are convinced that after an examination of the many original sources, the reliability of this test will be self-evident. This strategy was planned in advance.

The agreement of these liberal intellectuals in absolute condemnation of religious extremism is remarkable. Sometimes they use the same arguments and the same sources and give identical answers, with differences only in individual style. This is true despite differences in social and political background.

The general conclusions that may be derived from the views quoted above are as follows:

SEPARATION OF RELIGION AND STATE

The liberal intellectuals demand a separation of religion from the state. They believe that clergy should deal with clerical issues and leave management of the affairs of state to the politicians. A *Shari'a* state should not be established because, notwithstanding its attraction for Muslims throughout the world, this would be a totalitarian state. What was appropriate for Muhammad and his companions is not necessarily right in our era. The Quran and the Sunna brought a high level of order and culture and, above all, glory to the Muslim world at the center of which were the Arabs. They even created an empire which defeated other great empires – Byzantine, Persian and others – before Islam appeared. But all these empires, including the Ottoman Empire, have crumbled over the generations. The last empire to survive, the Soviet Union, which had supported the Arabs, collapsed like a house of cards just a few years ago, and only one superpower remains, the United States, and it is not an empire.

THE IRRELEVANCE OF THE CALIPHATE

To liberal intellectuals, the institution of the caliphate, which was at the core of an Islamic *Shari'a* state, has lost its relevance today. Liberal intellectuals have spoken out in various ways against this institution because it leads to an absolute dictatorship of one who would make all the fateful decisions. They aspire to greater democratization and, almost without exception, they draw a dismal picture of what was wrought by the institution of the caliphate over the generations. They forcefully claim that it is not a binding institution and is not one of the principles of Islam, as is claimed by the fundamentalists. The institution of the caliphate, in their view, is corrupt and corrupting, and it is inconceivable that the Muslim world in general and Egypt in particular would return to the dark ages. They look toward democracy as the only solution to the critical social problems of Egypt. The Shura, which the fundamentalists claim is the height of democracy in Islam and constitutes a check on the dictatorship of the caliph, has never met these expectations and its powers have only ever been theoretical. From the moment the *bay'a* was given, that is, when the caliph was appointed, the task of the members of the Shura was finished and they could be dispersed. Even the method of choosing the first four caliphs was not uniform in Islam, until the Umayyad dynasty decided the caliphate should be determined according to heredity and not the Shura. Actually neither the Quran nor the Hadith establishes any single method for selecting the caliph. It was left to the Muslims to choose the best system for administering the affairs of the *Umma*. Not only the liberal intellectuals repudiate the institution of the caliphate, but so do the avowedly religious leaders, clergy and *'ulama* of al-Azhar, who refute the claim that the caliphate is one of the principles of Islam and therefore binding on Muslims. At most, therefore, the institution symbolizes the longing of Muslims for the glorious past of the Arabs and the Muslims who ruled the world in an era that has long since passed.

NON-MUSLIM BELIEVERS IN A SHARI'A STATE

The liberal intellectuals query the status and fate of non-Muslim believers in a *Shari'a* state headed by a caliph. These non-Muslim believers would comprise Jews (very few of whom are left in Egypt or the Arab world) and Christian Copts, millions of whom live in Egypt. Would they again become a lower-class religious minority? The secular state has given them 'full' civil rights and freed them from paying the *jizya* – a head tax supplement to the regular taxes.

THE CONCEPT OF NATIONAL IDENTITY

A *Shari'a* state and the institution of the caliphate, the intellectuals point out, actually negate the concept of national identity and belonging to a homeland state. Is it conceivable to give preference to the distant Muslim in India or in China over the Coptic nearby in Egypt, just because the latter is not a Muslim? What about service in the army? The Copt serves beside the Muslim in the Egyptian Army, but would he not have equal rights with the Muslim soldiers in his country? During war, the jihad in the Islamic sense becomes the draft. Sometimes the term 'jihad' is even used as an alternative to 'war' in the modern Arab or Islamic state. How can this paradox be resolved?

FUNDAMENTALISTS AND EGYPT'S CURRENT PROBLEMS

Besides broad general slogans such as 'Islam is the solution', do the fundamentalists have a specific plan to solve Egypt's current problems? ask the liberal intellectuals. Islam is an integral part of Egyptian society, and has a place of honor in the heart of the people. But what is required is a comprehensive program to solve the problems. Religion in the heart and prayers in the mosque are one thing, but a comprehensive plan and daily action are something quite different. One must behave and act according to the rules of modern economics, with banks that charge interest, and detailed plans of action. The intellectuals claim that they believe with all their hearts in the centrality of Islam, but a *Shari'a* state in Egypt would not solve the problems of a country connected by the umbilical cord of foreign relations to the external world. Problems demand long-range planning and a detailed solution, and this does not come from a magic wand. This has been proved, they claim, in the Sudan of Numeiri and the Sudan of Hasan al-Turabi, which conspire with Iran against Egypt.

PUNISHMENT IN A *SHARI'A* STATE

A *Shari'a* state will carry out the punishments of *hudud* called for by the Quran against thieves, adulterers, etc., such as cutting off hands, stoning and so forth, and this, the liberal intellectuals point out, would only add disabled people to Islamic society which is itself in such need of rehabilitation.

THE ROLE OF EDUCATION AND SCIENCE

Only by deepening education and embracing science and technology, the liberal intellectuals aver, can Egypt stride toward a better future. It is claimed that all the sciences already appear in the Quran and the Hadith and this claim is correct in the general sense, but what is required is a precise itemization. Religious precepts should be accommodated to the spirit of the times so that Egypt will not lag behind the powerful progress being made in the West. The Prophet Muhammed himself said: 'Pursue science, even if it is in China.' The people of China were not then Muslim and yet he advocated trudging all the way to that distant land to acquire knowledge. The intellectuals also contend that not all sins are attributable to Western culture, technology and science. People should select the good from the West and throw away the chaff, and not remain preoccupied with outdated interpretations. The fertile cooperation between the Muslim exegetes from the end of the nineteenth century until the mid-twentieth century who did not repudiate Western science brought prosperity in all fields. Casting religion in opposition to international developments in science and technology brings only damage to Egypt.

Part III
Democratic Reforms and Fundamentalism

11 Epilogue

The exploits of the militant Islamic groups in Egypt are escalating. A week does not pass without acts of terrorism against the government, the security forces, intellectuals, journalists who oppose religious extremism, ministers, former ministers and others. Even the Prime Minister, Atif Sidqi, was miraculously unharmed by a car bomb set by Islamic terrorists in November 1993 which exploded when his entourage passed through Heliopolis near Cairo. In the past few years there have been attempted assassinations of six current or former Interior Ministers and a senior journalist, Makram Muhammad Ahmad. In October 1990, Rif'at al-Mahjub, Chairman of the Egyptian Parliament, was murdered. In June 1992, the renowned intellectual, Faraj Fuda, was murdered. In May 1993, an attempt was made on the life of the Communications Minister, Safwat al-Sharif. Attacks have been made on dozens of senior police officers and hundreds of policemen, who represent the ruling regime to the fundamentalists. There have been frequent attacks on Copts and Coptic churches, property and businesses, as well as assaults on tourists to the historic sites of Upper Egypt. Centers of entertainment in the heart of Cairo were attacked, as well as coffee houses and video shops.[1]

In the course of an interview with the author in May 1993 the well-known Egyptian intellectual, sociologist Saad Eddin Ibrahim, noted that the amount of terrorism in the previous two decades had been limited, so that the average Egyptian citizen was unaware of it or ignored it. The phenomenon assumed dramatic proportions in 1992–93, and as a result stirred up emotions in Egypt. Terrorism in the 1970s had been limited to four districts, while in the 1990s it had spread to more than 14. The number of victims in the first three months of 1993 was equal to the number of victims in the whole of 1992. The number of victims in 1992 was four times the number the previous year. This substantial rise in the number of victims has aroused deep trepidation. The fact that Islamic terrorism is spreading extensively among the young, who are on average younger than ever is of signal importance. The average age of Islamic terrorists in the 1970s was 28. Today it is 21. Furthermore, 85 per cent of the fundamentalists in the 1970s were university students or graduates, but in recent years 60 per cent of high school students have joined their ranks. Also, Islamic terrorism has spread from the big cities to smaller cities, towns and villages, and thus the rural areas have become an integral part of the phenomenon of terrorism.

Members of terrorist groups come from the lower middle class or from those close to the poverty line. They feel that their standard of living is threatened and that, even after having completed high school or university they have a bleak future. This is also true of the Copts. To escape their deep frustration and the bitter fate that awaits them, the Muslims join Islamic extremist groups which help them earn a livelihood, and religion becomes for them a banner under which they may protest against the socio-economic and political oppression, as they have no other way whatsoever in which to influence the government to improve their lot.

A new source of extremists has arisen in recent years with increase in the number of unlicensed housing developments being constructed, for which the state has not prepared the necessary infrastructure, such as water, electricity, health, schools and so on. The residents of these housing developments are either immigrants from villages who have come to work in the cities, but who could not find housing near their place of work, or second- or third-generation city-dwellers who have not been able to find reasonable housing, and therefore have moved to the developments. Today in Egypt there are some 300 unplanned housing developments with a population of ten million. About 170 of the 300 are located in metropolitan Cairo, that is, in Cairo, Giza, and Shubra al-Haima in the south of al-Qalyubiyya. Thus, surrounding the capital city of Cairo which has a current population of 16 million, there is a relatively new belt of poverty of almost five million in addition to the poverty areas which already exist in Cairo. These housing developments soon turn into slums which breed frustration, extremism, violence and criminal gangs.

The government was not fully aware of this situation until recently, when it began to provide basic services and facilities, both in Upper Egypt and in the belt of poverty surrounding Cairo. It also began to create modest sources of employment, but these were too little too late, because the sums allocated from the national budget were inadequate to address this problem. The government could only give first aid, not full treatment, though the move was in the right direction. In recent years, Egypt has received massive assistance from the United States and other countries, a significant portion of which has been applied to expansion of the infrastructure in areas such as transportation, education, housing, health and welfare. However, the rapid population growth – one million births every eight months – means that everything that the government invests is almost instantly absorbed. The government of the late President Sadat began to establish satellite cities outside Cairo and in other districts, including the Sinai, with the objective of resettling urban dwellers but there was no massive influx of residents to these areas. Since then, large investments have flowed into Egypt, and these have raised the capacity for industrial and agricultural production, hence increasing economic growth by a significant percentage. Some estimate the growth to be six per cent, with the rate of inflation decreasing to about ten per cent and the national deficit down to 3.5 per cent. As noted, all this is the result of a massive infusion of capital from outside Egypt and the cancelling of debts in the amount of billions of dollars. Foreign currency reserves have recently increased and today stand at about $11 billion, and these help to keep the Egyptian economy stable without additional decreases due to population growth. These reserves also permit importation of vital goods, sufficient quantities of which are now available.

Despite these significant achievements, the economic situation of the average Egyptian has not markedly improved. The current population of Egypt is over 60 million, and although annual economic growth is relatively high, it cannot keep pace with the population increase. For many years the government has attempted unsuccessfully, to reduce the birth rate. In the years 1991–92, the birth rate did indeed decrease by about 150,000 a year, and indications are that this small decrease reflects a longer-term trend.

The Egyptian government woke up to the danger posed by religious extremism only as a result of the murder of the intellectual Faraj Fuda. It then began an unprecedented hunt for concentrations of fundamentalists in greater Cairo and Upper Egypt. This was accompanied by an extensive information campaign directed against fundamentalist terrorism through books and educational materials, a campaign in which the best minds in Egypt, including even religious leaders, participated. The Egyptian press and the state media – both written and broadcast – were involved. At the international book fair in Cairo in early 1993, symposia against terrorism were organized; bans which had been issued by al-Azhar against the books of famous intellectuals such as Justice Ashmawi and Faraj Fuda were lifted, and their works again appeared on the shelves of the fair. In October 1992, President Husni Mubarak issued a presidential order, the equivalent of a law, which permits the trial of fundamentalists in military court, although they are civilians, and allows for summary proceedings, which do not give the right of appeal to higher courts. From then until late 1993, dozens of death sentences were issued against violent fundamentalist activists, and more than 25 have been executed.

The question now posed is whether these measures – attacking fundamentalists, a concentrated program of arrests, the trial and execution of the most violent among them – are sufficient. The view of Dr Fuad Zakariyya is:

> The problem under consideration concerns the future of the entire nation. This is a problem that cannot be solved by administrative measures or trials. First and foremost, this is a problem that must be resolved in the minds of people, or it will continue to burn again and again. And this burning could be much more dangerous next time. Why is the Egyptian nation so divided in its views? Every group thinks in a different mentality, and ignores groups different from it or treats them derisively, and does not see any benefit in dialogue with them. The apparent reason is fear and mistrust.[2]

This attitude is shared by most of the intellectuals interviewed by the author in late May 1993 in Cairo, including Husain Ahmad Amin, 'Abd al-'Azim Ramadan, Anis Mansur, Saad Eddin Ibrahim and many others. Some feel that the educational system must be completely reformed, by means of totally revising the curriculum, replacing all the teachers who support fundamentalism, and completely changing the programs broadcast on television, radio and the other media. This is, of course, in addition to improving the standard of living and saving the youth from militant Islamic gangs. Again the question arises, can such dramatic programs be implemented in the current state of Egypt today? And if implementation is begun, will results be visible in the foreseeable future? Despite the obstacles, it seems possible to begin the process, just as economic growth rebounded and increased in the early 1990s following the troubling decline in the late 1980s.[3]

Mubarak's government moved slowly and deliberately in instituting reforms during his first two terms of office (about 12 years). He did not want to take dramatic measures as his two predecessors, Nasir and Sadat, had done. Having established and stabilized his position as undisputed leader, he may now logically seize the momentum in his third term of office. And although the Egyptian people view him as hesitant, he enjoys broad public support and is considered honest and fully committed to the good of the people. The international situation has been helpful to him, especially since the 1991 Gulf War. Mubarak's joining of the Arab coalition, alongside the international coalition headed by the United States, to wage war against Saddam Husain of Iraq, who had occupied Kuwait and was compelled by force of arms to abandon it, raised the prestige of Egypt as an important and stabilizing power in the region.

Dr Saad Eddin Ibrahim wrote in the May 1993 edition of the journal *Al-Mujtama' al-Madani* ['civil society'], that while the country was taken up in the 1970s by the process of liberation (the October 1973 war), and thereafter by the process of peace, it was completely preoccupied during this period with finding economic solutions to the ills of Egypt. But the fundamentalists were working quietly and *en masse* to take control of the minds of the younger generation by continual brainwashing. Terrorism penetrated all the teachers' colleges of Cairo and the provincial cities, and those who had been recruited there were then hired as schoolteachers. In other words, fundamentalists were taking mass control of the education of millions of schoolchildren in the elementary and high schools throughout Egypt. This is the danger that threatens Egypt. The authorities did not notice the drama taking place under their noses, and thus, by default, permitted the creation, over time of a huge reserve army of educators espousing violent extremism against the state. Ibrahim notes that the hard core of fundamentalists does not exceed 10,000 today, while the periphery encompasses several hundred thousand. But this is nothing compared with what can be expected from this army of fundamentalist educators in Egypt in the coming years. These extremist elements were not content with recruiting male schoolchildren, but they also recruited schoolgirls, some as young as ten years of age. These girls held stormy demonstrations in their high school in Qalyub during Ramadan in February 1993, and they violently attacked Copts and set fire to a wing of the church in the city.

Having noted the socio-economic situation and the problems of

education, we turn now to the challenge to the Egyptian government in the realms of democracy and civil rights as a result of fundamentalist terrorism. During Nasir's regime, all parties in Egypt
were abolished, including the Wafd, which was popular and liberal
in character, and Nasir held power by virtue of his military junta
and officers. He also created a unified political body, the United
Socialists, to provide legitimacy to his rule. Liberalism and democracy, which had prospered until the late 1950s, were virtually
paralysed during the Nasir era. While it is true that Nasir fought the
Muslim Brothers and religious extremists, the blow he dealt to the
liberals, who had enjoyed relative democracy until then, was far
worse. Nasir, as is known, nationalized all the media and personally
appointed the editors of newspapers and the heads of the media.
Liberal journalists and authors could not act freely, except those
who toed the party line and praised his regime. Under the subjugation and torture of this era, fundamentalist activity was suppressed.
Some escaped to Saudi Arabia and other Arab countries and some
to the west. The religious faith of those in prison was heightened,
and they awaited their opportunity for revenge. Hatred for Nasir's
regime nurtured religious extremism in the underground and in the
prisons, in a fervor that was hitherto unknown in Egypt (see
Chapter 3).

The late President Sadat, after suppressing the Nasirist centers of
power which had opposed his presidency in May 1971, sought
legitimacy for his regime. He released the Muslim Brothers from
prison in order to gain their support, and divided the Socialist
Union into three wings – left, right and center – with Sadat himself
leading the central wing in an attempt at democratization. Following the October War, the three wings became the three civilian
parties which represented the political left, right and center. Hence,
Sadat was the first to democratize the Egyptian political system,
after a hiatus of an entire generation.

During the rule of Mubarak, from October 1981, additional
progress has been made in democratizing the Egyptian political
system. After a dozen years of his rule, there are 13 political parties.
Mubarak does not allow religious groups to organize into parties,
neither the Muslim Brothers nor the Copts. He even prevented the
formation of a Nasirist party until the elections of 1991. In the 1984
elections, Mubarak allowed the Muslim Brothers to join existing
parties, and they joined the Wafd, which they abandoned for another
party in the next elections. In the 1987 election, there were 50

representatives of the Muslim Brothers in the People's Council, but they did not constitute an independent body. Mubarak attempted to conduct talks with the Muslim Brothers who were considered moderates, to grant them legitimacy, but he soon broke off the talks when he realized that their views concerning opposition to the existing government and support for a full Islamic state, including replacement of the constitution with the Islamic *Shari'a* and appointment of a caliph, were identical to those of the extremists (*see* Chapter 4). The National Democratic Party, Mubarak's party, has been the dominant force in Parliament throughout his rule. Despite the proliferation of other parties, none is likely to rival it in power in the foreseeable future. During Mubarak's term, considerable freedom of the press has been established. With one or two exceptions, Mubarak has not used his power to revoke the license of any periodical. The Egyptian press today is thought of as the freest in the third world. There are periodicals which harshly criticize the government, senior figures and even the president himself, with impunity. This is a complete reversal of the position during the two previous presidencies. Mubarak has had to consider how to protect his rule and democracy at the same time.

The problem is that Islamic terrorism which spread in Egypt in previous years has set obstacles in the way of Mubarak's efforts to give more freedom. To fundamentalists, all means to seize power and control are legitimate. They have already taken control of most of the university student councils and most trade unions. The government is currently trying to keep them out of these centers of power. In early 1993, a presidential order was issued stating that if a quorum of 30 per cent does not vote in the elections of any association, the government can appoint the members of the governing council or board of that association. This is in fact what happened to the Bar Association, which had been controlled by religious extremists until May 1993. This measure is, of course, anti-democratic, and journalists and authors have raised their voices in protest, calling it a setback for democracy. However, the government, supported by the non-extremist majority of the population, seems to have had no choice but to implement this measure. It seems that some measures of democratization will inevitably lead to a situation in which the fundamentalists will take control of some institutions. On the other hand, orders such as the one cited are anti-democratic. The government is thus on the horns of a dilemma, with conflicts in the liberalization that it strives for.

In early December 1993, the opposition press in Egypt reported that the Civil Rights Committee of Egypt had protested at the torture and execution of fundamentalists who murdered senior police officers, including an important security official. An extremist Islamic organization claimed responsibility for the killings, which had been carried out in revenge for the hanging of three key fundamentalists. The question arises as to whether this act serves to create *shahada* [martyrs] and a vicious cycle of executions and murders. There were also reports at this time of restrictions on foreign journalists in Egypt to prevent reporting in the foreign press of the government's war on fundamentalists. In addition, several foreign publications were confiscated for publishing articles about human rights violations in Egypt, such as the *Middle East Times* and *Cairo Today*.

Of further concern is the lack of contenders for the position of president, which resulted in the unopposed election of Mubarak, a process which appears anti-democratic to those educated in the ways of western democracy. The absence of challengers to Mubarak engenders apathy in the voters, which was manifested in his election to a third term in October 1993. Only ten per cent of those with the right to vote participated in the elections, a figure which is low by any standards. Moreover, although the existing constitution limited a president to two terms, Mubarak was able to run for a third after the passage of enabling legislation in the People's Council. With all the contradictions in attitudes about democratizing Egypt, this appears to be the middle path which befits an Egypt that is battling terrorism on the one hand, and aspiring to stability on the other.

The anti-democratic element is of the very essence of the Islamic groups. They completely deny democracy, but will thoroughly exploit the relative democracy that exists in order to gain power, in addition to employing violent means. If and when these groups take power, no trace of democracy will remain, as may be seen in the two states where this has already happened, the Sudan of Hasan al-Turabi and Iran.

The liberal intellectuals of Egypt are constantly striving, sometimes at great personal risk, to repel the extremist Islamic attempts to establish a *Shari'a* state and to return to the period of the forefathers and to stagnation. Professor Shimon Shamir, an expert on Egyptian affairs and someone who has served in Egypt in various capacities, writes:

For a while, the Nasirist revolution paralyzed Egyptian liberalism, but as the revolution declined, liberalism renewed itself and proved its vitality. After the revolution, Islamic fundamentalism began its efforts to uproot this intellectual movement in the Egyptian community, but even in the face of this challenge, the liberals showed their resilience. Organic ties bind liberals of all types in one ongoing continuum and this continuum is bound to the fabric of Egyptian society. The vitality of the system of beliefs of Egyptian liberalism is revealed in the dialectical process which reflects the fact that liberalism is one of the basic options regularly presented to Egyptian society, which continues to seek its way in the modern world.[4]

When this article was published in 1989, it seemed that Egyptian liberalism was in continuous retreat before the Islamic tidal wave and that the government was endeavouring to prove that it was no less Islamic than the groups that claimed to represent the true Islam. The government appeased the extremists and did not deflect their attacks against the intellectuals, and thus the influence of the liberals waned. How ironic it is that liberalism in Egypt made gains after the murder of one of the foremost intellectuals, Faraj Fuda, when the government realized the staggering dimensions of Islamic terrorism, and began to do battle with it. One measure, as already mentioned was the recruitment of intellectuals for the widespread education campaign against fundamentalism. Thus, in retrospect, Professor Shamir was right, to an extent, in seeing the centrality of the liberal option in Egypt.

As we saw in the early chapters of this book, the reforms in Islam at the end of the nineteenth century and during the first half of this century were led by conspicuously religious leaders and men of letters who had absorbed Western culture at the height of its glory, which catalysed progress and wide cultural awakening. The vast majority at the time, including some religious leaders, accepted the separation of church and state. It was then also acceptable to borrow values from the West in matters of legislation, parties, education, culture, science, technology and so on, and these were central elements in Egyptian society. Today, however, Western-style liberalism is viewed by religious fanatics as hateful, corruptive and anti-Islam. Educated Egyptian youth steer clear of these values. The author and journalist Fathi Ghanim provides a telling description of the situation of today's young people in the period preceding the murder of Sadat, in his book *Al-Afial* ['the elephants'] with the profile of the young hero of his story, Husain Yusuf Mansur:

Youth his age from every background and type are drawn to the underground. Underground activity satisfies their need for adventure, their
dreams of glory and danger. The fervent appetites of adolescent youth
yearn to defeat everything, but from my experience I also found that
youth are hungry for blind obedience. With all the physical and spiritual
resources at their command, they are searching for a focus that they can
respect to the point of sanctification, to give devotion and to take refuge
. . . What remains for the boy who loses his respect for school, for his
principal and his teachers, and for all those his senior . . . He sits there as
they exchange curses among them. Their words are no different from
the stories of theft and corruption that they hurl at their friends the
moment they turn their backs . . . The boy who is faced with such
change around him rebels at everything and at all conventions. He
erupts in order to destroy everything, even if he ends up destroying it
only in his imagination. But he loses his equilibrium when he is envel-
oped in a sense of desolation. Inside he wants to return to security, to
stability, and to the refuge for which he is searching, and therefore he
turns to underground activity with all the sense of awe about it, the wild
glory that envelops it, the secrecy and the concealment, working
together with other anonymous people, total obedience to orders and
instructions from an unknown supreme command which issues holy
orders that must be obeyed, and that you must not go easy on anyone
who does not obey them . . . as he will lose his life. Tyranny and
terrorism. Indeed . . . But this is a situation that is clear, stable, black
and white, with no two-ways-about-it. That's what attracts youth.[5]

Similarly, Dr Fuad Zakariyya writes:

The murder of Sadat by a jihad organization, according to the special
claims expressed, was essentially the murder of modernity which is an
integral part of us all, that is of the enlightened intellectuals, the murder
of the modern period completely and of the progress for liberation that
humanity has achieved in this period. It was not their desire to murder
Sadat alone, but they wished to murder Newton, Galileo, Qasim Amin,
Taha Husain, and everyone who participated in the modernization of
society and who lifted the fog from its eyes. Indeed, it was the murder of
everyone who thinks critically and who does not rely on obedience
and blind devotion. Their goal was to murder all the principles that
humanity has struggled to attain, against all the tyrants of all times and
against the distorters of thought of every type and kind.[6]

Anis Mansur wrote:

Life has two faces – religion and politics. Every clergyman has a policy
for application of his religion, and every politician believes in the need
to implement his philosophy. Each one desires power for himself . . .
The reason for all the political struggles is religious, and for all the
religious wars is political . . . The terrorist did not err who revealed

himself to the nineteenth century and said, I cannot correct my fathers, my forefathers, and my sons, but I can only destroy them! No war ever erupted without carrying the name of God . . . Death is on His behalf.[7]

History reminds us that war is the product of a popular social movement . . . The periods of ceasefire and peace have been very brief . . . And just as wars developed from the use of stones to the use of bombs and lasers; and just as people conduct wars out of a fear of wars; thus religious terrorism rises and falls, appears and hides . . . I am not saying that we are facing a disaster in the Middle East because of religious extremism, but that we are at the heart of the disaster, in the eye of the tornado. Therefore we do not know where we are in terms of the direction of the disaster. Wherever we look we see only blood and fire or people who say – There is no God but Allah and Muhammad is his Messenger . . . A paradise for zealots . . . But are the zealots only Shi'ites? No, they are only Sunnis . . . And the mills of hatred and animosity are grinding up the innocent.[8]

It is illuminating to read the imaginary announcement number 10 written by Husain Ahmad Amin in the name of the Islamic Revolutionary Command, as if it had taken power in Egypt three months after the outbreak of the revolution, in which he reports to the Islamic nation on the achievements of the revolution. And what are the achievements of the three-month-old revolution as imagined by Amin? First is the beheading of intellectuals – Zaki Najib Mahmud, Yusuf Idris, Fuad Zakariyya, Louis 'Awadh, Alfred Faraj, Faraj Fuda, and Husain Ahmad Amin (the writer himself) – all in the first week of the revolution; the beheading of thousands during the first month; and the beheading of another 2,800 a week after the imaginary announcement. There is also the execution of the prime minister of the new Islamic state, the Shaikh Salih Farmawi (perhaps a reference to Shaikh Mutawalli Shaarawi) who had been appointed prime minister because of his activity on behalf of Islam, and who refused to admit his crimes, but the security men forced him 'or a voice like his' to record on tape the details of his crimes. And what were his crimes? The books and video tapes which were found, so to speak, in his house. Afterwards, his assistant Taha al-Badi'i was executed for issuing a *fatwa* that ruled that revealing the sole of the foot of a woman is not nakedness and that the acquisition of photographs of people is not impure. Some of those who were executed despite their adherence to Islam had asked for civil rights for the Copts, and had allowed a woman to show both her eyes through the veil rather than just one! And so on.'[9] Amin, like other intellectuals, left no doubt as to the identity of the Islamic rule that would take power.

The question arises as to whether these intellectuals did not contribute to this situation by their debates with the religious fanatics. Instead of stating clearly and unequivocally the need to separate religion and state, and eschewing any attempts to relate the discussion to explanations in the Quran or the Hadith, they cite from the liberal facets of Islam, relying on some verses and the Hadiths. Instead of saying that there had indeed once been Islamic governments which had applied the *Shari'a* throughout the Islamic periods, as there had been Christian governments in Europe several hundred years ago, but that such regimes had passed from the modern world, they seek to 'bend' tradition in their favor. They generally emphasize in their writings that the *Shari'a* suits every time and place. Their wriggling, however, does not help. One cannot state that he favors application of the *Shari'a*, but. . . This is a recipe for failure.

An additional question concerns the influence of these liberals. The intellectuals listed by Amin in his announcement, to which dozens more with varying degrees of importance could be added, could not provide a counterbalance to the religious fanatics with the masses thronged behind them. Until the murder of Faraj Fuda, the liberals seem to have waged a rearguard action. Recall the battle fought by Tawfiq al-Hakim against the religious leaders. He was in an inferior position and was forced into a full retreat, despite the aura that surrounded him all his life. The influence of the intellectuals would not be strongly felt even if each were of national or international stature, because their philosophy was not generally acceptable to the hardliners among the Muslim masses. The cultural terrain of Egypt these days is not the same as that of of the first half of this century.

It is not our intention to engage in prophecy about the future of Egyptian society; on the contrary, this study examines the ongoing phenomenon. We would be remiss in intellectual integrity, however, if we were to desist from giving a cautious evaluation of the character of Egyptian society in the future. Values like democracy, culture and science, even with preaching on their behalf, will not grow on fertile soil if the fundamental problems of Egypt are not resolved. In this context, we quote Naguib Mahfouz who wrote in 1987 in his weekly column in *Al-Ahram*:

Our problems in the face of the challenges are the type that could be called labor pains. Because the laws which hamper our democratic development, our inability to give food and shelter to the population, the weakness of education which threatens our young people, the lack of creative employment opportunities and a sufficient wage, air pollution, the dirt of our cities, the corruption of administration and conscience, the absence of law and order and the weakening of identity; all these are symptoms of an unhealthy congenital disease. Our birth to the reality of the world is similar to this. It closed off our orientation to reality. As for our fundamental problem, it is cultural. It is the problem of backwardness in the era, of being immersed in a morass of economic, social, and cultural problems. This backwardness requires that we imitate the developing nations in everything, from how we slice our bread to our taste, in spite of our uniqueness. Surrender and hunger constantly terrify us. Humiliation and alienation dwell within us. Perhaps we must first feel the tragedy deeply. This feeling must keep our conscience from nodding off to sleep, must sadden our souls, and must enable the pain to penetrate the marrow of our bones. This must be the feeling of everyone, big and small, men and women, for us to expect hope for the revolution despite the reality and to leap toward changes in everything – administration, sanity, and a desire for a inspired life. It does not matter how much time we need to reach what we aspire to nor the distance that we must travel. The important thing is that we live the struggle hour by hour, day by day, and that no matter what, the struggle is better than giving up in despair. Toil is better than being helpless and unrecognized. We must be fully aware, must absorb power in order to work, to free ourselves from the fetters of governments which bind the intellect and the soul. We must challenge the period in which we fell to the bottom through inattention and laziness. We must know that if we do not leap forward in strength from within ourselves, no one will extend a helping hand. If we do not distance death by our lofty aspirations, no one will mourn us. At the end, we get only what we deserve. And fate, in most cases, is what we write with our own hands.[10]

Egypt at the end of the 1980s was closing itself off from the culture and values of the west. During Sadat's time, a clause was introduced which said that the *Shari'a* was the source of the Egyptian constitution. Just a few years ago, the teaching of Darwin's theory of evolution was abolished from the curriculum as it 'desecrated the holiness of the first man in the Quran that Allah bequeathed to him the earth and the fullness thereof.' Egypt strode toward more radicalization. The role of the liberal intellectuals in the western world was held by shaikhs and *'ulama* who have a doctorate degree and who use the title doctor rather than shaikh in order to attract the hesitating and vacillating youth. Those who preach application of the *Shari'a*, both moderates and extremists, made good use of the relative openness of the regime. In the 1987 elections, their power increased from 15 to 45 representatives in the People's Council, out of a coalition of some 60 representatives. They learned from the experience of the past and seek to attain their goals quietly but steadfastly as the soil is prepared for them by many forces. The more the government is open to them with the strengthening of democracy, the stronger they get. We see this in the Algerian experience. The success of the Front for Islamic Rescue headed by Shaikh 'Abbas al-Madani in the democratic elections held in Algeria in 1992 shocked the Algerian government, which was forced to revoke the election results and to throw the leader of the Front into prison, leading to murders on both sides. It was also proven in Jordan's 1991 parliamentary elections, with religious circles winning 40 per cent of the vote and the growing influence of the Muslim Brothers and Hamas, to say nothing of the increase in terror by the Hamas and Islamic Jihad organizations in Gaza and the West Bank, which have penetrated into Israel and the Israeli settlements in the Territories despite the negotiations between Israel and the Palestinians that began with the signing of the Oslo Accords. This is, of course, in addition to the ongoing terrorism of the Shi'ite organization Hizbullah in southern Lebanon, which is aided by massive Iranian support and covert support from Syria.

To be fair, however, it must be acknowledged that this expression of Islam by militant Islamic organizations, which is so dangerous for Israel and the West, is not the same relatively liberal Islam witnessed throughout history. The clerics of Islam were comparatively moderate until the twentieth century, and, with the exception of isolated cases, Jews and Christians in Islamic countries lived in harmony with Muslims, with cooperation in many fields, particularly business and commerce. The slaughter of Jews and foreigners in the name of Islam was less acceptable in the past, and in any event was never so cruel as in the countries of Europe, such as France and England, a few centuries ago, and certainly never approached the horrors of Nazi Germany in the dark era of the Second World War. In Arab countries relations with Jews and Christians were tolerant largely because of the influence of the Hanafite school that prevailed in the days of the Ottoman Empire in most of the Arab and Islamic lands under its domain. Judaism and Christianity were tolerated as fellow religions in the spirit of the Quran, which recognized *ahl al-kitab* [the people of the book]. There were even periods when Jewish communities flourished in certain Islamic countries, enjoying autonomy in the administration of their communal and religious lives. Extremism against other religions, and in particular Judaism, began to escalate at the end of the first third of the twentieth century, with the rise of Nazism in Europe and the growth of pan-Arabism and pan-Islam. Historically, Islam showed a more humanistic and tolerant face toward minorities, and in particular toward Judaism, than is realized by non-Muslims and by Western countries today.

Egypt appears to be on the threshold of a positive turning-point, in terms of both openness toward Israel and relations with the west. The mutual recognition of Israel and the Palestine Liberation Organization and the signing of the Declaration of Principles between them in Washington on 13 September 1993 assigned to Egypt an important role of mediation between the two sides to implement the agreement, side by side with the United States. This agreement also justified retroactively the peace agreement between Egypt and Israel, both internally and in the eyes of other Arab countries. The agreement between Israel and the Palestinians might also lead to agreements with other Arab states and to a new page of history involving a shining and prosperous Middle East. Left-wingers who opposed peace with Israel and who were allied with the fundamentalists have begun, very slowly and cautiously, to ease their opposition. Some have even visited Israel and conducted a fruitful dialogue with Israeli intellectuals. There is a reasonable chance that terrorism will decrease, at least in the foreseeable future, in the wake of the drastic measures taken by the government of Egypt. The dream of peace and prosperity may become a reality.

Of course there is no certainty in this; the Middle East has known many vicissitudes. What appears to be correct today could change tomorrow. Egypt, like most Islamic states, has not yet escaped the dangerous cycle of religious extremism and terrorism. And we have already noted that militant fundamentalists lie in wait for every opportunity. The President of Egypt and other senior politicians are still in the gunsights of the militant fundamentalists. The drama is not over.

A stable Egypt is critical for stability in the Middle East and also possibly in the free world generally, and hence should have the support of the free world. Presumably the United States today will not address human rights issues as it did with the Shah of Iran, which *inter alia* helped bring Khomeini to power with a regime much more controversial and anti-democratic than there was before. The measures taken by Mubarak in his battle against fundamentalism in Egypt are an unfortunate necessity, even though they contain anti-democratic elements and violations of human rights. However, caution and wise rule on the inside together with financial aid from abroad could lead to greater stability. Egypt is at the very modest beginning of resolution of its difficult problems. All beginnings are difficult and it has already been said that a long journey begins with one small step. The new era that is dawning for Egypt could well continue this path.

NOTES

1. *Strategic Report of Al-Ahram* (Center for Strategic Reports of *Al-Ahram*, 1992), pp. 375–98 and Egyptian newspapers.
2. Zakariyya, *Al-Haqiqa wal-Wahm*, pp. 123–4.
3. The decline in the 1980s was dramatic: in 1984, economic growth was 8.0 billion Egyptian Pounds; in 1985 it was 7.4; in 1986 it fell to 4.8; in 1987 to 4.2; in 1988 to 2.2; and in 1989 it dropped to 2.0. The data are from the Economist Intelligence Unit, *Egypt, Country Report No. 4* (1989), p. 2.
4. Shimon Shamir, 'Neo-liberalism in the Period After the Revolution', *Zemannim – A History Quarterly*, Fall 1989, No. 52, pp. 63–72.
5. Fathi Ghanim, *Al-Afial* [The elephants] (Cairo, 1981).
6. Fuad Zakariyya, *Al-Haqiqa wal-Wahm*, pp. 94–5.
7. Anis Mansur, *Al-Din wal-Dinamit* [Religion and dynamite] (Cairo, 1988), pp. 500–1.
8. Ibid., pp. 1–4.
9. Husain Ahmad Amin, *Al-Islam fi 'Alam Mutaghayyir*, pp. 287–307.
10. Naguib Mahfouz, *'Al-Wa'y al-Manshood'* [The required consciousness], *Al-Ahram*, 29 Oct. 1987.

Bibliography

WORKS IN ARABIC

'Abd al-Fattah, Nabil, *Al-Mushaf wal-Saif* [The book and the sword: the struggle between religion and state], (Cairo, 1984).

Abd al-Rahman, Dr 'Umar, *Kalimat Haqq: Murafa'at al-Doctor 'Umar 'Abd al-Rahman fi Qadiyyat al-Jihad* [A word of truth: the defense of Dr 'Umar 'Abd al-Rahman in the al-Jihad trial], (Cairo, 1987).

'Abd al-Raziq, Shaikh 'Ali, *al-Islam wa-Usul al-Hukm* (Islam and the fundamentals of government), Beirut, n.d.

Abu Isma'il, Salih, *Al-Shahada fi Qadiyyat al-Jihad* [Testimony about the jihad] (Cairo, 1984).

Abu al-Majd, Dr Ahmad Kamal, *Hiwar la Muwajaha* [Dialogue, not confrontation] (Cairo, 1988).

Adham, Isma'il and Naji Ibrahim, *Tawfiq al-Hakim* (Cairo, 1945).

Ahmad, Dr Rif'at Sayyid, *Al-Islambuli: Ruya Jadida Li-Tanzim al-Jihad* [Islambuli, a new view of the Jihad Organization] (Cairo, 1988).

—— *Limada Qatalu al-Sadat: Qissat Tanzim al-Jihad* [Why they killed Sadat: the story of the Jihad Organization] (Cairo, 1989).

'Ali, Kamal Hasan, *Muhariboon wa-Mufawidoon* [Warriors and negotiators] (Cairo, 1986).

'Amara, Dr Muhammad, *Al-Islam: Qadaya al-'Asr* [Islam: problems of modern times] (Beirut, 1984).

—— *Al-Islam wal-Mustaqbal* [Islam and the future] (Beirut, 2nd edition, 1986).

—— *Al-Islaman wal-Thawra* [The two Islams and the revolution] (Beirut, 3rd edition, 1988).

—— *Jamal al-Din al-Afghani al-Muftara 'Alayhi* [Jamal al-Din al-Afghani, the slandered] (Beirut, 1984).

—— *Tayyarat al-Fikr al-Islami* [Streams in Islamic thought] (Beirut, 1985).

Amin, Husain Ahmad, *Dalil al-Muslim al-Hazin* [Guide for the sad Muslim] (Cairo, 1987).

—— *Fi Bayt Ahmad Amin* [In the home of Ahmad Amin] (Cairo, 1989).

—— *Al-Islam fi 'Alam Mutaghayyir* [Islam in a changing world] (Cairo, 1988).

Amin, Husain Ahmad *et al.*, *Al-Tasamuh al-Dini wal-Tafahum Bayn al-Mu'taqadat* [Religious apologetics and interfaith understanding] (Cairo, 1986).

Amin, Dr Jalal, *Nahwa Tafsir Jadid li-Azmat al-Iqtisad wal-Mujtama' fi Misr* [Toward a new explanation of the economic and social crisis in Egypt] (Cairo, 1989).

al-Ashmawi, Muhammad Sa'id, *Al-Islam al-Siyasi* [Political Islam] (Cairo, 1987).

—— *Jawhar al-Islam* [The essence of Islam] (Cairo, 1984).

—— *Al-Khilafa al-Islamiyya* [The Islamic caliphate] (Cairo, 1990).

—— *Ma'alim al-Islam* [Milestones of Islam] (Cairo, 1989).

—— *Al-Riba wal-Faida fi al-Islam* [Usury and benefit in Islam] (Cairo, 1988).

—— *Ruh al-'Adala* [The spirit of justice] (Cairo, 1986).

—— *al-Shari'a al-Islamiyya wal-Qanun al-Islami* [Islamic law and Egyptian law] (Cairo, 1988).

'Awadh, Dr Louis, *Aqni'at al-Nasiriyya al-Sab'a* [The seven masks of Nasirism] (Cairo, 1987).

—— *Tarikh al-Fikr al-Misri al-Hadith* [The history of contemporary Egyptian thought] (Cairo, 1980), Vol. 1, and (Cairo, 1983), Vol. 2.

'Aziz, 'Abd al-Ghaffar (head of 'Ulama Seminary) (ed.), *Man Qatal Faraj Fuda* [Who killed Faraj Fuda?] (Cairo, 1992).

Badawi, Jamal, *Al-fitna al-Taifiyya fi Misr* [Communal strife in Egypt] (Cairo, 1992).

Bahaa al-Din, Ahmad, *Muhawarati Ma'a al-Sadat* [My dialogues with Sadat] (Cairo, 1987).

al-Bishri, Tariq, *al-Muslimun wal-Aqbat fi Itar al-Jama'a al-Wataniyya* [The Muslims and the Copts in the national society] (Beirut, 1982).

Dhaif, Shawqi, *Al-Adab al-Arabi fi Misr* [Arab literature in Egypt] (Cairo [undated]).

Fahmi, Isma'il, *Al-Tafawud min Ajl al-Salam* [Negotiating for peace] (Cairo, 1985).

Fuda, Dr Faraj, *Al-Haqiqa al-Ghaiba* [The absent truth] (Cairo, 1986).

—— *Hatta la Yakoun Kalaman fi al-Hawaa* [So it won't be just talk] (Cairo, 1992).

—— *Al-Irhab* [The terror] (Cairo, 1988).

—— *Al-Mal'ub* [The swindled] (Cairo, 1988).

—— *Al-Nadir* [The warning] (Cairo, 1989).

—— *Nakoun aw la Nakoun* [To be or not to be] (Cairo, 1992).

—— *Qabl al-Suqut* [Before the fall] (Cairo, 1985).

—— *Al-Wafd wal-Mustaqbal* [The Wafd and the future] (Cairo, 1983).

—— et al., *Al-Taifiyya ila Ayn* [Whither sectarianism?] (Cairo, 1987).

Galal, Dr Muhammad Na'man, *Al-Tayyarat al-Fikriyya fi Misr al-Mu'asira* [Currents of thought in modern Egypt] (Cairo, 1987).

Ghanim, Fathi, *Al-Afial* [The elephants] (Cairo, 1981).

al-Ghazali, Muhammad, *Miat Saal 'An al-Islam* [One hundred questions about Islam] (Cairo, two parts, 3rd edition, June 1987).

al-Ghazali, Zainab, *Ayyam min Hayati* [Days from my life] (Beirut, 1980).

Habib, Dr Rafiq, *Al-Masihiyya al-Siyasiyya fi Misr* [Political Christianity in Egypt] (Cairo, 1990).

Haikal, Muhammad Hasanain, *Kharif al-Ghadah* [Autumn of the anger] (Beirut, 1986).

al-Hakim, Tawfiq, *Al-Ahadith al-Arba'a* [The four conversations] (Cairo, 1983).

—— *'Awdat al-Wa'y* [Return of recognition] (Cairo, 1975).

—— *Fi al-Waqt al-Dai'* [In lost time] (Cairo, 1983).

—— *Muhammad: Sira Hiwariyya* [Muhammad: his history in dialogue] (Cairo, 1936).

—— *Al-Ta'aduliyya ma' al-Islam* [The equilibrium with Islam] (Cairo, 1983).

—— *Tahta Shams al-Fikr* [Under the sun of meditation] (Cairo, 1982).

—— *Yaqzat al-Fikr* [The awakening of thought] (Cairo, 1933).

Hamuda, Adil, *Al-hijra ila al-'Unf* [The *hijra* to violence] (Cairo, 1987).

—— *Ightiyal al-Sadat* [The assassination of Sadat] (Cairo, 2nd edition, 1985).

—— *Qanabil wa-Masahif* [Grenades and holy books] (Cairo, 1985).

—— *Sayyid Qutb* (Cairo, 1987).

Hanfi, Dr Hasan, *Al-Din wal-Thawra fi Misr* [Religion and the revolution in Egypt] (Cairo, 1989).

Hanna, Dr Milad, *Al-a'mida al-Sab'a lil-Shakhsiyya al-Misriyya* [The seven pillars of the Egyptian personality] (Cairo, 1989).

Hasanain, Dr 'Ali, *Hatta la Ta'ud al-Shari'a Nassan Shakliyyan* [So that the *Shari'a* will not remain a formal text] (Cairo, 1985).

al-Hudaibi, Hasan, *Du'at la Qudat* [Preachers not judges] (International Islamic Association for Student Organizations, 1977).

Huwaidi, Fahmi, *Iran min al-Dakhil* [Iran from the inside] (Cairo, 1987).

—— *Muwatinun la Dimmiyyun* [Natives not under the protection of Islam] (Cairo, 1986).

—— *Al-Tadayyun al-Manqus* [Blemished religiosity] (Cairo, 2nd edition, 1988).

Ibrahim, Husain Tawfiq, 'Zahirat al-'Unf al-Siyasi fi Misr' [The phenomenon of political violence in Egypt], *Al-Mustaqbal al-Arabi*, No. 117, 1988, pp. 26–59.

Ibrahim, Saad Eddin, *Taammulat fi Masalat al-Aqalliyyat* [Thoughts about minorities] (Cairo, 1992).

Ibrahim, Saad Eddin, ed., *Misr fi Rub' Qarn* [Egypt over 25 years] (Beirut, 1981).

Idris, Yusuf, *Intiba'at Mustafizza* [Provocative impressions] (Cairo, 1986).

al-Jundi, Anwar, *al-Yaqza al-Islamiyya fi Muwajahat al-Isti'mar*, [The Islamic awakening in confrontation with imperialism] (Dar al-I'tisam, Cairo [undated]).

Kailani, Muhammad Sa'id, *Al-Adab al-Qubti Qadiman wa-Hadithan* [Past and recent Coptic literature] (Cairo [undated]).

Madgur, Rajab, *Al-Takfir wal-Hijra Wajhan li-wajn* [Accusations of apostasy and the *hijra* face to face], with examination and study by Dr 'Ali Grisha (Cairo, 1985).

Ma'had al-Qadaa li-Dubbat al-Shurta [Institute for the police command in Egypt], *Al-Aathar al-Ijtima'iyya al-Salbiyya lil-Tatarif* [the negative social effects of extremism] (Cairo, 1987), Vol. 1.

al-Mahdawi, Tariq, *Al-Ikhwan al-Muslimun 'ala Madhbah al-Munawara* [The Muslim Brothers on the altar of maneuvering] (Cairo, 1986).

Mahfouz, Naguib, *Awlad Haritna* [Our neighborhood children] (Beirut, 5th edition, 1986).

—— *Al-Tanzin al-Sirri* [The secret organization], story from a book by the same name; Hebrew translation: Sagiv, David, *The View Toward Egypt* (Erez Biton, ed.), 1989, pp. 31–7.

—— *Al-Tasawwur al-Fanni fi al-Quran li-Sayyid Qutb* [Artistic perception in the Quran of Sayyid Qutb], 'Al-Hilal', Cairo, December 1988 (an article written in 1945).

—— *Yawma Qutila al-Za'im* [The day the leader was assassinated] (Cairo, 1983).

Mahmoud, 'Ali 'Abd al-Halim, *Wasail al-Tarbiya 'Ind al-Ikhwan al-Muslmin* [Educational methods of the Muslim Brothers] (Cairo, 1989).

Mahmud, Zaki Najib, *Fi Tahdith al-Thaqafa al-Arabiyya* [About modernization of Arab culture] (Beirut, 1987).

—— *Ruiya Islamiyya* [An Islamic viewpoint] (Beirut, 1987).

Mansur, Anis, *Al-Din wal-Dinamit* [Religion and dynamite] (Cairo, 1988).

—— *Fi al-Siyasa* [In politics] (Beirut, 1982).

Mardini, Zuhair, *Al-Ladudan: al-Wafd wal-Ikwan* [The two rivals: the Wafd and the Brothers] (Beirut, 1986).

al-Mawdudi, Abu al-A'la, *Al-Qanun al-Islami wa-Turuq tanfidhuhu* [Islamic law and its implementation], translated from English (Cairo, [undated]).

Mitchell, Dr Richard, *Al-Ikhwan al-Muslimun* [The Muslim Brothers], translation from English, with Arabic introduction by Salih 'Issa (Cairo, 1977).

al-Muhafadha, 'Ali, *Al-Ittijahat al-Fikriyya 'Ind al-'Arab fi 'Asr al-Nahdha 1798–1914* [Thoughts and directions of the Arabs in the Renaissance] (Beirut, 1987).

al-Najjar, Husain Fawzi, *Al-Dawla wal-Hukm fi al-Islam* (State and rule in Islam] (Cairo, 1985).

—— *Al-Islam wal-Siyasa* [Islam and politics] (Cairo, 1977).

Ni'mat-Allah, Gunaina, *Tanzim al-Jihad – Hal Huwa al-Badil fi Misr* [The Jihad Organization – is it an alternative in Egypt?], introduction by Dr Saad Eddin Ibrahim (Cairo, 1988).

Qutb, Sayyid, *Fi Zilal al-Quran* [In the shadow of the Quran] (Cairo).

—— *Al-Islam wa-Mushkilat al-Hadara* [Islam and problems of culture] (7th edition, 1988).

—— *Kasais al-Tasawwur al-Islami* [Characteristics of the Islamic perception], (Beirut, 10th edition, 1988).

—— *Ma'alim fi al-Tariq* [Milestones] (Beirut, 1982).

—— ''*Al Naguib Mahfouz*', [On Naguib Mahfouz], in *Al-Hilal* (Cairo, December 1988), and articles about Mahfouz written in the 1940s.

—— *Al-Naqd al-Adabi wa-Mahahijuhn* [Literary criticism and its methods] (Beirut, 6th edition, 1990).

—— *Al-Tasawwur al-fanni fi al-Quran* [Artistic perception in the Quran] (Beirut, 7th edition, 1982).

Ramadan, 'Abd al-'Azim, *Al-Ikhwan al-Muslimun wal-Tanzim al-Sirri* [The Muslim Brothers and the secret organization] (Cairo, 1982).

—— *Misr fi 'Ahd al-Sadat* [Egypt during Sadat] (anthology of articles, 2 volumes, Cairo, 1986, 1989).

—— *Tahtim al-Aaliha* [Smashing idols] (Cairo, two volumes, 1986).

Rida, Shaikh Muhammad Rashid, *Al-Khilafa* [The caliphate] (Cairo, new edition, 1988).

Sabri, Musa, *Al-Sadat: Al-Haqiqqa wal-ustura* [Sadat: the truth and the legend] (Cairo, 1985).

al-Sadat, Anwar, *Al-Bahth 'An al-That* [Search for myself] (Cairo, 1978).

Sadiq, Liwaa Hasan, *Judhur al-fitna al-Taifiyya fi al-firaq al-Islamiyya* [The roots of strife between Islamic sects] (Cairo, 1988).

al-Shinnawi, Fahmi, *Nahwa Islam Siyasi* [Toward a political Islam] (Cairo, 1985).

Shnuda, Zaki, *Qubti Shahid 'Ala al-'Asr* [Coptic witness to the era] (Cairo, 1992).

Shukri, Ghali, *Thawrat al-Mu'tazil: Dirasa fi Adab Tawfiq al-Hakim* [Revolt of the loner: studies in the literature of Taqfiq al-Hakim] (Beirut, 2nd edition, 1973).

al-Tawil, Muhammad, *Lu'bat al-Umam wa-'Abd al-Nasir* [The game of nations and 'Abd al-Nasir] (Cairo, 1986).

al-Tawila, 'Abd al-Sattar, *Azmat al-Yasar al-Misri* [The crisis of the Egyptian left] (Cairo, 1987).

—— *al-Sadat fi Israil* [Sadat in Israel] (Cairo, 1978).

—— *Umaraa al-Irhab* [The *amirs* of terrorism] (Cairo, 1992).

Zakariyya, Dr Fuad, *Al-Haqiqa wal-wahm fi al-Haraka al-Islamiyya al-Mu'asira* [Truth and fantasy in the contemporary Islamic movement] (Cairo, 2nd edition, 1986).

—— *Kam 'Umr al-Ghadab: Haikal wa-Azmat al-'Aql al-'Arabi* [What is the lifespan of anger: Haikal and the crisis of Arab thought] (Cairo, 2nd edition, 1984).

—— *Al-Sahwa al-Islamiyya fi Mizan al-'Aql* [The Islamic awakening in the scales of mind] (Cairo, 1989).

al-Zarkali, Khair al-din, *Al-A'lam: Qamus Tarajum Ashhar al-Rijal wal-Arab* [The distinguished dictionary of the most known men and women] (Beirut, 3rd edition, 1969).

WORKS IN ENGLISH

Abdelnasser, Walid M., *The Islamic Movement in Egypt: Perceptions of International Relations, 1967–1981* (A publication of the Graduate Institute of International Studies – Geneva Series, November 1993).

Ajami, Fuad, *The Arab Predicament* (Cambridge, UK, 1981).

Ayubi, Nazih N.M., 'The Political Revival of Islam: The Case of Egypt', *Int. J. Middle East Stud.* 12 (1980), USA, pp. 481–99.

Binder, Leonard, *Islamic Liberalism* (Chicago, 1988).

Chitman, E.J., *The Coptic Community in Egypt* (Durham, 1986).

Dekmejian, R. Hrair, *Islam in Revolution* (Syracuse, NY, 1985).

Edgar, Adrienna L., 'The Islamic Opposition in Egypt and Africa', *Journal of Arab Affairs*, Vol. 6, No. 1 (1987), pp. 82–110.

Encyclopaedia of Islam (new edition, reprint, Leiden, 1965).

Gershoni, Israel, *An Intellectual Source for the Revolution: Tawfiq al-Hakim's Social and Political Critique 1933–1945* (The Dayan Center, Tel Aviv, June 1987).

Gilsenan, Michael, 'Apprehensions of Islam', *Middle East Report*, July–August 1988 (USA).

Guillaume, Alfred, *Islam* (Edinburgh, 1952).

Haddad, Yvonne Y., 'Islamic "Awakening" in Egypt', *Arab Studies Quarterly*, Vol. 9, No. 3 (1987), pp. 234–59.

Haim, Sylvia G., 'Sayyid Qutb', *Asian and African Studies*, Vol. 16, No. 1 (March 1982), pp. 147–56.

Hourani, Albert, *Arabic Thought in the Liberal Age 1798–1939*, (Cambridge, rev. edition, 1984).

Ibrahim, Saad Eddin, 'Anatomy of Egypt's Militant Islamic Groups', *Int. J. Middle East Stud.*, 12 (1980), pp. 423–53.

—— 'Egypt's Islamic activism in the 1980s'. *Third World Quarterly* 10, 2 (April 1988), pp. 632–57.

Kedourie, Elie, *Islam in the Modern World* (London, 1980).

Kepel, Gilles, *The Prophet and Pharaoh*(translated from French) (London, 1985).

Kupferschmidt, Uri M., 'Reformist and Militant Islam in Urban and Rural Egypt', *Middle Eastern Studies* (Haifa), pp. 403–18.

Landau, Jacob M., *The Politics of Pan-Islam* (Oxford, 1990).

Lazarus-Yafeh, H. 'Some Differences Between Judaism and Islam as Two Religions of Law', *Religion* 14 (1984), pp. 175–91.

Lewis, Bernard, *Islam in History* (London, 1973).

Matthee, Rudi, 'Jamal al-Din al-Afghani and the Egyptian National Debate', *Int. J. Middle East Stud.*, 21 (1989), pp. 151–69.

Mikhail, Kyriakos, *Copts and Moslems Under British Control* (London, 1911).

al-Najjar, Fawzi M., 'Egypt's Laws of Personal Status', *Arab Studies Quarterly*, Vol. 10, No. 3 (1988), pp. 299–317.

Nettler, Ronald L., *Past Trials and Present Tribulations* (Oxford, 1987).

Ni'mat-Allah, Gunaina, 'The "Jihad" – An "Islamic Alternative" in Egypt', *Papers in Social Science*, Vol. 9, Monograph 2, Summer 1988 (Cairo).

Peters, Rudolph, *Islam and Colonialism: The Doctrine of Jihad in Modern History* (The Hague, 1979).

Quandt, William B. (ed.), *The Middle East: Ten Years After Camp David* (Washington, 1988).

Rivlin, Paul, *The Liberalization of the Egyptian Economy* (Tel Aviv, 1981).

Safran, Nadav, *Egypt in Search of Political Community* (Cambridge, UK, 1961).

Sagiv, David, 'Judge Ashmawi and Militant Islam in Egypt', *Middle Eastern Studies*, Vol. 28, No. 3 (July 1992), pp. 531–46.

Shamir, Shimon (ed.), *Self-Views in Historical Perspective* (Tel Aviv, 1981).

Shepard, William E., 'Islam as a "System" in the Later Writings of Sayyid Qutb', *Middle Eastern Studies*, Vol. 24, No. 1 (January 1989), pp. 31–50.

Somekh, Sasson, *The Changing Rhythm: A Study of Najib Mahfuz's Novels* (Leiden, 1973).

Tritton, A.S., *Islam, Belief and Practices* (London, 1951).

Vatikiotis, P.J., *Islam and the State* (London, New York, Sydney, 1987).

Warburg, Gabriel R. and Gilbar, Gad G. (eds.), *Studies in Islamic Society* (Haifa, 1984).

Watt, Montgomery W., *Islamic Fundamentalism and Modernity* (London and New York, 1988).

Winter, Michael, *Society and Religion in Early Ottoman Egypt* (New Brunswick, NJ, 1982).

Yadlin, Rivka, *Egyptian Opposition: The Boundaries of National Consensus* (Jerusalem, 1989).

WORKS IN HEBREW

Altman, Israel, *Islamic Opposition Groups During Sadat's Regime* (Shiloah Institute, Tel Aviv University, 1978).

Ayalon, Ami (ed.), *Government and Opposition in Egypt*(Tel Aviv, 1983–84).

Ayalon, Amos, *The Finding of Egypt* (Schocken Publications, Jerusalem and Tel Aviv, 1980).

Balas, Shimon, *Arabic Literature in the Shadow of the War* (Am Oved, Tel Aviv, 1978).

Flint, Eli, editor: Eli Rekhess, *Institutes of Higher Education in Egypt* (Shiloah Institute, Tel Aviv University, 1979).

Gal, Itzhak, *The Economy of Egypt in the Face of the Arab Sanctions* (Shiloah Institute, Tel Aviv University, 1980).

Gershoni, Israel, *Egypt Between Uniqueness and Unity* (Hakibbutz Hameuchad Publications, Israel, 1979–80).

Gibb, H.A.R., *New Trends in Islam* (translated from English: Michael Schwartz) (Am Oved, Tel Aviv, 1976).

Harkabi, Yehoshafat, Yehushua Porath and Shmuel Moreh, *The Arab-Israeli Conflict in the Mirror of Arab Literature* (Truman Institute and Van Leer Institute, Jerusalem, 1975).

Keening, Hans, *Journey in Egypt* (translated: Nurit Adar) (Jerusalem, 1980).

Lazarus-Yafeh, Hava, 'Is there new religious thinking among the clergymen of al-Azhar today?' in Gabriel Bar (ed.), *The 'Ulama and Religious Problems in the Muslim World* (Magnes Press, Jerusalem, 1971).

Lazarus-Yafeh, Hava (ed.), *Studies in the History of the Arabs and Islam* (Tel Aviv, 1980).

LeMans, Henry, *Islam* (translated from French: Efraim Harpaz and Yoseph Yoel Rivlin) (Jerusalem, 1966–67).

Lewis, Bernard, *The Arabs in History* (translated: Yonatan Ratosh) (Tel Aviv, 1955).

—— *Leaves of History* (Hebrew editor: Rachel Simon) (Jerusalem, 1988).

—— *The Middle East and the West* (translated: Eliakim Rubenstein) (Tel Aviv, 1972).

Mansur, Yaakov (ed.), *Studies in Arabic and Islam* (Bar-Ilan University, Ramat Gan, 1973–74).

Meital, Yoram, *Agricultural Cooperation Between Israel and Egypt 1980–1984* (Tel Aviv University, 1986).

Milson, Menachem, *Intellectuals in the Arab World in the Middle Ages and the Modern Era* (Van Leer Institute, Jerusalem, 1973).

Rivlin, Yosef Yoel (translator), *al-Quran* (Dvir Publications, 3rd edition, 1974–75).

Sagiv, David, 'Dialogue with God: The Debate Between Tawfiq al-Hakim and Religious Zealots', in Erez Biton (ed.), *The View Toward Egypt* (Apiryon, 1989), pp. 75–85.

—— 'Who Owns Egypt? Muslim-Copt Relations', *Davar*, 7 May 1993.

Shamir, Shimon, *History of the Arabs in the Middle East in the Modern Era* (Tel-Aviv, 1987).

—— 'Neo-liberalism in the Period After the Revolution', *Zemannim – A History Quarterly*, No. 52 (Fall 1989), pp. 63–72.

Sivan, Emmanuel, *Arab Political Myths* (Am Oved, Tel Aviv, 1988).

—— *Islamic Fanatics* (Am Oved, Tel Aviv, 1986).

Somekh, Sasson, 'Husain Fawzi: Egyptian Author and Scientist', *Keshet*, No. 69 (Fall 1975), pp. 138–58.

Winter, Michael, *Developments in the Structure of the Educational System in Egypt in the 1970s* (Shiloah Institute, Tel Aviv University, 1981).

—— 'The Mawalid in Egypt from the Beginning of the Eighteenth Century to the Mid-Twentieth Century', in Gabriel Bar (ed.), *The 'Ulama and Religious Problems in the Muslim World* (Magnes Press, Jerusalem, 1971).

Yadlin, Rivka, *Arrogant and Exploitive Genius* (Jerusalem, 1987–88).

Zeliger, M., *Camp David Agreements and their Political Context* (Policy Publications, The Hebrew University of Jerusalem, 1987).

Zemach, David (ed.), *Articles on the Works of Tawfiq al-Hakim: Tawfiq al-Hakim and the Legend of the Ivory Tower*, (al-Shuruq Press, Israel, 1970).

Index

For Product Safety Concerns and Information please contact our EU
representative GPSR@taylorandfrancis.com
Taylor & Francis Verlag GmbH, Kaufingerstraße 24, 80331 München, Germany

9 781138 991828